THE ANCIENT
GREEKS
IN THEIR OWN WORDS

MATTHEW DILLON

SUTTON PUBLISHING

First published in the United Kingdom in 2002 by
Sutton Publishing Limited · Phoenix Mill
Thrupp · Stroud · Gloucestershire · GL5 2BU

British Library Cataloguing in Publication Data
A catalogue record for this book is available from the British Library.

ISBN 0-7509-2715-1

Typeset in 11/13 pt Sabon.
Typesetting and origination by
Sutton Publishing Limited.
Printed and bound in England by
J.H. Haynes & Co. Ltd, Sparkford.

Contents

Preface

I would like to thank Rupert Harding of Sutton Publishing for first inviting me to write this book. I hope his original aim of providing a series of extracts at once both interesting and informative about the ancient Greeks is met by this volume. The editors at Sutton have been most patient while this volume has been delayed by ever-increasing teaching duties.

Not every aspect of the ancient Greeks or ancient Greece is covered by the passages translated here, but I hope that they give enough information to provide at least a broad overview of the main features of Greek society and the sorts of things that the Greeks themselves considered important. This is in no sense a political history but aims to reveal something about the nature and characteristics of the Greeks themselves.

The passages translated are chosen mainly from well-known authors in order to encourage readers towards further exploration in the main works of Greek literature. I have tried to keep the translations as close as possible to the original Greek but I have not hesitated to modify them for sense when this is required. The process of selecting extracts is difficult from a corpus of writings numbering in the hundreds of thousands of words. If the choice seems idiosyncratic and eclectic, then this is the responsibility of the author. Comments on the passages are kept to a minimum, as I wanted the Greeks to speak 'in their own words'.

I have translated poetry as poetry to help convey the 'flavour' of the text. Sometimes this means that the line numbering does not exactly correspond with the original, as some re-ordering of words and phrases is necessary for a smooth translation, but on the whole the line numbering matches that of the original texts. In rendering Greek names into English I have largely used traditional forms, such as Achilles rather than the exact transliteration Achilleus, which I think will be more familiar to the reader. Some names, however, are closer to the original, but I have usually aimed to make them recognisable rather than alien. Perhaps this volume will encourage some readers to commence the study of the ancient Greek language.

I need (again) to thank my wife for taking time out of her own heavy academic duties to proofread this volume. Thankfully we both share a love for ancient Greece. For my daughter Sophia who asks, 'Haven't you finished that book yet?', and my son Isaiah who comes into the study and lays out my Greek texts on the floor to make 'roads', much love.

Matthew Dillon
Armidale, Australia, February 2002

Introduction

Man is but the dream of a shadow.

Pindar, *Pythian Victory Ode*, 8.95–6.

Pindar immediately arrests our attention here, drawing us towards a consideration of the ancient Greeks, and in a few words beckoning us towards their contemplation of the human spirit and its potential. Materially their temples are able even in their ruined state to speak to us about their religious aspirations. But their words reveal much more, defining the human spirit and speaking eternal truths.

Ancient Greece was the crucible of western civilisation. Most of what is known about the ancient Greeks comes from their writings, particularly in the archaic and classical periods, which lasted from about 800 BC to 336 BC. Archaeology is important, particularly when it yields the remains of houses, domestic items, works of art, graves and inscriptions. But on the whole it is writers such as Herodotus, Thucydides and Xenophon who provide the history of this period, with poets such as Aeschylus, Sophocles, Euripides, Pindar and Bacchylides revealing the ethos and customs of the Greeks.

Many of these writers were conscious of their own abilities. Thucydides wrote that his work was destined for posterity, to last for all time, while Pindar says of himself, Fragment 152: 'My voice is sweeter than honeycombs toiled over by bees.' There can be no better way to learn about the Greeks than by reading what they wrote about themselves: what concerned them most, what behaviour they found acceptable (and what unacceptable), what interested them, what they feared and what pre-occupied them.

But who were the ancient Greeks? Ancient Greece consisted of the Greek mainland itself, as well as Crete and the Aegean islands, just as it does today. But in addition the Greeks had in two main waves of colonisation spread elsewhere. From about 1200 to 1000 BC, the Greeks settled the coast of what is now Turkey, giving rise to magnificent cities such as Miletus, Ephesus and Didyma; the remains of these and other Greek cities are particularly impressive. There was a second wave of colonisation from about 800 to 600 BC when the Greeks settled the shores of the Black Sea,

Sicily and southern Italy, with some colonies as far away as modern-day France (notably modern Marseilles) and Cyrene in Libya.

But like all societies, there were radical differences between not just various groups of Greeks but also between those living within the same city. The Greeks were not a homogenous group but lived in thousands of different communities, each recognisably Greek but also with local customs and other distinguishing features. Today, the remains of Greek temples from Naples in Italy to Ephesus in Turkey bear witness to this greater Greek world. But more than ruins are left behind. The Greeks produced the first outpouring of western literature, beginning with the poet Homer, the favourite of the Greeks themselves throughout their history. (In fact, over twenty Greek cities claimed to be his birthplace.) He and other poets believed that their works were the result of divine inspiration by the nine Muses, goddesses of poetic inspiration. The words of the Greeks included in this volume come not just from Greeks in Athens, but from those who lived in Asia Minor, on the Aegean islands, in Syracuse and Egypt. Over a cultural world several thousands of kilometres wide, they give voice to all that was best – and worst – in Greek civilisation.

Greece itself is often described as a country dominated by hills, mountains and small plains and this is true to some degree, but there is fertile soil. Thucydides wrote of the various waves of invasion of Greece, in which the best land was conquered by newcomers. Thucydides, 1.2.3, 5: '[1.2.3] It was always the best land that experienced changes of inhabitants, the land now called Thessaly and Boeotia, and most of the Peloponnese, except for Arcadia, and the most fertile areas of the rest of Greece . . . [1.2.5] But the area around Athens from the earliest times, because of its thinness of soil, was undisturbed and always inhabited by the same race of men.' Sparta itself nestles in a bowl, and the snow of Mount Taygetus is visible from nearly any direction. Homer describes it in the *Odyssey*, 4.1: 'Sparta lying in a hollow, full of ravines'.

In mainland Greece there are numerous mountain ranges often hemming in small or medium-sized plains. In the middle of such a plain, usually clustered around a hilly outcrop of rock, was the city. Many cities had such a centre and the Greeks called it an acropolis, of which that at Athens is an excellent example. On it stands the temple of the Parthenon, dedicated to the virgin goddess Athena; it still dominates the modern city's skyline. And, as at Athens, the acropolis of an area was often the first place of settlement, and then as towns and cities grew, the people lived in houses clustered around its base and the acropolis became public property, where temples were built and often political meetings were held.

Ancient Greece was dominated by what is called the city-state, which the Greeks called the *polis*. Greece was not in any sense a 'nation', but rather a cultural phenomenon, something like the western European world, where there are separate governments that, however, share a common religious, political and economic heritage. The modern political building-block is the nation. In ancient Greece, its equivalent was the city-state. The *polis* was a small city by modern standards. There were literally hundreds of Greek cities, some of them no more than small towns. Greek city-states had their own armies, calendars, currencies and local variations on the main political systems of democracy, aristocracy or oligarchy. Different cities had different names for the months and common dating was non-existent.

Athens, with its 30,000 male citizens, was the largest Greek city-state, followed by Syracuse in Sicily, which had about 20,000 citizens. A city-state was ideally, in Greek eyes, an autonomous political unit. The city with its associated amenities was the high-point of Greek civilisation, and for the Greeks life without the city was unimaginable. Athens and Sparta were the main cities of ancient Greece, but there were many differences between them, not just physically but also in terms of temperament, characteristics and outlook.

At the conference of Sparta and its allies in 432 BC when it was debated whether to go to war or not against the Athenians, the delegates from Corinth attempted to goad the Spartans into action by unfavourably comparing them with the Athenians. The contrasts might be overdrawn but hold true on the whole: the Athenians were dynamic and resourceful, the Spartans (who never numbered more than 10,000, and this figure gradually decreased) tried to stay at home as much as possible and did not take risks, as they had a large servile population, the *helots*, to control. In their speech at Sparta, the Corinthians made the following points. Thucydides, 1.70.1–9:

(1.70.1) You Spartans have never considered what sort of men the Athenians are and how completely different from you are the men you will fight against. (1.70.2) They are without a doubt innovators, and quick to make their plans and to accomplish in reality what they have thought out, but you preserve simply what you have, and come up with nothing new, and in what you actually undertake don't complete what has to be done. (1.70.3) And in addition, the Athenians are reckless beyond their capabilities, risking danger beyond their judgement, and are confident even in crises. But for you it is the case that you undertake less than your power allows, you distrust what your judgement is certain of, and think you will never escape from your crises. (1.70.4) And again, they are unhesitating while you procrastinate, they are abroad while you are the greatest 'stay-at-homes'. They believe that by being abroad they will gain something, while you think that if you go out on campaign you will damage what you have already. (1.70.5) If they are victorious over their enemies they advance over the greatest distance, and when they are defeated give ground as little as possible.

(1.70.6) Furthermore, they use their bodies on behalf of the city as if they were somebody else's, but their minds as most intimately their own for activities on her behalf. (1.70.7) And when they plan something but fail to achieve it they feel they have been robbed of their rightful possessions, and whenever they go after something and take possession of it, they consider they have achieved only a small thing compared with what the future will bring, and if they might fail in an undertaking, they make up for the loss by forming expectations for other things. For to them alone, having is the same as hoping in whatever they plan, due to the quickness with which they act upon their decisions. (1.70.8) At all this they labour with toils and dangers throughout their lives, and have little enjoyment of what they have as they are always acquiring more and they consider that there is no holiday except to do what has to be done, and that untroubled peace is no less a disaster than laborious activity. So if someone summing up the Athenians were to say that they were born neither to have peace themselves nor to allow it to other men, he would speak correctly.

So Athenian and Spartan characteristics were very different. In addition, the Athenians were wealthy and adorned their city with magnificent temples, such as the Parthenon mentioned above. Sparta, however, was lacking in financial resources and the modern visitor will not find any impressive remains from the classical period. But this is exactly what Thucydides predicted. In fact, Sparta was not a 'city' in the true sense of the word, but was made up of five unwalled separate villages, and its temples were rudimentary. Thucydides, 1.10.2:

If the city of the Spartans were to be deserted, and only the temples and the foundations of the buildings survived, I would imagine that there would be a strong disbelief after a long time had passed among the people of that time that the power of the Spartans was as great as their fame. However, they occupy two-fifths of the Peloponnese, and have leadership over all of it, as well as many allies in other places. But as Sparta is not constructed as a compact unit, and is not adorned with beautiful temples and buildings, but is inhabited in villages, according to the old Greek fashion, it would appear more inferior than it is. But if Athens were to be similarly deserted, its power would seem to be twice as great as it is, from the appearance of the city which met the eye.

Thucydides' history is taken up with the long struggle, known now as the Peloponnesian War (431–404 BC), that took place between Sparta and Athens. Sparta won, and deprived Athens of her empire of island states that she had ruled since 479 BC. But Athens was not politically destroyed by its loss in the Peloponnesian War, and always remained the pre-eminent Greek state culturally and intellectually. It was always an important player in Greek affairs, and in the second half of the fourth century BC was the main opponent of the power of Macedon, first ruled by Philip II and then by his son Alexander the Great.

Another major player in Greek history was the city of Corinth, an important participant in the Battle of Salamis in 480 BC and advocate of war against Athens in 432 BC. Herodotus, Thucydides and Xenophon preserve most of what is known of Corinth's history; it produced no major writers itself. The Isthmus of Corinth, a narrow strip of land 6 km wide, was the land gateway between southern Greece, the Peloponnese, and the rest of the mainland. Immediately beyond the Isthmus was the city of Megara, and not far beyond it Athens. The Isthmus was the invasion route for the Spartans in their expeditions against Athens in the late sixth century BC and again during the Peloponnesian War. Its importance is described by Thucydides, 1.13.5:

For the Corinthians occupied a city on the Isthmus and had always had a trading centre there, because the Greeks – both those in the Peloponnese and those outside it – in the past had dealings with each other more by land than sea, and they passed through the Isthmus. The Corinthians were powerful because of their wealth, as even the early poets illustrate, who gave it the epithet 'wealthy'. When the Greeks took to the sea more, the Corinthians acquired ships and rooted out piracy, and provided a market for both sea and land trade, and the city became powerful from money revenues.

Corinth sent out numerous colonies in the seventh and sixth centuries BC, and none was more successful than Syracuse in Sicily, whose war-like tyrants often held sway over many of the Greek cities on the island, so much so that Pindar could describe the city as a shrine to Ares, the blood-thirsty god of war, where even the horses love to go to war! Pindar, *Pythian Victory Ode*, 2.1–2:

Great city of Syracuse, shrine of Ares, plunged deep in war,
divine raiser of men and horses which exult in the iron of battle.

Sicily became famous for its horses bred on its rich open plains, and one of the main pleasures of Syracuse's tyrants was entering chariot teams in the great contests of the motherland. The poets Pindar and Bacchylides wrote victory odes in their honour. Here Bacchylides praises the tyrant Hieron for his victory in 470 BC at the games held at Delphi (the Pythian games) every four years; the Greeks believed that Delphi in central Greece was the navel of the earth. Hieron did not drive the chariot team himself, but had a trained charioteer to do this. Bacchylides, *Victory Ode*, 4.1–6:

> Golden-haired Apollo
> still loves the Syracusan city
> and honours Hieron, just ruler of his city;
> for the third time beside the navel of the high-cliffed land of Delphi
> he is sung as a Pythian victor
> through the excellence of his swift-footed horses.

Elsewhere, Bacchylides describes Hieron (Bacchylides, *Victory Ode*, 5.1–2): 'General, well endowed by fortune, of the chariot-whirled Syracusans.' Most Greeks may have thought that Delphi was the navel of the earth but for the Athenians their own city was the centre of the universe. One fifth-century comic poet summed it all up. Lysippus, Fragment 8:

> If you haven't seen Athens, you're a blockhead;
> if you've seen her and you're not captivated, a donkey;
> if you love it here but go away, a pack-ass.

The reader may well have gathered by now that the Greeks were not a united race. In fact in Sicily the Greeks spent as much energy fighting among themselves as attacking the natives, the Sicels, and the Carthaginians, who also laid claim to the island. The city-state was an independent unit and, as such, political fragmentation rather than unity was the reality. Although the Greeks were bound together by their common religion, customs and language, there were nevertheless local variations. There were different dialects and accents; the Athenians thought Spartan and Boeotian accents funny. In a fragmentary play of Sophocles, a character, probably Helen, notices and comments on the accent of another speaker. Sophocles, *The Demand for Helen's Return*, Fragment 176:

> Something in his tongue
> addresses me, to detect a Spartan way of talking.

The conflict between Athens and Sparta in the fifth century BC was a case of the clash of two very different societies, with Athens open, democratic and cosmopolitan, a crucible for intellectual activity (though Socrates' execution in 399 BC somewhat qualifies this), while Sparta was closed, conservative, ascetic, militaristic, and xenophobic (even occasionally expelling all foreigners from Sparta). Euripides in his play *Andromache* produced in 425 BC, six years after Sparta declared war on Athens, expressed the hatred that many Athenians must have felt for Sparta during the Peloponnesian War. Euripides, *Andromache*, 445–9:

Inhabitants of Sparta, most hateful of mortals
to all mankind, treacherous schemers, plotters,
masters of falsehoods, skilled contrivers of wrongs,
thinking nothing sound but every thing that is twisted,
unjust is your prosperity in Greece.

But there was much more to this civilisation than political rivalry. In this volume it is the culture of the Greeks that will be explored, examining their society, its beliefs and customs, through the words of the Greeks themselves, and observing the balance that they successfully struck between good and excess. For them, life was to be lived to the full, but there could be too much of a 'good thing'. Pindar, *Hymn*, 35b:

The wise also have praised without qualification the saying,
'Nothing in excess.'

However, the Greeks were not 'prudes', and life was to be enjoyed, as the same author told his *listeners*. Pindar, *Encomion*, 126:

Don't cut back on fun in your life: it's best
by a long shot for a man to have a happy life.

Yes, *listeners*. Much of Greek literature in the archaic and classical periods was not written down to be privately read but to be spoken out loud. Herodotus' massive work of history was originally *read out* in sections to an audience; Pindar composed victory odes to be *sung* at Olympia and other athletic centres, and in the houses of the victors. Homer was *sung* by a skilled bard to an audience that never tired of hearing about the Trojan War, and schoolboys were set the task of memorising his epics. All the great tragedies of Aeschylus, Sophocles and Euripides were *performed* before audiences, whose concerns and fears are reflected in these plays. Much of Greek literature is poetry, considered to be the gift of the nine Muses, goddesses of song and music, who dwelt on Mount Pieria, north of Mount Olympus. Bacchylides, *Victory Ode*, 19.1–8:

An infinite highway
of ambrosial songs there is
for whoever obtains gifts
from the Muses of Mount Pieria,
whose songs   5
the violet-eyed maidens,
the Graces bearing garlands,
dress with honour.

From this 'infinite highway' of poetry, as well as ordinary prose, this volume selects what is hopefully a representative collection of extracts to open up the lives of the Greeks to our scrutiny, using what they themselves wrote to arrive at an understanding of what Greek society and culture was like. It may be the case that 'Man is only breath and shadow' (Sophocles, *Ajax the Locrian*, Fragment 13) but in the case of the Greeks they were a people who have cast a long benevolent shadow over western civilisation and so the world, and whose 'breath' of words continues to fascinate and exert an influence. Despite the distance of time (over 2,750 years in the case of Homer) and an alien yet surprisingly familiar culture, the Greeks do speak to us – in their own words.

ONE

Gods and Mortals

One race of men, one of gods: but from a single mother, Earth,
we both take breath. But a sundering power completely separates us.
For one race is of nothing, but for the other race bronze heaven remains
    a safe haven forever.
Notwithstanding that, our nature is a bit like that of the immortal gods
either in greatness of mind or in our nature,
although we don't know either by day or by night
what course Destiny has inscribed for us to run.

                            Pindar, *Nemean Victory Ode*, 6.1–7.

For the ancient Greeks there was a gulf between the race of immortal gods and that of mortals: one did not know death but the other was well acquainted with it. There was something divine about mortals, however, as the Greeks saw it, in their gifts of intellect and their emotional capacities. But in the classical period there was no possibility that mortals could aspire to divinity, and as the story of Polycrates shows, the gods guarded their prerogatives carefully. For a mortal to become like the gods was an act of hybris ('outrage'), punished by the gods with nemesis ('destruction').

But the gods were not overly negative. They could be supplicated with prayer and sacrifice. The slaughter of animals in a ritual context was in fact the main way in which the Greeks worshipped the gods, who were thought of either as attending the sacrifice itself, or as enjoying the aroma of the cooking while on Mount Olympus, their home. Victims were usually led in procession to the altar, and the frieze of the Parthenon, the main temple on the acropolis of Athens, shows many animals being led to sacrifice (see illustration 1.1).

The relationship between mortals and immortals was in many ways reciprocal. The Greeks believed that the gods expected to be worshipped, but in return mortals could legitimately call upon the gods for assistance, reminding the gods of past favours mortals had done for them. This is precisely how the priest Chryses calls upon Apollo's assistance when the Greeks will not return his daughter to him, as will be seen in the first passage below.

'Gods', of course, implies more than one god, and Greek religion was polytheistic in nature, with numerous deities, each of which tended to have particular areas of speciality. There were twelve main gods, the Olympians, who dwelt on Mount Olympus. Zeus was the chief god, controller of weather, generalissimo of the other gods and protector of guests and strangers (among other things). As Pindar wrote, 'Everything is in the hands of Zeus' (Pindar, *Pythian Victory Ode*, 2.49). His consort was Hera, patron of marriage. Hades and Poseidon, Zeus' brothers, had charge of the underworld and sea respectively, though Poseidon was also the god of horses and earthquakes. Demeter, Zeus' sister, was responsible for agriculture, and was the goddess who presided over the Eleusinian Mysteries with their promise of a better afterlife. Her daughter Persephone was abducted by Hades and became his wife and queen of the underworld. Aphrodite was the goddess of sensuality and sexuality, but also watched over the transition of girls to womanhood. She is often contrasted with Athena, the virgin goddess and protector of Athens, who had martial qualities but was also patron of weaving and crafts. However, the two are shown sitting and chatting amicably, arm in arm, on the east frieze of the Parthenon of the Athenian acropolis.

Apollo was god of prophecy, and also of plagues, and it is his arrows that spread the plague among the Greeks at Troy to punish them for their treatment of Chryses, his priest. Artemis, Apollo's twin sister, was also skilled with arrows; she was a virgin goddess of the hunt, and also the protector of women in childbirth. Hephaestus was the god of metal work, and the Sicilians believed that volcanic Mount Etna was his furnace. Despised among even the gods was Ares, the god of war, delighting in bloodshed and gore, with no real interest in who won or lost. Hermes, with his winged sandals, was the messenger of the gods, but also a trickster and a thief. Other important gods included Dionysus, the god of wine, and Asclepius the healer, while the goddess Hecate presided over sorcery and magic.

There was a general lack of written texts; there was no Hebrew Torah or Christian Bible. Herodotus notes that Homer and Hesiod compiled the stories of the gods, but this was in no sense a theology, or a statement of principles and practices. It is sometimes said that Greek religion was not ethical in orientation; it was not pre-occupied with ideas of good or morality. In fact, some philosophers criticised the ways in which Homer and Hesiod depicted the gods as an anthropomorphic (made in human form) group of adulterous, devious egotists. But the gods were concerned with wickedness, even if their justice might be slow and take several generations to come to fruition. Zeus in particular was the god of justice, and the writings of Hesiod are especially concerned with divine interest in human wrongdoing.

For guidance in various matters, from whether or not to found a colony to how to overcome childlessness, the Greeks resorted directly to the gods. They believed that Zeus communicated his will through the god Apollo, who in turn spoke at Delphi through the medium of a woman priest, the Pythia. Delphi was the most important oracular site in Greece. Trophonius also had an oracle at nearby Lebadea, and in western Greece at Acheron the very souls of the dead themselves could be consulted.

The dead, as Odysseus sees when he consults them, have a miserable existence which only a few can escape, or at least this is the case in the Homeric epics. Death, as in all societies, was the ultimate human tragedy, but even more so when one died before one's time, and for a parent to bury a child, particularly an adult one, was considered (as now) an especially bitter fate. A poignant scene on an Athenian vase shows a deceased boy bidding farewell to his mother and taking his go-cart with him into the afterlife, as Charon the ferryman of dead souls waits in his boat to take him to Hades (see illustration 1.2). But the Eleusinian Mysteries promised the initiated an escape from the dreariness of Hades. While some writers were pessimistic about life and growing old, the Greeks did not have a morbid fascination with death, nor did they engage in any form of fatalism (or nihilism). They enjoyed feasts and games for the gods, and lived their private lives to the full. The gods loved feasting and entertainment and what their lives had to offer, and in this way the gods reflected their human worshippers.

PRAYER AND DIVINE VENGEANCE

The Greeks have been at the walls of Troy for nine years, unsuccessful in their attempts to take the city. The *Iliad* opens in the tenth year with a plague sent by the god Apollo to punish the Greeks (the Achaeans) for the way in which his priest Chryses has been treated. His daughter had been captured by the Greeks in a raid, and was part of Agamemnon's booty. He is the leader of the Greeks, and like Menelaus is the son of Atreus, and hates Calchas the seer for the advice that he gives below. Agamemnon demands that if he gives up the priest's daughter he must have another woman as his prize, and insists that Achilles, the great hero, give up his prize (the woman Brisis) to him. So begins a fearful argument, and Achilles refuses to fight in battle anymore. Homer, *Iliad*, 1.8–32:

Which of the gods brought these two into contention?
It was the son of Leto and Zeus, Apollo, for angry against king
   Agamemnon
he aroused the foul pestilence throughout the army, and the people
   were perishing,

10

for the son of Atreus had dishonoured Chryses, Apollo's priest:
for Chryses came to the swift ships of the Achaeans
bearing a ransom beyond reckoning to free his daughter,
carrying in his hands the ribbons of far-shooting Apollo
on a golden staff, and entreated all the Achaeans,   15
but especially the two sons of Atreus, the marshals of the army:

'Sons of Atreus and you other well-greaved Achaeans,
to you may the gods who have their homes on Olympus grant
that you sack Priam's city, and have a fine return home:
but give back to me my beloved daughter, and take the ransom,   20
honouring Apollo the far-shooting son of Zeus.'

Then all the rest of the Achaeans cried out in agreement,
to honour the priest and to accept the splendid ransom:
but this pleased not the heart of Agamemnon, son of Atreus,
but he sent Chryses harshly away, laying a forceful command
   upon him: 25

'Do not let me, old man, find you by the hollow ships
neither dallying now nor later on coming again,
in case your staff and the ribbons of the god not protect you.
I will not set her free: before that happens old age will befall her
in my house in Argos, far from her father-land   30
plying the loom and sharing my bed.
But leave, do not anger me, so that you may go safer.'

Agamemnon's refusal was to have dire consequences for the Greeks.
Chryses prays to Apollo, who hears his priest. This is the earliest recorded
Greek prayer, and several features of it are important. Chryses addressed
Apollo by his cult epithets (such as Smintheus in line 39), and this was
normal in Greek prayers. The person praying addressed the god, sending
the prayer in the right direction: there were many gods, and the prayer
must go to the right one. More importantly, Chryses reminds the god of
past services; the old priest now, so to speak, calls in his debts. A bronze
statue shows a young man lifting his hands in prayer to the gods
(illustration 1.4). Greek men would not kneel before the gods: that was a
position of worship adopted only by women. The god acknowledges
Chryses' piety, with dreadful consequences for the Greek army. Homer,
Iliad, 1.33–129:

So Agamemnon spoke, and the old man was gripped with fear and
   obeyed his word;
he went silently along the shore of the loud-roaring sea:

and fervently the old man as he went along alone prayed to 35
Lord Apollo, whom lovely-haired Leto bore:

'Hear me, you of the silver bow, who bestrides Chryse
and sacred Cilla, and rule Tenedos in might,
Smintheus, if ever it pleased you that I built your temple,
or if ever I burned to you fat thigh pieces 40
of bulls and of goats, accomplish for me this desire:
let the Danaans repay my tears by your arrows.'

So he spoke praying, and Phoebus Apollo heard him,
and he came down from the peaks of Olympus, angry of heart,
bearing on his shoulders the bow and covered quiver. 45
The arrows rattled on the shoulders of the striding,
wrathful god, and he came like the night.
Then he sat down away from the ships, and loosed an arrow:
a terrible twang resounded from the silver bow.
First he attacked the mules and the swift-footed dogs, 50
and then loosening the piercing arrow against the men themselves
he struck: and the crowded pyres of the corpses burned densely.

Nine days throughout the army the god's arrows flew,
but on the tenth Achilles summoned the people to assembly,
for the white-armed goddess Hera put it into his mind to do so: 55
for she pitied the Danaans, seeing them dying.
And when they were collected together and assembled,
Achilles fleet of foot stood up among them and spoke:

'Son of Atreus, now I think we, driven back,
will return home, if we can escape death, 60
if indeed war and plague alike are to slaughter the Achaeans.
But, come, let us consult a soothsayer or priest,
or even a dream-interpreter, for even a dream comes from Zeus,
who can explain why Phoebus Apollo is so wrathful,
whether he blames us because of an unfulfilled vow or sacrifice, 65
and if perhaps by the aroma of lambs and unblemished goats
he is willing to ward off from us this destruction.'

When he'd finished speaking he sat down at once: and from among
  them
Calchas son of Thestor stood up, the best of the diviners,
who had knowledge of what was, what was to be, and what
  had been, 70
who had guided the Achaean ships into Ilion

through the prophetic arts given to him by Phoebus Apollo.
With good intentions he addressed them, advising so:
'Achilles, loved by Zeus, you ask me to explain
the anger of lord Apollo, who strikes from far away.   75
So I will speak: but take heed and swear to me
that you will willingly defend me with words and hands.
For I think that I will make angry a man who rules
mightily over all the Argives and whom the Achaeans obey.
For a king is too strong when he is angry with a lesser man,   80
and even if on the day itself he swallows down his anger
afterwards he holds a grudge until it finds fulfilment in his heart.
So tell me if you will keep me safe.'

Fleet of foot Achilles said in answer to him:
'Have courage, and speak, whatever prophecy you know.   85
For by Apollo, loved by Zeus, to whom you pray Calchas,
revealing the oracles to the Danaans,
no one while I live and have sight on the earth
will lay heavy hands on you beside the hollow ships,
out of all the Danaans, not even if it is Agamemnon you speak of,   90
who now claims to be by far the best of the Achaeans.'

And then the faultless seer took courage and said:
'It is not because of either a vow or a sacrifice that Apollo blames us,
but because of the priest whom Agamemnon dishonoured,
not giving back his daughter and not accepting the ransom: 95
because of this the far-shooter gives grief and will go on doing so
nor will he drive away the dreadful plague from the Danaans
until we give to the dear father the quick-glancing maiden
without a price-tag, without a ransom, and also lead a sacred
    sacrifice
to Chryse: then we might appease and persuade him.'   100

When he had spoken so he sat down again, and among them
    stood up
heroic, wide-ruling Agamemnon, son of Atreus,
angered: great rage his black soul completely
filled, and his eyes were like blazing fires.
He spoke to Calchas first, his visage baneful: 105

'Seer of evil, not once have you prophesied a good thing to me:
always your heart delights in evil prophecy,
not ever yet have you spoken a propitious word or brought such to
    pass.

And now in the assembly of the Danaans you prophesy that
it is on account of this that the far-shooter afflicts them: 110
because I would not accept the splendid ransom
for the girl Chrysis, since I greatly desire to have her
in my house. For I prefer her over Clytemnestra
my wedded wife, since she is not inferior to her,
neither in build nor in stature, nor in intellect or handiwork. 115
But even so I am willing to give her back, if this is the better course:
for I want my people to be preserved and not perish.
However, get ready for me at once a prize so that not I alone
of the Argives am without one; that would not be fitting:
for all of you are witnesses that my prize goes elsewhere.' 120

Then swift-footed god-like Achilles answered him:
'Most glorious son of Atreus, most acquisitive of men,
how will the great-hearted Achaeans give you a prize?
For we don't know of any common treasure hoard lying around,
but what we captured from the cities is distributed, 125
and it isn't right to take this back from the people.
But now give the girl back to the god Apollo, and the Achaeans
shall repay you three or four times, if ever Zeus
will give us the well-walled city of Troy to sack.'

PRAYER AND SACRIFICE

Achilles has to give up his prize, Brisis, to Agamemnon, and so withdraws
from the fighting in a fit of temper. The Greeks experience several disasters
in battle, and Agamemnon attempts to win him over. The Greek hero
Phoenix attempts to persuade Achilles to accept Agamemnon's gifts and
return to the battle outside Troy. Homer, *Iliad*, 9.499–514:

And mortals with incenses and pious offerings
and with libation and the aroma of the sacrifice 500
supplicating the gods turn their anger aside when anyone might
    transgress and sin.
For Prayers are the daughters of great Zeus,
they are lame, shrivelled, and cast their eyes sideways,
and are mindful to go after Ate, goddess of ruin and sin,
Ate, both mighty and swift of feet, who so greatly 505
outdistances the Prayers, arriving first in every land
harming men: and the Prayers come after as healers.
He who shall revere these daughters of Zeus as they approach near,
him they will greatly advantage, and they hear his prayers:

but if someone denies and stubbornly refuses them,   510
departing, they pray to Zeus son of Cronus
that Ate will at once follow him, so that being hurt he might pay the
    penalty.
So, Achilles, grant you also that the daughters of Zeus receive
honour, such as bends the mind of other good men.

Telemachus has come to 'sandy Pylus' to find out any information he can
about his father Odysseus and his return from Troy. There he finds Nestor
on the beach sacrificing black bulls to Poseidon. Nestor entertains him; the
next day at dawn another sacrifice, this time to Athena, is held before
Telemachus sets out for Sparta to visit Menelaus and see if he also has any
news of Odysseus. The lustral water was used to wash the hands of the
main presider over the sacrifice (line 440); here the barley in the basket was
tossed on the victim's head to make it nod, so assenting to its own
destruction: the gods were not pleased with unwilling victims. These details
of sacrifices are shown on numerous Greek vases (see illustration 1.3). It
was often the duty of young girls to carry this basket. The horns of the
victim could be covered in gold foil so that the beast had a more pleasing
appearance. In the museum at Delphi, the remains of gold foil that covered
an entire beast can be seen: a magnificent offering to the god there, Apollo.
Homer, *Odyssey*, 3.430–63, 470–2:

So Nestor commanded, and they all scampered to their tasks. The
    cow was brought   430
from the plain, and from the even-keeled, swift ship
came the companions of great-hearted Telemachus; the smith arrived
carrying in his arms his bronze tools, the gear of his trade,
anvil and hammer and the well-made tongs
with which he worked the gold. And Athena came   435
to receive the sacrifice. And the old charioteer Nestor dished out
the gold. The smith prepared and fashioned it over the horns of
    the cow
so that the goddess would delight when she saw the offering.
And Stratius and god-like Echephron led the cow by its horns.
And Aretus came from the storeroom carrying the lustral water
    for them   440
in a bowl decorated with flowers, and in his other hand barley grain
in a basket. Thrasymedes, staunch in battle, stood ready
with the sharp axe in his hands to cut down the cow.
And Perseus held the bowl to catch the blood. The old charioteer
    Nestor

commenced the sacrifice, washing his hands and sprinkling the
   barley.   445
Praying earnestly to Athena he made a first offering of hairs from the
   cow's head, throwing them into the fire.

Now when they had prayed and strewn the barley grain over the
   beast,
immediately Thrasymedes, the high-hearted son of Nestor, standing
   near
struck the blow: the axe severed the tendons of the neck, and loosed
the strength of the cow. The women screamed the sacrificial
   ululation,   450
both the daughters and daughters-in-law and the venerable wife of
   Nestor,
Eurydice, the oldest of the daughters of Clymenus.
And then the men lifted the cow from the broad-wayed earth and
   held it
as Peisistratus, leader of men, cut its throat. And when
the black blood had flowed from her, and the life fled the bones,   455
they quickly butchered the carcass, and immediately sliced out the
   thighs,
doing everything in proper order, and covered them,
making a double layer of fat, and arranged raw flesh on them.
Then the old man burned this on shavings of wood and poured
   sparkling wine
over them: the young men beside him held five-pronged forks in
   their hands.   460
But when the thighs were completely consumed in the flames and
   they had tasted the entrails,
they carved the rest up into pieces and placed it on spits,
roasting it, holding the pointed spits in their hands.   463

Now when they had roasted the outer flesh and drawn it off
   the spits,   470
they sat down and fell to the feast: and high-hearted men waited
on them, pouring wine into golden goblets.

Hesiod gives advice on the importance of approaching the gods in
prayer with clean hands: Hesiod, *Works and Days*, 724–6:

Don't ever pour a libation of sparkling wine after dawn with unwashed
   hands

to Zeus nor to any other of the immortal gods: 725
for they will not give ear to you, but will spit your prayers back
    at you.

Sacrifices established a relationship between the worshippers and the gods.
Some argued that they could do much more, but Plato is critical of practices
that claim a greater efficacy for sacrifices. Plato, *Republic*, 364b–5a:

(364b) But the most amazing of all these stories concern the gods and
virtue, and how it is the gods who consign misfortunes and a wretched
life to many good men, and the opposite fate to wicked men. Begging
priests and soothsayers knock on the doors of the wealthy, persuading
them that sacrifices and incantations have furnished them with power
from the gods, so that any wrong which he himself has committed, or his
ancestors, (364c) can be atoned for through pleasant festivals, and also if
he wishes to harm an enemy for a small price he will be able to harm
both just and unjust alike, with magic lore and binding spells, with which
they claim they can persuade the gods to serve them. And for all these
claims they quote evidence from the poets, and about the easiness of
doing wrong they cite Hesiod:

Wrong can be chosen easily and in plenty
(364d) the road to her is smooth, and she lives nearby:
but the gods have placed sweat on the road of virtue,

and a certain long, steep road. Others quote Homer as a witness to the
misleading of gods by men, since he also wrote:

The gods themselves are moved by prayers
and men entreating with sacrifices and appeasing vows
(364e) and libations and the aroma of burnt sacrifices turn aside the
    wrath
of the gods whenever anyone has transgressed and sinned.

And they pull out a host of books by Orpheus and Musaeus, descendants
as they claim of the Moon and the Muses, which they employ in their
rituals, persuading not just individuals but also cities that there are both
remissions and purifications from wrong-doings through sacrifices and
pleasant enjoyments for those still living, (365a) and also for the dead,
which they call initiations, which deliver us from evil in the hereafter, but
that a terrible fate is in store for those who haven't sacrificed.

Greek religion was based on the assumption that the gods did have an
individual relationship with those who honoured them, and did come to

their worshippers' assistance in return for prayer, sacrifice and reverence. Menander here places in the mouth of a character a deliberate satire on philosophic ideas about the gods. Menander, *The Arbitrators*, 1084–99:

Onesimus: Do you think that the gods lead such a leisured existence
as to apportion bad and good daily   1085
to each person, Smicrines?

Smicrines: What are you saying?

Onesimus: I'll show you clearly. There are, to speak in rough figures,
all up one thousand cities. In each of these
there lives thirty thousand men. Can the gods
punish or preserve each one of them? How?   1090
That would make the life of the gods hard work.
You'll ask: 'Don't the gods spare us a thought?'
They've given to abide with each man a guardian:
his character. This is on duty inside us,
punishing those who treat it badly   1095
and guarding those who treat it well. This is our god,
the one responsible for each man's doing
good or bad. In order to prosper,
please it by doing nothing harmful or stupid.

THE SOULS OF THE DEAD AND THE UNDERWORLD

The suitors for Penelope's hand, who had wooed her in Odysseus' absence, have been slain by him on his return to his home. The psyche (the soul or spirit) of each is now guided by Hermes to Hades. Elsewhere (but not in this passage) he is called Hermes Psychopompus, the 'soul leader'. Homer, *Odyssey*, 24.1–18:

Hermes summoned the souls of the suitors.
He held in his hands his beautiful golden wand
with which he enchants the eyes of those he wishes,
while others he awakens from their sleep.
Rousing the souls with this he led them, and they followed with
      shrill cries.   5
As when bats in the depths of a wondrous cave
fly about crying shrilly, when one of them has fallen from the
chain of bats on the rock, with which they cling to each other,
so the souls went with him crying shrilly: and Hermes the Healer
led them down through the dank pathways.   10

They journeyed past the streams of Ocean, and the White Rock,
and went by the gates of the Sun and the land of dreams,
and quickly arrived at the field of asphodel
where dwell the souls, phantoms of men whose toil has ended.
Here they came upon the soul of Achilles, son of Peleus   15
and Patroclus and Antilochus without rival
and of Ajax, who best was in appearance and build
out of all the Greeks, next after the peerless son of Peleus.

Zeus made a race of heroes, who fought at Troy: some went down to Hades, but others had a happier afterlife, and were physically assumed ('translated') to a better place, the Isles of the Blessed, where they enjoyed a utopian immortality. Hesiod, *Works and Days*, 168–73:

To others father Zeus, son of Cronus, settled at the ends of the earth
and gave life and habitation unlike that of men,
and there they live with untroubled heart   170
in the Isles of the Blessed along the shore of deep-eddying Ocean,
contented heroes, for whom honey-sweet fruit
the grain-yielding fields bear copiously thrice a year.

The sorceress Circe advises Odysseus that before proceeding on his homeward journey he must consult the spirits of the dead at Acheron, in order to speak to Teiresias the seer. Although the actual ritual here described by Homer does not appear to have been practised by the Greeks of classical times, there was an oracle of the dead at Acheron (in southern Epirus on the west coast of northern Greece), where consultants called up the dead and received advice. The ruins of the nekyomanteion, oracle of the dead, can still be seen there. The remains of metal machinery there were once thought to have been part of an elaborate contrivance used by the priests to fake the appearances of ghosts, but the metal pieces have now been identified as catapault parts. The Greeks did not need to fabricate their religion in any way. The black ram is typical of the black-animal offerings often made to the deities of the underworld (line 33). Erebus is the place of the dead (line 37); Aeaea was the island of Circe (line 70). Here Odysseus describes his consultation. Homer, *Odyssey*, 11.23–80:

Here Perimedes and Eurylochus held the victims,
and I, drawing the sharp sword from beside my thigh,
dug a pit, a cubit in length in both directions,   25
and poured around it a libation to all the dead,

first one of honey mixed in milk, and after that one of sweet wine,
and the third of water. And over it I sprinkled white barley.
Fervently I implored the feeble heads of the dead,
that returning to Ithaca I would sacrifice in my palace a cow   30
that had not calved, the best I had, and pile up the altar with fine
    gifts,
and that separately to Teiresias alone I would sacrifice a ram,
completely black, the prize ram of my flocks.
And when with both vows and prayers I had supplicated
the tribes of the dead, taking the sheep I slit their throats   35
over the pit, and their dark-coloured blood flowed. The souls
of the dead who have gone below gathered from out of Erebus:
brides and young unmarried men and old men worn out with toil,
and tender virgins with hearts bearing fresh sorrow,
and many wounded with bronze spears, men slain in war   40
wearing their battle-gear stained with gore.
These crowded around the pit on all sides
with unspeakable shrieking: and pale terror gripped me.
Then I urged on and ordered my companions
to skin the sheep, those that lay there slaughtered   45
with the pitiless bronze, and to burn them, and to pray to the gods,
to mighty Hades and his consort dread Persephone.
Myself, drawing the sharp sword from beside my thigh, I
squatted there, not allowing the feeble heads of the dead
to come nearer the blood, until I had questioned Teiresias.   50

The first to come was the soul of my companion Elpenor:
for not yet had he been buried beneath the broad earth
for we had left his corpse behind in Circe's palace,
and he was unmourned and unburied, since another task urged
    us on.
When I saw him I burst into tears, and my heart pitied him,   55
and I spoke out loud to him, addressing him with winged words:

'Elpenor, how did you come under the murky gloom?
You've come quicker on foot than I in my black ship.'

I said this, and groaning he answered me with a word: 'Son
    of Laertes,
Odysseus of the many ruses, sprung from the race of Zeus,   60
an evil destiny of a god undid me, and immeasurable wine.
When I had laid down on Circe's palace roof to sleep, I didn't think
when I went to descend back down the long ladder,

but fell straight off the roof: and my neck
was broken off the spine, and my soul fled down to Hades.   65

Now I beg you, by those we left behind, who are not present,
by your wife and father, who reared you as a baby,
and Telemachus, your son, whom you left an only child in your
   palace:
for I know that going from here, out of the house of Hades,
you will put in again at Circe's island of Aeaea in your well-built
   ship: 70
there, then, I call upon you lord not to forget me.
Don't abandon me unmourned and unwept, going and departing
from there, in case I become a cause of wrath to you from the gods,
but burn me in my armour, whatever is mine,
and pile up a memorial for me, by the shore of the olive-grey sea,   75
and for those that will come after, to learn of me, a wretched man.
Complete these things for me, and plant my oar on the mound,
with which I rowed when I was alive among my companions.'
He said this, and I replying said to him,
'Wretched man, I'll complete and do all these things.'   80

Odysseus' mother comes up, but she cannot recognise her son; he cries
and is full of pity for her: she was alive when he left for Troy but died
during his travels. Nevertheless he will not let her taste the blood until
he speaks to Teiresias. The seer makes many predictions, and then
Odysseus asks how he might speak to his mother; she refers to the
practice of cremation (line 220). Homer, *Odyssey*, 11.140–53:

But come, tell me this Teiresias, and answer truthfully: 140
I see the soul of my departed mother:
she is sitting quietly near the blood, and doesn't
deign to see or talk to her own son.
Tell me, lord, how can she recognise that it is me?'

So I spoke, and he answered me in reply: 145
'Easy is the word that I will say, and will place in your mind.
Whomever of the dead who have gone below you'll allow
to draw near the blood, that one will speak to you truthfully,
and to whom you begrudge this, he will then go back again.'

Having said this the soul of lord Teiresias went within   150
the house of Hades, when he had spoken his prophecies:
then I waited there, steadfast, until my mother came
to drink the dark-coloured blood. At once she recognised me.

Odysseus and his mother exchange news, and she reassures him of his wife's faithfulness. He tries three times to embrace his mother, and fails; in his distress he asks her why this is so. Homer, *Odyssey*, 11.204–22:

> But I was troubled in my mind and wished
> to embrace the soul of my departed mother.   205
> Three times I lunged towards her, my heart desiring to grasp her,
> three times out of my hands like a shadow or a dream
> she flew. And the pain grew sharper within my heart,
> and I spoke to her, addressing her with winged words:
>
> 'My mother, why don't you now remain still for me, desiring to
>   embrace you,   210
> so that even in the house of Hades we might throw our loving arms
> around each other and have our fill of chill lamenting?
> Or is this just a phantom which dread Persephone conjures up for me
> so that I might mourn and groan still more?'
>
> I said this, and immediately my stately mother replied: 215
> 'Ah me, my child, ill-fated above all other men,
> Persephone the daughter of Zeus doesn't cheat you in any way,
> but this is the natural way for mortals, when one dies.
> For no longer do the sinews keep the flesh and bones together,
> but the mighty prowess of the blazing fire conquers   220
> as soon as the spirit leaves the white bones,
> and the spirit like a dream flits about and flies away.

Odysseus goes on to speak to other souls of the dead. After this, he sees the torture chambers of hell. In mainstream Greek religion, the dead were not punished for the sins of this life. For all alike, except for particular heroes, a dreary existence in the afterlife was their lot. The main exception were the initiates in the Eleusinian Mysteries, who were thought to have a happy existence after death. But there were several mythical figures punished in Hades. In the *Odyssey*, Tityus, Tantalus and Sisyphus are all subjected to various tortures of a refined kind. All had violated Zeus' laws and these figures and their punishments were meant as a warning to others. Tantalus is 'tantalised' for eternity. Homer, *Odyssey*, 11.576–600:

> I saw Tityus, son of glorious Earth,
> lying on the ground, stretched over nine acres,
> and two vultures sat on either side tearing at his liver, plunging inside
> his bowels, and he could not beat them away with his hands.

For he had accosted Leto, the glorious consort of Zeus, as she   580
journeyed through Panopeus of the beautiful countryside, toward
   Pytho.

And I saw Tantalus enduring strong torments,
standing in a pool with the water nearly up to his chin.
Parched, he would make as if to drink, but he could not take and
   drink any:
for as often as the old man stooped desiring to drink,   585
as often would the water disappear, sucked away, and at his feet
the black earth would appear, dried up by some divine power.
And trees, their foliage high up, produced abundant fruit above
   his head,
pear, pomegranate and apple trees with their shiny fruit,
and sweet fig and flourishing olive trees: 590
but as often as the old man stretched out with his hands to
   grasp them
the wind tossed them to the shadowy clouds.

And I also saw Sisyphus enduring strong torments,
lifting up a gigantic boulder with both hands.
Truly, with both hands and feet braced against   595
the boulder he would push it up to the crest of a hill, but then
   whenever
it was about to roll over the top, then its mighty weight turned it
   back again:
then again to the level ground the ruthless stone rolled.
But he would again strain, pushing it up, and the sweat
rolled down his limbs, and a cloud of dust rose over his head.   600

The tyrant Periander of Corinth also consulted the oracle of the dead at
Acheron (as had Odysseus), and the spirit of his dead wife gave him
information about some money that he had buried but the location of
which he had forgotten. He had killed his wife, then slept with her.
Herodotus, 5.92η1–4:

(5.92η1) In a single day Periander stripped all the women of Corinth
because of his wife Melissa. (5.92η2) Periander had sent envoys to the
oracle of the dead on the river Acheron in Thesprotia about a deposit of
money which a friend had left in his care, but the ghost of his wife
Melissa said that she would not by sign or word reveal where in the
ground the deposit lay. For she was both cold and naked: the clothes he
had buried with her had not been burned and so were of no use to her.

And she said the witness to the truth of what she said was that Periander had put his loaves into a cold oven.

(5.92η3) When this was reported back to Periander by the envoys the token (of the loaves and bread) was true for him, as he had slept with Melissa's corpse. He immediately, after receiving the message, issued a proclamation that every woman in Corinth should come to the temple of Hera. The women rushed to the temple in their best clothes as if to a festival, and Periander, who had secretly posted some of his guards, had them all stripped, every one of them – both freeborn women and servants – and their clothes collected into a pit and burnt, while he prayed to Melissa. (5.92η4) When he had done this he sent a second message, and the ghost of Melissa revealed in what place the deposit lay.

VIEWS ON THE AFTERLIFE

Here is a pessimistic outlook on life, which is evident in other Greek writing as well: it is best not to be born at all, but if one is born, die and get to Hades as quickly as possible. Theognis, 425–8:

It's best of all not to be born upon the earth
and not to behold the rays of the penetrating sun;
but if born, to pass as quickly as possible through the gates of Hades
and to lie under a great mound of heaped-up earth.

Sophocles sees the Eleusinian Mysteries as an escape for the dead from the dreariness of Hades and, negatively, that for those who have not been initiated, Hades 'is evil'. The Eleusinian Mysteries were secret rites, not to be divulged under penalty of death. The goddess Demeter promised the initiates a happy afterlife, completely different from that of the other souls in Hades as seen by Odysseus. Sophocles, Fragment 837:

Three times blessed are those mortal men who having seen these rites
journey to the halls of Hades. These alone
have life there, for others everything there is wretched.

Those who have seen the rites of the Eleusinian Mysteries will fare better than others in Hades (Pindar refers to the rites as 'these things'). Pindar, Fragment 137:

Blessed is anyone who goes under the earth having seen these things:
he knows the end of life,
he knows its Zeus-given beginnings.

Pindar, however, has several other ideas about the afterlife. This version is quite idyllic. (Some of the text is missing in line 4.) Pindar, *Threnos*, 7:

> They below enjoy the strength of the sun
> while it is night-time here,
> and in meadows scarlet with roses before their city
> . . . there is the shade of incense trees, and trees laden with golden
>   fruit;
> some with horses and others in athletic feats, some with draughts
> and others with the lyre do amuse themselves,
> and among them absolute happiness flowers, flourishing
> while perfumes waft over the beloved place,
> and always they mingle incense of various kinds
> with fire seen from afar on the altars of the gods.

Pindar in this passage describes an afterlife that might simply be the work of his imagination, involving a cycle of six existences, three on earth and three in Hades, which results – if the individual has the strength and courage to avoid committing injustice – in an existence in a land where the sun never sets. Pindar, *Olympian Victory Ode*, 2.57–76:

> The helpless spirits of the dead immediately pay the penalty there
> as the sins committed in this realm of Zeus here
> are judged by one under the earth
> pronouncing judgement with hateful necessity.   60
>
> But for eternity good men have the sun
> during both day and night of equal length
> and receive a life of lesser toil, not troubling the earth
> or the water of the sea with the strength of their hand
> for the sake of a paltry livelihood, but those who happily kept
>   their oaths   65
> spend a tearless aeon dwelling in the presence of the gods
> but the others endure not-to-be-looked-upon toil.
>
> As many as have the strength to abide three times in Hades and on
>   earth
> keeping their soul pure from all wrongful deeds
> journey the road of Zeus to the tower of his father Cronus   70
> where the winds of ocean blow around the Isles of the Blessed
> and flowers blaze of gold, some of them from glossy trees on dry
>   land
> others nourished by the water –

they weave these into chains for their hands, and garlands,
doing so in obedience to the strict counsels of Rhadamanthys 75
whom the great father Cronus keeps ready at hand.

Sophocles reflects the notion of a dismal afterlife, the general lack of a
belief in reincarnation and the need to remember that 'you only live once'.
Sophocles, *Acrisius*, Fragment 67:

My child, life is a gift sweeter than any other:
for it isn't possible for the same person to die twice.

Anacreon was not keen to die and refers to the fear of old people when
death is at the door. Tartarus came to mean Hades, but originally was an
abyss beneath Hades itself. Anacreon, 395:

Grey indeed are my temples
and my head white,
the gracefulness of younger years
is with me no longer, aged are my teeth,
and not many years 5
remain of sweet life.
That is why I let tears fall
often, fearing Tartarus,
for the dark corner of Hades is dreadful
and the road descending to it perilous: 10
for without a doubt
whoever goes down does not come up again.

Life is a festival, but one can outstay one's welcome. Menander,
Fragment 871:

Think of the time of which I speak
as a festival, the time we spend above:
the crowd, the market-place, thieves, gamblers, amusements:
best to be the first to return to your lodgings –
you'll have spending money and no enemy.
The one who spends a longer time grows weary and is ruined,
grows old miserably and becomes poor;
he wanders about finding enemies, is plotted against from somewhere
    or other
and doesn't die a happy death when his time is up.

FUNERALS AND MOURNING

Achilles has killed Hector for slaughtering his beloved companion Patroclus, and has humiliated Hector's corpse by dragging it in the dust. Returning to the ships and to the body of Patroclus, Achilles holds a feast around his friend's corpse, stretching out Hector's naked body in the dust before it. After the feasting, Achilles lays down for the night and the spirit of Patroclus appears to him. The Myrmidons were Achilles' men (line 60). Homer, *Iliad*, 23.30–4, 59–107:

Many sleek bulls struggled around the iron as they were
    slaughtered,   30
many sheep and bleating goats,
and many white-tusked swine rolling with fat
were stretched out and singed over the flame of Hephaestus:
and all around the corpse the blood could be scooped up in cups.   34

The son of Peleus, Achilles, lay down along the shore of the thundering
    sea,
groaning heavily among the many Myrmidons   60
in an open space, where the surf crashed on the shore:
when sleep overwhelmed him, loosening the sorrows of his heart,
sweetly pouring around him – for his glistening limbs were very weary
from chasing Hector toward blustery Ilion –
there appeared to him the ghost of wretched Patroclus,   65
in every way resembling him, in size, beautiful eyes,
and voice, and the very clothes he wore on his body:
and he stood over Achilles' head, and spoke a word to him.

'Ah Achilles, you sleep, and you have forgotten me.
You were not so careless of me while I lived, but now are so in
    death: 70
bury me as soon as possible, so I will enter the gates of Hades.
The spirits, the phantoms of men whose toil has ended, keep me at a
    distance,
not yet will they allow me to join them beyond the river Styx,
but I wander in vain through the wide-gated house of Hades.
I beg you with my tears, give me your hand, for not ever again   75
will I return from Hades, when once you have given me the rites of the
    funeral fire.
For never again living, sitting apart from our dear companions
will we make plans together, but for me the hateful fate
allotted to me at birth has opened its jaws,
and you also have your own destiny, god-like Achilles,   80

to be killed under the wall of the prosperous Trojans.
There is another matter which I'll speak of and put to you, if you'll listen
   to me.

Don't bury my bones separately from yours, Achilles,
but together, just as we were raised in your house,
when Menoetius brought me from Opoeis as a little boy   85
to your house because of a baneful manslaughter,
on the day I killed the son of Amphidamus;
I was only a child, and did not do it intentionally, being angry over a
   game of dice.
There the horseman Peleus received me into his dwelling
and raised me carefully and named me your servant.   90
So also let the one golden two-handled urn,
the one your lady mother gave you, enclose together the bones of us
   two.'

Then swift-footed Achilles answered him:
'Why do you come to me here, beloved head,
and order me to do each of these things? But I certainly will   95
accomplish everything for you, and I will obey as you command.
Yet, stand closer to me: let's embrace each other even if just
for a little while, and take our fill of pitiful mourning.'

Saying this he reached out with his loving arms,
but couldn't embrace him: the spirit crying shrilly went back   100
under the earth like a wisp of smoke. Achilles leapt up in amazement,
clapped his hands together, and spoke a word of mourning:

'Ah, how strange, there is something even in the house of Hades,
a spirit and an image, though the mind is not at all in it.
For the whole night the spirit of wretched Patroclus   105
has stood over me both weeping and wailing,
and instructed me about each thing, and it was amazing how like to him
   it was.'

'The greatest funeral of them all' would be an apt description for
Alexander's mourning for his friend Hephaestion; it can be compared to
that of Achilles for Patroclus. But Alexander had much greater resources at
his disposal, and the mourning was clearly extravagant. Hephaestion died
in 324 BC at Ecbatana, halfway between the Caspian Sea and the Persian
Gulf, nearly 1,000 km from the coast of Asia Minor (now Turkey).
Asclepius was the god of healing (7.14.5); Arrian mentions the story of the
Hellespont, which Xerxes punished because a storm there destroyed his

bridge of boats across it in his invasion of Greece (7.14.5). The oracle of Ammon at Siwah in Egypt had previously declared Alexander a god, but denied the same status to Hephaestion (7.14.7). Alexander's mourning was clearly excessive by classical Greek standards: the Greeks would lay a corpse out for mourning while it was still at home. Women were the most energetic and vocal mourners, while men were meant to mourn quietly and with restraint (see illustration 1.5). Arrian, *The Expedition of Alexander*, 7.14.1–10:

(7.14.1) At Ecbatana Alexander performed a sacrifice, as was his usual practice after some favourable outcome, and also held an athletic and musical competition, and had an orgy of drinking with his companions. It was at this time that Hephaestion became sick. On the seventh day of his illness they say that the stadium was crowded, for there were athletic contests for boys on that day. But when Alexander was told that Hephaestion was very sick, he quickly left, but when he reached him, Hephaestion was no longer alive.

(7.14.2) Different historians have written different things about Alexander's grief. All writers relate one thing: his mourning was great. As to his actions, the writers differ, depending on whether they are in favour of Hephaestion or bear hatred towards him, or even against Alexander himself. (7.14.3) Of those who narrated scandalous accounts of the mourning, some seem to me to have thought such things as Alexander did or spoke out of excessive grief for his most loved of all men to be to his credit, others that it was to his discredit and not fitting for a king or Alexander.

Some write that for most of the day he lay on top of the body of his friend weeping, and would not be separated from him, until his companions dragged him off by force. (7.14.4) Others write that he lay on the body all day and night. Still others write that he hanged the doctor Glaucias for giving Hephaestion a noxious drug, others that Glaucias saw Hephaestion drinking far too much but did nothing about it. I don't find it implausible that Alexander cut his hair in memory of the dead, and various other things, in imitation of Achilles, with whom – ever since he was a boy – he had felt a sense of rivalry. (7.14.5) Some also write that Alexander himself drove the cart in which the body was carried, but I myself put no faith in such a statement. Others say that he ordered the shrine of Asclepius at Ecbatana to be completely obliterated, something a barbarian might do but in no way worthy of Alexander, but rather of Xerxes' arrogance toward the divine and the chains which they say he let down into the Hellespont, to punish it, so to speak.

(7.14.6) But something else written down seems to me not completely outside the bounds of the probable: when Alexander went to Babylon, several ambassadors from Greece met him on the way, and there were some ambassadors from Epidaurus among these. They got what they wanted from Alexander, and he gave them a dedication to take to Asclepius, but he did say, 'Asclepius has not been fair to me, he didn't save my friend, who I held as dear as my own life.' (7.14.7) Most write that he commanded that sacrifices always be made to Hephaestion as a hero. Others say that he sent to the oracle of the god Ammon in Egypt enquiring if he permitted sacrifice to Hephaestion as to a god. But the god refused.

(7.14.8) The following, however, is agreed to by all. For three days after Hephaestion's death Alexander didn't taste food or take care of himself, but lay either weeping or silently grieving. He ordered Hephaestion's pyre to be prepared in Babylon at a cost of ten thousand talents, though some writers say even more. (7.14.9) He commanded mourning to be made throughout the entire territory of the barbarians. Many of Alexander's companions out of respect for him dedicated both themselves and their armour to the dead Hephaestion. Eumenes was the first to commence this practice; he (of whom I said a little earlier) had argued with Hephaestion, and did this so that Alexander might not think that he was happy that Hephaestion had died.

(7.14.10) Alexander did not appoint anyone to take Hephaestion's place as commander of the cavalry made up of Alexander's companions, so that Hephaestion's name would not disappear from the squadron, but it was still called 'Hephaestion's Squadron', and the image made of Hephaestion would still be carried before it. Alexander made plans for athletic and musical contests with a great crowd of competitors; these were more conspicuous in the amount of money lavished on them than any held previously, for he made arrangements for a total of three thousand competitors. And these, a short time later, they say, competed at Alexander's own funeral.

The death of Alexander the Great in 323 BC provoked a revolt by the Greeks against the Macedonians, in the so-called Lamian War, in which Athens and Aetolia led the Greeks. The Macedonians were victorious in 322 BC. The Athenian orator and politician Hyperides composed and spoke the eulogy for the Athenian dead. Hyperides, 6, *Funeral Oration*, 41–3:

(6.41) It is no doubt perhaps difficult to offer words of sympathy to those enduring such sufferings as these. For griefs are not lulled by speech or law, but each man's nature and the love he had for the departed define the extent of grief. Nevertheless, we have to take courage, and withdraw from grief as much as possible, and bear in mind not only the death of those who have died, but also the virtue which they have left behind as their heritage. (6.42) For if they have suffered things worthy of our lamentation, they have earned the greatest of praises. If they have not shared in a ripe old age, they have achieved instead a glory that is timeless, and are also supremely fortunate. For as many of them as were childless when they died, the praises of the Greeks will be immortal children for them. And as many as have left children behind, their country's goodwill will serve their children as a guardian. (6.43) Moreover if death is like not existing, they have been set free from the bondage of sicknesses and griefs and of all the other things which assault our human existence. But if in Hades we have perception, and are looked after by some god, as we are given to understand, surely those who lost their lives coming to the aid of the gods' worship when it was being threatened will receive the greatest solicitude from the god.

INSCRIPTIONS ON GRAVES

Inscriptions on graves in modern western cemeteries are sometimes confined to simply a name and the relevant dates, of birth and death, of the deceased, though sometimes more information is supplied. Greek grave inscriptions could be similarly short, but sometimes did give some details about the deceased. An example of a brief one is Xenwares of Tiryns in the Peloponnese, dating to the sixth century BC, whose name was inscribed on a column (set up on his grave) which 'speaks' to the reader. P. Friedländer, *Epigrammata. Greek Inscriptions in Verse* (London, 1948), no. 1: 'I am the column of Xenwares, son of Meixis, placed on his grave.' Some funerary inscriptions offer some autobiographical information, such as this tomb inscription from Corinth, of the sixth century BC. Friedländer, *Epigrammata*, no. 2: 'This is the grave-mound of Dweinias, whom the insatiable sea destroyed.' From the island of Corcyra off western Greece from the sixth century BC comes this inscription praising a dead warrior. Friedländer, *Epigrammata*, no. 25:

> This is the tomb of Arniadas. Bright-eyed Ares destroyed him
> fighting by the ships at the streams of the Aratthus
> showing great valour among the groans and shouts.

From Athens in the middle of the sixth century BC the tombstone of another soldier killed in war addresses the passer-by, and urges him to work hard. Friedländer, *Epigrammata*, no. 135:

Whether he is a man from this city or a stranger coming from elsewhere
let him lament before he passes by for Tetichus, a good man,
overcome in battle destroying the prime of his youth:
after bitterly lamenting this, go on to good tasks.

HYBRIS, NEMESIS, AND POLYCRATES' RING

Only the gods were meant to be all-successful, and even they, including
Zeus, did not always get their own way. Polycrates rebelled against the
Persians, became tyrant of Samos (532–522 BC) and ruled over several
other Aegean islands. He repelled an attack by the Spartans, who had a
habit of deposing tyrants throughout Greece and installing pro-Spartan
oligarchies. He concluded an alliance with Amasis, King of Egypt, and they
exchanged presents. The Persians eventually tricked Polycrates into coming
to the mainland, where they crucified him. The story of Polycrates and the
ring is justly famous, and finds many parallels in European folklore. The
tale is not meant to be historical, and it is doubtful that Amasis
corresponded with Polycrates about his success. But it is didactic and
moralising, warning of the dangers of hybris and the god's jealousy of
mortals who through great success become god-like. Herodotus,
3.40.1–43.2:

(3.40.1) Now, somehow the great good fortune of Polycrates did not
escape Amasis' notice, and he was concerned about it. And when even
more good-fortune still occurred to Polycrates, Amasis wrote this on
papyrus and sent it to Samos:

> 'Amasis says this to Polycrates. (3.40.2) It is a pleasure to learn that a
> friend and ally is prospering. But your outstanding successes don't
> please me, as I know how jealous the gods are and so I wish both for
> myself, and those I hold dear to me, that in some things they have
> good fortune but that in others they might stumble, and in this way to
> pass through life with its ups and downs, rather than achieving
> everything with good fortune. (3.40.3) For I know from what I've
> heard in conversation that there is no one who didn't finally come to
> an utterly bad end after having an unbroken chain of success. Now, be
> guided by me and do as follows about your good fortune: (3.40.4)
> think of whatever you might find to be most valuable to you and at
> the loss of which you will be particularly grieved in your soul, and
> throw this thing away so that it will no longer come among men. If
> after this your successes do not occur alternating with disasters, make
> amends in the way prescribed by me.'

(3.41.1) Polycrates, reading the letter and taking into consideration that Amasis had given him good advice, sought for which of his valuables would grieve him most if it was lost, and looking around found this: he had a seal-ring which he wore, an emerald stone set in gold, the work of Theodorus son of Telecles of Samos. (3.41.2) So when he had made the decision to throw this away, he did as follows: he fully manned a fifty-oared ship and went on board, and then ordered them to put out to sea. And when the ship was some distance from Samos, taking off the seal-ring he hurled it into the sea, in full view of everyone who was sailing with him. When he'd done this he sailed back to the island, and when he got home he grieved at his misfortune.

(3.42.1) But on the fifth or sixth day after this, it so happened that these events occurred to him. A fisherman landing a large and magnificent fish thought it good enough to give to Polycrates as a present. Carrying it to the doors of Polycrates' palace, he said that he wanted an audience with him, and when he was granted this he said, giving him the fish, (3.42.2) 'O king, when I landed this fish I didn't think it right to take it to market, even though I am only a working man (and could do with the money), but I thought that it was good enough for both you and your kingship. So carrying the fish here, I give it to you.' Polycrates was delighted with his sentiments, and replied as follows:

'You have done very well and I am doubly grateful, for both the words and the gift, and I invite you to dinner.' (3.42.3) And the fisherman, considering this to be a great honour, went home. But the palace servants, cutting the fish open, found in its gut the seal-ring of Polycrates. (3.42.4) When they saw it they quickly took it, bearing it joyfully to Polycrates, and giving him the seal-ring they told him how it had been found. As he saw the hands of the gods in this, he wrote in a letter everything that he had done, and what had happened to him, and having written this dispatched it to Egypt.

(3.43.1) When Amasis read the letter that came from Polycrates, he realised that it was impossible for someone to rescue another man from his intended destiny, and that Polycrates, having good fortune in all things even to regaining what he had thrown away, was destined to come to a bad end. (3.43.2) He sent a messenger to Samos, to Polycrates, and said that he was breaking off their alliance. He did this so that when a catastrophic and enormous misfortune overtook Polycrates, Amasis himself might not feel grief in his soul, as he would if he had still been a close friend.

SORCERY AND MAGIC

Telemachus, Odysseus' son, has arrived at the palace of Menelaus and Helen in Sparta; the company becomes saddened, thinking of what may have become of Odysseus. Helen decides to cheer them up by administering a potion in their drinks. There is no real evidence that the Greeks knew of opiates or hallucinogenic drugs, but they did make use of medicines, herbal concoctions and potions, especially love potions. The Greeks would have the wine in a large mixing bowl (a krater), into which water was poured to dilute it. Helen throws her drug into this, so that as each drinker has his wine poured, he imbibes it. Helen had spent time in Egypt; the Egyptians, for the Greeks, were the embodiment of ancient wisdom. Homer, *Odyssey*, 4.219–31:

> Then Helen, born to Zeus, thought of something else.
> At once she cast a drug into the wine which they were drinking,   220
>   both banishing pain and quieting anger, causing one to forget all
>   evils.
> Whoever gulps this down, when it is mixed in the bowl,
> on that day would not let a tear roll down his cheeks,
> not even if his mother and father lay there dead,
> not even if in front of him men slew his brother or beloved son   225
> with the sword, and he saw it with his own eyes.
> Such cunning drugs the daughter of Zeus possessed,
> good drugs, ones which Polydamna, the wife of Thon, an Egyptian
>   woman,
> had given her, for in that place the bounteous lands yield many
>   drugs,
> of which when mixed, many are excellent, and many baneful: 230
> every man is a doctor, knowing more than all other men.

The encounter between Odysseus (and his companions) and the goddess and sorceress Circe occupies Book 10 of the *Odyssey*. The book reflects the Greeks' interest in potions, drugs and magic. Homer, *Odyssey*, 10.229–48:

> They cried out, calling to Circe.
> And coming out straightaway, she opened the shining doors   230
> and asked them in: all in their ignorance followed her.
> But Eurylochus remained outside, suspecting foul play.
> Circe brought them inside and sat them on couches and stately
>   chairs,
> blending for them cheese and barley and pale honey mixed
> with Pramnian wine, but into this food stirred   235

malevolent drugs so that they would completely forget their fatherland.
When she had given them this and they had drunk it, then at once
she struck them with her wand and shut them up in the animal pens.
And they had the heads, voice, bristles and form of pigs,
but their minds were unchanged, and just as they had been before.   240
So crying they were penned in, and Circe
threw them acorns, ilex and the fruit of the cornel-tree,
such food as pigs sleeping on the ground always eat.

But Eurylochus immediately returned to the swift, black ship
to bring news of his companions and their dreadful fate.   245
But he wasn't able to get a word out, eager though he was,
his heart stricken with terrible anguish, and both of his eyes
were awash with tears, his soul possessed with lamentation.

Odysseus with the help of Hermes is immune to the goddess's potion, and persuades her to transform his men back into their human form. Odysseus is speaking. Homer, *Odyssey*, 10.388–99:

I said this, and Circe went through the palace, holding her wand
in her hand, and opened the doors of the animal pen, and she
drove my companions out, looking like nine-year-old hogs.   390
So they stood opposite her, and she went among them
smearing each one with another drug. The bristles
fell away from their limbs, which the other baneful drug
had grown on them, the one which queenly Circe had given them.
They were transformed into men immediately, but younger   395
than before and more handsome and taller to look at.
They recognised me, and each of them clasped my hands.
A longing for lamentation overtook us all, and the palace around us
echoed with a dreadful din: and the goddess herself was moved
   to pity.

Helen and Circe's drugs may have been the stuff of fiction, but the sorceress of Theocritus' *Idyll* 2 is obviously modelled on an actual practitioner, and love magic was clearly practised by the women of ancient Greece. One of her main devices is a 'magic wheel', a device consisting of a bird, usually identified as the wryneck, attached to a small wheel, which would be turned; by sympathetic enchantment it was hoped that the beloved would be similarly 'turned' to the lover. Here the woman performing the sorcery (with the aid of her assistant Thestylis) aims to restore the faded attentions of her lover Delphis. Next to nothing is known

about 'golden-haired Perimede', but she was clearly a sorceress (line 16).
Theocritus, *Idyll 2*, *The Sorceress*, 1–62, 159–66:

Where are my bay-leaves? Bring them, Thestylis. And where are my
   magic potions?
Put a wreath around the bowl with the best purple-red wool,
so that I will bind my man, my love, who is so cruel,
who hasn't even visited me for twelve days, the wretch,
and doesn't know whether I am dead or alive;   5
he, monster, hasn't knocked on my door. Surely Eros and Aphrodite
have carried off his quick fancy to someone else.
In the morning I will go to Timagetus' wrestling ground
and see him, and I'll complain about how he treats me.
And now I will bind him with spells of flame. But Selena   10
shine brightly: for to you, moon-goddess, I will croon softly,
and to Hecate beneath the earth, making even the dogs tremble
as she goes among the tomb-barrows of the dead and the dark-red
   blood.
Greetings, infernal Hecate, and be with me to the end,
making these drugs of mine not weaker than those of Circe   15
or of Medea or of golden-haired Perimede.

My magic-wheel, draw you the man to my house.

First, the barley-groats are consumed on the fire. But strew them,
Thestylis. Poor wretch, to where have your wits flown? Loathsome
   one,
have I become even to you an object of malicious gloating?   20
Strew them, and say as you do so: 'I strew Delphis' bones.'

My magic-wheel, draw you the man to my house.

Delphis has grieved me. And I for Delphis this bay
do burn. And as the bay-leaves cackle loudly, catching fire
and quickly perishing and we don't see even their ash,   25
so also may the flesh of Delphis be utterly consumed in the flame.

My magic-wheel, draw you the man to my house.

Now I'll burn the husks of bran, and Artemis you can
rouse the adamant things of Hades and also anything else which is as
   immoveable –
Thestylis, the dogs bay for us through the town: 30
the goddess Hecate is at the cross-roads: quickly, sound the bronze.

My magic-wheel, draw you the man to my house.

Look, the sea is silent, the winds are quiet:
yet do not silence the grief in my breast,
but I am all consumed with fire for that man who   35
instead of a wife has made me a sorry wretch, a virgin no longer.

My magic-wheel, draw you the man to my house.

As I this bees-wax melt with the help of the goddess Hecate,
so at once may Delphis son of Myndus melt with love.
As the bronze magic spinning-top turns about with Aphrodite's
      help   40
so may that man turn about my doors.

My magic-wheel, draw you the man to my house.

Three times I pour a libation, and three times I say this, lady:
whether it be a woman or man that lies with Delphis,
may he forget them just as much as once they say   45
Theseus, with Dia, forgot fair-haired Ariadne.

My magic-wheel, draw you the man to my house.

The thorn-apple herb for which all foals
and swift mares run mad on the mountain is from Arcadia.
So may I see Delphis, and may he come to this house   50
from the splendid wrestling school like one possessed.

My magic-wheel, draw you the man to my house.

This fringe which Delphis lost from his cloak
I now pluck and throw into the cruel fire.
Alas, grievous Love, why do you cling closely to me like a leach   55
of the marshes sucking all the dark blood of my body?

My magic-wheel, draw you the man to my house.

I will grind up a lizard and in the morning bring him an evil
      potion.
But now, Thestylis, take these herbs and smear them over
his door-posts while it is still dark   60
and say, murmuring, 'I kneed the bones of Delphis.'

My magic-wheel, draw you the man to my house.

Now with my magic potions I will bind him, yet if he still
grieves me, he'll be knocking on the gate of Hades, by the Fates: 160
such wicked drugs I guard for him in my chest,
learning them, Lady Hecate, from an Assyrian stranger.

But farewell you and turn your horses to the ocean,
Lady: and I'll bear my yearning as I have endured it until now.
Farewell, Selene brightly-throned, farewell all the 165
other stars that pursue the silent chariot of Night.

SUPERSTITION AND THE SUPERSTITIOUS MAN

All ancient Greeks, with the exception of a few philosopher atheists, believed both in the gods and that they sent omens or signs to help humans decide on courses of action. But there was also a notion that it was possible to give prophetic significance to phenomena that had no importance, or for someone to be too influenced by divination. In this passage, Theophrastus paints a comic picture of the man who sees a portent in just about everything, and who is obsessed with purification but in particular is concerned with the malevolent powers of the underworld goddess of magic, spells and sorcery, Hecate, who was thought to be exceptionally powerful at crossroads. Sabazius was an exotic deity, especially associated with snakes (4). The Hermaphrodites (and this, incidentally, is the first occurrence of the word in the Greek language) were double-sided stone sculptures with a male and female face on opposite sides (see 10). They were thought to be lucky. Puppies were sacrificed to Hecate; killed, they were then rubbed onto those in need of purification (see 13). In Boeotia, the sacrificed dog would be cut in two and those needing purification would walk between the two halves. Theophrastus, *Characters*, 16, *Superstition*:

(16.1) It's obvious: superstition would appear to be cowardice about the gods. The superstitious man is the sort of fellow who, (16.2) when he sees a crow, will wash his hands, sprinkle himself all over with holy water, put a bay-leaf in his mouth, and go about that way for the day. (16.3) If a weasel crosses his path, he won't go further on until someone passes by, or he throws three stones across the road. (16.4) If he sees a red-brown snake in the house, he calls upon Sabazius, but if it is a sacred snake, he straightaway founds a shrine at the very place.

(16.5) When he passes the oiled stones at the meeting of three roads he liberally pours oil onto them from his carry-flask, and falling on his knees prostrates himself before he goes on his way. (16.6) If a mouse chews through a sack of barley, he goes to an omen interpreter and asks for advice, and if he is told to give the sack to the cobblers to mend, he pays no attention to this, but performs an averting sacrifice.

(16.7) He often purifies his house, saying that Hecate has put it under an enchantment. (16.8) If owls hoot as he is walking, he panics, and cries out, 'Athena is mightier!' (16.9) He won't step on a grave, or view a corpse or a woman in childbirth, but he says it is wiser for him not to incur pollution.

(16.10) On the fourth and seventh days in each month he orders those in the house to boil wine, then goes out and buys myrtle, frankincense and cakes, and coming back spends the rest of the day crowning the Hermaphrodites with wreaths.

(16.11) Whenever he has a dream, he consults the professional dream interpreters, the soothsayers and the omen expounders, asking to which god or goddess he should pray. Each month he goes to the Instructors in Orphism to be initiated, with his wife; but if she can't spare the time, he takes the nurse and the children. (16.12) It would seem that when people are sprinkling themselves fastidiously at the sea, he is there. (16.13) And if ever at the crossroads he sees someone wreathed with garlic, he goes away and washes around his head, and summoning priestesses he orders that they perform a complete purification with a sea-onion or puppy. (16.14) If he sees a madman or epileptic he spits down into his own chest.

HYMNS TO THE GODDESSES

Hymns were written to both gods and goddesses. The most important of these are those called the 'Homeric Hymns' (not written by Homer but in antiquity credited to him) and those of Callimachus. In the following hymn Callimachus describes some of Artemis' chief attributes. Callimachus, *Hymn to Artemis* (3), 1–25:

We sing to Artemis (it is not easy for singers to forget her)
whose interests lie in the bow and hare shooting
and the spacious dance-floor and amusements in the mountains,
and we commence when sitting on her father's knees
as a little maiden she addressed the one who had sired her with
    this request: 5

'Give me to keep eternal virginity to prize, father,
and let me have many names, so that Apollo will not be as good as me.
Give me arrows and a bow; wait, father, I don't ask you to give me
the quiver or great bow personally, the Cyclopes will craft for me
arrows and a well-curved bow at once.   10
But do allow me to be the 'Bringer of Light' and to wear a man's
    tunic,
with a coloured hem, reaching to my knees, so that I can slaughter
    wild-beasts.

And grant me sixty daughters of Ocean as a choir,
all nine years old, all girls not yet wearing the girdle of puberty.
And grant me twenty river nymphs of Amnisus to be my
    handmaids,   15
to look after my high hunter's boots, and when I've finished
shooting lynx and deer to take care of my swift hounds.
And grant to me all the mountains: and give to me whichever city
you chose: for Artemis rarely goes to town.
I will live in the mountains, and I will have dealings with mortals   20
only when women are struck with the sharp pains of childbirth
and call upon me for help. The Fates,
when I was first born, assigned me as woman's helper
just as my mother Leto did not suffer either when she gave birth
    to me
or was pregnant, but without effort pushed me out of her body.'   25

One of Callimachus' hymns describes Demeter's worship in a women-only rite. The women have been abstaining from food and drink, just as Demeter fasted from grief when she could not find her daughter Persephone, who had been abducted by Hades. The ritual cry of the women, 'Demeter, greatly welcome, feeder of many, bringer of many measures of grain', brings us to the language of the street, and the actual voices of fasting women are heard, echoing down thousands of years to us. Women are otherwise mute to posterity, except for the ritual cry that it was their task to make when the axe struck the victim at a sacrifice: '*ololyge*' they would cry, announcing the sacrifice to the gods. Spring and the harvest are white because of the growing barley (line 122). Callimachus, *Hymn to Demeter* (6), 1–6, 118–38:

As the sacred basket comes greet it women:
'Demeter, greatly welcome, feeder of many, bringer of many measures
    of grain'.
As the sacred basket comes, look upon it only from ground level,
    uninitiated ones,
and don't look at it from a roof or from on high,
neither a child nor a woman nor a girl who has cut her hair,   5
nor even when we spit from parched, hungry mouths.

Sing young women not yet wed, cry out mothers,
'Demeter, greatly welcome, feeder of many, bringer of many measures
    of grain'.
As the four white horses carry the sacred basket,   120

so to us the great goddess who rules far and wide will come
bringing white spring, and white harvest, and winter
and autumn, and preserve us until next year.
And as we walk the city bare-footed and with unbound hair
so may our foot and head be completely unharmed always   125
and as the basket bearers bear baskets full of gold,
may we gain plentiful gold.

As far as the town-hall let the uninitiated go,
but the initiated can walk as far as the shrine of the goddess,
as many as are less than sixty years old. Those who are heavy
    with child   130
and she who stretches out her hand in pain to Eileithyia the
    goddess of birth,
it is enough that they go as far as their legs will carry them. And to
    them Demeter
will give all things, overflowing, just as if they had made it to her
    shrine.

Hail, goddess, and preserve this city in harmony
and in prosperity, and in the fields bear everything in abundance.   135
Nourish our oxen, bear us flocks, bear us ears of grain, bring us the
    harvest,
preserve also the peace so that he who sows might also reap.
Be gracious to me, you who are earnestly prayed to, great queen
    among goddesses.

The *Homeric Hymn to Aphrodite* celebrates three goddesses. Line 23 is
a riddle: how was Hestia (goddess of the hearth) both first and last to be
born of Cronus? Cronus was destined to be overthrown by his children,
so he swallowed them each as they were born. Hestia was swallowed
first, so ended up on the bottom of Cronus' stomach while the other
children as they were successively eaten came on top of her: when Cronus
was forced to regurgitate his children, Hestia, at the bottom of his
stomach, came up last: so she was 'born' last. For an explanation of the
aegis (line 8), see the glossary. Hestia as goddess of the hearth receives a
tasty piece of any food consumed in the house (line 30). *The Homeric
Hymn to Aphrodite* (5), 1–41:

Muse, tell me the works of pure golden Aphrodite,
who often dwells in Cyprus, who rouses in the gods sweet passion
and who conquers the tribes of mortal men
the birds in heaven and all the wild beasts,

as well as the many creatures the land rears, and as many as are of
    the sea:

all these love the deeds of Cytherea [Aphrodite] with her beautiful
    crown.

Yet there are three hearts not in her power to persuade or beguile:
the daughter of Zeus who bears the aegis, bright-eyed Athena:
for she has no delight in the works of golden Aphrodite,
but loves wars and the handiwork of Ares   10
in combats and battles, and also working at beautiful crafts.
She it was who first taught earthly craftsmen
to make war-chariots and carts inlaid with bronze.
She also teaches soft-skinned young girls household skills
and imparts in each one's mind useful skills.   15
Nor is Aphrodite who loves laughter able to subdue in love
Artemis noisy in the chase with her golden arrow-shafts.
For Artemis loves to twang her bow and slay beasts in the
    mountains,
and loves lyres and choruses and piercing shouts and
shady woods and the cities of upright men.   20
And the modest maiden Hestia does not love the works of
    Aphrodite,
she was the first born of wily Cronus,
and also the last, by the will of aegis-bearing Zeus,
a lady whom Poseidon and Apollo wanted to marry.
But she was very unwilling, and sternly rejected them.   25
She swore a mighty oath, which has been fulfilled,
touching the head of her father, Zeus who holds the aegis,
that she would be a virgin all her days, peerless among the goddesses.
Zeus her father gave her a great honour in place of marriage
and she sits in the middle of the house, and she takes the choicest
    portion.   30
In all the temples of the gods she is honoured
and among all mortal men she is the most senior of goddesses.

These three – Athena, Artemis, Hestia – Aphrodite cannot persuade
    or beguile their hearts:
but of all others, nothing has escaped Aphrodite
neither among the blessed gods nor mortal men.   35
And she even leads astray the heart of Zeus who loves to thunder
he who is the greatest of all and has the greatest share of honour.
Whenever she wishes she bewitches even his shrewd heart
and easily couples him with mortal women,

without Hera's knowledge, his sister-wife,
the most beautiful among the immortal goddesses.

DELPHI AND PROPHECY

Xenophon of Athens sought the advice of the Delphic oracle before setting
out to Asia Minor on an expedition to support the rebellion of Cyrus,
which ended with Cyrus' death in battle in 401 BC. The god spoke through
the medium of a woman priest, the Pythia. It was a common question to
ask to which gods one needed to pray and sacrifice to gain a particular end.
Many of Delphi's oracles were in fact 'prescriptions', advising the
worshipper of the best way to attain their needs. The Cyrus referred to here
is not the founder of the Persian empire. Xenophon, *Anabasis*, 3.1.4–7:

(3.1.4) In the army there was a certain Athenian, Xenophon, who wasn't a
general or a captain or a common soldier, who had accompanied the
expedition because Proxenus an old guest-friend had sent for him at home.
Proxenus had promised him that, if he would go, he would make Cyrus his
friend. Proxenus said he considered Cyrus was of more benefit to him than
his own country. (3.1.5) Xenophon, reading the letter, went to Socrates the
Athenian about the journey, and Socrates suspecting that his becoming a
friend of Cyrus might be a ground for accusation against him by the city, as
it seemed that Cyrus had eagerly assisted the Spartans in their war against
Athens, advised Xenophon to go to Delphi to seek the advice of the god
about the journey. (3.1.6) So Xenophon went, and asked Apollo to which
of the gods he should sacrifice and pray so that he might most finely and
successfully undertake the journey he was contemplating, and how having
successfully accomplished it he might return safely. Apollo told him to
which gods he had to sacrifice. (3.1.7) When Xenophon arrived back from
Delphi, he told Socrates the oracle. When he heard it Socrates criticised
him that he had not first asked whether it was better for him to make the
journey or to stay, but himself decided that he was going and enquired
about this thing: how he might best make the journey.

Ion the temple servant tells the chorus of women who have accompanied
their mistress Creusa to Delphi what they need to do to consult the oracle.
Euripides, *Ion*, 226–9:

Ion: If you have sacrificed the holy cake before the temple
and wish to consult Apollo,
proceed into the temple. Do not, without first
slaughtering a sheep, enter the innermost chamber of the temple.

Ion speaks to Creusa; unknown to both, he is her child by Apollo; she had abandoned Ion at his birth. She and her husband Xuthus want assistance with their childlessness. Euripides, *Ion*, 299–304:

> *Ion:* Have you come with your husband, or alone, to the oracle?
>
> *Creusa:* With my husband. He is detained, at the shrine of
> Trophonius.   300
>
> *Ion:* Is he simply visiting or seeking oracles?
>
> *Creusa:* From Trophonius and Apollo he wishes to find out one thing.
>
> *Ion:* Have you come to Delphi to seek an oracle about crops, or about what?
>
> *Creusa:* We are without children, although we have been married for some time.

When something unusual happened, the Greeks would often consult an oracular centre, such as Delphi, and ask for a ritual prescription about which god to sacrifice or pray to in order to avert a calamity or disaster. The following oracle and reply indicate a typical formula of an enquiry. Demosthenes, 43 (*Against Macartatus*), 66:

> *Enquiry:* The Athenian people enquire about the sign which has appeared in the heavens, what the Athenians ought to do, or to which god they should sacrifice and pray, so that the sign will turn out for the best.
>
> *Reply:* Concerning the sign in the heavens, it is advantageous for the Athenians to sacrifice, with accompanying good omens, to Zeus 'Most High', Athena 'Most High', Heracles, Apollo 'The Saviour', to send offerings to the Amphiones, and sacrifice with good fortune to Apollo god of the ways, Leto and Artemis, and fill the streets with the smell of burnt sacrifice, to provide bowls of wine and organise choruses, and to wear garlands according to ancestral practice in honour of the Olympian gods and goddesses, holding up their right and left arms, to offer public thanksgiving according to ancestral practice, and to Erechtheus, your founding hero, make sacrifices and gifts, according to ancestral practice. For the dead, on the appointed day, their relatives are to make offerings according to the usual practice.

Plutarch, who was a priest at Delphi, describes a consultation that went horribly wrong and ended up with the Pythia dying. Apollo would not necessarily give an oracle even on the one day a month set aside for his consultations. The sacrificial sheep had, as in all such ceremonies, to assent to its destruction by nodding its head when water or barley grains were tossed onto it. If it did not, it was a bad omen. The following was an atypical consultation. Plutarch, *Moralia*, 438a–c:

> (438a) A foreign religious delegation had arrived, and it is said that the sacrificial victim remained unmoved by the first libations, and was not amenable. The priests persisted, wanting to please, (438b) and only when the priests had rained water down on it and deluged it did the victim give in. So how did the Pythia react? She went down into the oracular shrine of the temple, they say, unwillingly and unenthusiastically. From her first responses it was immediately clear that her voice was rough and she was not prophesying properly, but was weighed down like a ship, possessed with an incoherent and malevolent spirit. Finally she became totally hysterical, and with a great fearful cry she rushed to the exit and threw herself down, so that not only the delegation but the prophet Nicander and the holy men who were present also fled. However, after a little while they went in and took up the Pythia, still conscious, (438c) and she lived for a few more days.

SANCTUARIES

The site of Lebadea in central Greece not far from Delphi is still an impressive one, with its springs and caves. It is easy to see how this came to be a place of oracular inspiration for the ancient Greeks. At Lebadea, the consultant sought an oracle from the hero Trophonius; heroes were 'chthonic', of the earth, where it was believed their powers resided. The complicated procedure leading up to the actual consultation was clearly important in establishing the right frame of mind for the consultant. Pausanias (writing in about the middle of the second century AD) had himself been a consultant, as he says at the very end of the passage. The need for the stout local boots (8) is made clear in (11): the enquirer has to force his feet through a narrow opening into the innermost sacred place. The person consulting the oracle is referred to as the 'descender', as they descended down into the oracle. Pausanias, 9.39.5–14:

> (9.39.5) What happens at the oracle of Lebadea is as follows. When someone decides to descend to the oracle of Trophonius, first he spends an appointed number of days in a certain building, sacred to the Good Spirit and Good Fortune. There he leads a certain way of life, among other ways for keeping pure abstaining from hot baths; the bathing place is the river Hercyna. There is meat in abundance from the sacrifices, for

the one who descends to the oracle sacrifices both to Trophonius himself and to the children of Trophonius, and to Apollo, Cronus, Zeus surnamed 'King', to Hera the Charioteer and to Demeter, whom they give the surname Europa and claim was the nurse of Trophonius.

(9.39.6) At each of the sacrifices a seer is present who examines the entrails of the sacrificial victim, and after the inspection prophesies to the person descending whether Trophonius will receive him favourably and propitiously. The entrails of the other sacrificial animals do not indicate the opinion of Trophonius so clearly as the ram, and on the night on which each consultant descends, he sacrifices one over a pit, invoking Agamedes. The previous sacrifices, performed propitiously, are of no account if the entrails of this ram do not wish to indicate the same. But if the ram's entrails agree, then the enquirer descends with high expectations, and descends as follows.

(9.39.7) Firstly, he is taken in the night to the river Hercyna, led by two boys about thirteen years old, named Hermae, with citizen parents, who after leading him there anoint him with olive oil and wash him. It is these boys who wash the descender and they are his attendants for just as many things as are necessary. From there he is taken by the priests, not immediately to the oracle, but to springs of water which are quite close to each other.

(9.39.8) Here he has to drink the water called 'of Forgetfulness', so that he might forget all the things he has been thinking about up to this point, and after this he immediately drinks the water 'of Memory', so that he remembers from this point on what he sees when he descends into the oracle. Having viewed the image which they say was made by Daedalus – it is not shown by the priests except to those intending to go to consult Trophonius – having seen this image and honoured it and also prayed, he goes to the oracle, wearing a linen tunic with ribbons around its waist, and wearing local boots.

(9.39.9) The oracle is beyond the grove, on the mountain. A wall of white marble surrounds it in a circle, the circumference of the wall is that of the smallest threshing floor, and the height is just a bit short of two cubits. On the wall are fixed spikes, of bronze, as are the crossbars holding them together, and between them a double-door has been built. Within this enclosure there is a chasm in the earth; it isn't natural but built skilfully and with very precise construction.

(9.39.10) The form of this structure is similar to that of a bread-oven. The width of the diameter amounts as far as one can guess to four cubits.

And the depth of the construction, as far as one could guess, is no more than eight cubits. No way of descent has been constructed to the bottom; when someone consults Trophonius they bring him a narrow, light ladder. Going down is a hole between the floor and the construction: its breadth is two outstretched spans of the hand, and the height appeared to be one span.

(9.39.11) The enquirer lies down on the ground, holding barley cakes kneaded with honey, and he goes into the opening feet first and then himself follows, struggling to get his knees into the opening. The rest of the body is immediately drawn in, just as the greatest and swiftest of rivers catching hold of a man in its eddy will suck him under. After this for those who have entered this innermost sacred place the future is not taught to each in one and the same way, but one sees it and another hears it. The return trip up for the enquirers is by the same opening, their feet coming out first.

(9.39.12) They say that no one making the descent has ever died, except for one of the body-guards of Demetrius. But they say this man did not perform the sacred rite, neither the customary ones nor the ones to consult the oracle, when he made his descent to consult the god, but was hoping to steal gold and silver from the innermost sacred place. It is said that this man's corpse appeared at another place, and was not thrown out at the sacred mouth. Other accounts are given about this man, but I have related the one most worth telling.

(9.39.13) After making his descent to Trophonius, the priests take the enquirer to the chair called Memory, which stands not far from the sacred innermost place, and sit him on it, and they ask him as he sits there what he has seen and learned. After learning (of his experience) the priests entrust him to the care of his associates. These pick him up and carry him, still possessed and terror-struck, not conscious either of himself or of what is around him, to the house in which he had lived recently with Fortune and Good Spirit. Afterwards, however, he will regain all his faculties, no less than before, and laughter will return to him.

(9.39.14) I am not writing hearsay, as I myself have enquired of Trophonius, and seen others doing so. It is required that those who have descended into the shrine of Trophonius write what they have heard or seen on a tablet which they dedicate to the god.

Sanctuaries could be nature reserves, valuable ecosystems with trees for shade and beauty. The whole sanctuary technically belonged to a god but was managed by the city or a priesthood. Laws against chopping down trees and dumping human and animal waste into sanctuaries are common and indicate that the Greek urban community did not have a pristine environment. This following law was promulgated by a priest of Apollo at Athens in the fourth century BC. The king archon was the chief religious official of Athens, elected each year. E. Kirchner (ed.), *Inscriptiones Graecae* vol. 2 (2nd edn, Berlin, 1913), no. 1362:

The priest of Apollo publicly proclaims and announces on his own behalf and on that of the *demes* and the Athenian people that it is prohibited to cut wood in the shrine of Apollo and to carry wood and branches, either dead sticks or with leaves, out of the shrine. If anyone is apprehended chopping or carrying out any of the prohibited items from the shrine, if it is a slave he will be given fifty lashes and the priest will hand him over, along with the name of his master, to the king archon and the city council, according to the terms of the decree of the council and the Athenian people. If it is a free man who is caught the priest and the *deme* official will impose a penalty of fifty *drachmas* on him, and give his name to the king archon and the council, according to the terms of the decree of the council and the Athenian people.

Theocritus describes the natural beauty of Delphi. The goddesses of Mount Helicon were the nine Muses. Theocritus, *Epigram*, 1:

The roses drenched with dew and that thick creeping thyme
which grows prostrate there belong to the goddesses of Helicon:
but the dark-foliaged bay Pythian Healer, Apollo, is for you
since this adorns the rock cliffs of Delphi:
and this white-horned he-goat who nibbles at the sprays   5
of the turpentine tree will stain the altar red with his blood.

Theocritus describes a sanctuary of the god Priapus, who was often associated with gardens; his cult roles included sexuality and human fertility, and he was frequently shown with an erection. Theocritus, *Epigram*, 4:

Turn down that lane, goatherd, and there by the oak trees
you will find a newly carved image in the wood of a fig:
it is legless, earless, with the bark still on it, but with a child begetting
member able to fulfil the works of Aphrodite of Cyprus.
A sacred enclosure surrounds it, and an eternal   5
spring flows from the rocks flourishing on all sides
with bay and myrtle and fragrant cypress,
around there a vine with its clusters of grapes spreads its tendrils,

and the blackbirds of spring with clear-voiced songs
pour out their various-noted honeyed tunes.   10
The tuneful nightingales reply with their warblings
and sing back with their honey-sweet voices.
Sit yourself down there and to grinning Priapus
pray that I'll lose my longing for Daphnis,
immediately offering to sacrifice a fine, young goat. But if he will   15
not consent, if I get Daphnis, I'll make three sacrifices:
for I'll slay a heifer, a hairy he-goat, and a lamb I have
kept in the pen. And may god be well-disposed toward you.

The Greeks had few private gardens; at most even wealthy homes would
have had a courtyard with perhaps a tree and a few plants. The narrow
streets of the big cities and the houses crowded close together cannot have
made for a pleasant environment. The Greeks, however, clearly loved
natural beauty, and this description of the sanctuary of the Erinyes (Furies)
at Colonus near Athens is justly famous, and indicates the Greeks'
appreciation of nature. The chorus of elderly Athenian men sing here;
Sophocles himself was from Colonus, about 2½ km north of the Athenian
acropolis. Sophocles, *Oedipus at Colonus*, 668–93:

Stranger, in this land of glorious horses
you have reached
white Colonus, where   670
the melodious nightingale warbles
in this its favourite haunt
under the green glens,
living in the wine-dark ivy
and the sacred foliage of the god   675
burgeoning with fruit unscorched by the sun
nor buffeted by the wind
of many winter storms, where the frenzied Dionysus
continually measures out his paces
with his divine nurses the nymphs.   680
The narcissus with its beautiful clusters
bedewed from heaven blooms each and every day,
the ancient crown of the great goddesses
Demeter and Persephone,
as well as the crocus that gleams like gold.   685
Nor are the sleepless springs
as they flow wanderingly
from the river Cephisus diminished,

but each and every day
it flows through the plains bringing life to   690
earth's swollen breast with pure moisture, nor is Colonus
unloved by the choruses of the Muses
nor by Aphrodite with her golden reins.

TWO

Husbands and Wives

Why are you shedding tears, Patroclus, like a baby girl
who running after her mother demands to be picked up,
clutching at her dress, and holding back her mother as she hurries on,
looking up at her crying until she picks her up?
You are just like such a little girl, Patroclus, letting your soft tears fall
    down.

Homer, Iliad, 16.7–11.

A young girl led a sheltered existence, close to her mother, and with few contacts with the outside world. When she grew older, and experienced puberty, her thoughts had to turn to marriage. For a young woman, marriage was crucial: a free citizen woman had no status and in a sense no existence except through her relationship with men, and so a young woman *had* to have a husband. There were no 'careers' for women except marriage, childbirth and rearing children. Marriage details were usually handled by those around her, and her husband might be the first man outside her family that a young marriageable woman had ever met, and he could well be a total stranger to her. Despite this, there was love between couples, and the bond between the two was important. While the wedding ceremony cemented the union, it is clear that the birth of the first child was regarded by husbands as the first real sign of intimacy and the success of the marital union.

Medea voices complaints about the fate of wives: women must 'purchase' their husbands, bringing a dowry provided by their father into the marriage, and she says a woman must 'take a master of our body' (Euripides, *Medea*, 233). Wives had to bend to the will of their husbands, and Clytemnestra advises her daughter Iphigenia: 'Think like your husband, changing the colour of your true thoughts, like a polyp on a rock' (Sophocles, *Iphigenia*, Fragment 307).

The Greek household might include not just the husband and wife, and their children, but also slaves and perhaps even a freed slave, as in the case of the household where a man had taken in his old freed nurse when he found her starving. The term *oikos* covered the household and its property, and the term *oikonomia* was given to the management of it: our term economy directly derives from this. In prosperous homes the wife was responsible for running many aspects of the household, especially the care of the slaves and the manufacture of clothes, and also small details such as where particular belongings were stored.

A household, an *oikos*, began when a man and a woman married. A wedding involved no particular ceremony or rites specifically recognised by law. Marriage took place when a man took his bride from her home to his own. This was made into a public display of their intentions in the form of the wedding procession (see illustration 2.1). A bride and groom would bathe separately before the wedding, often drawing the water for the wedding bath from a sacred spring. Presents would be given to the bride for the occasion. She was often quite young and might have only just experienced puberty, while her husband was generally several years older than her, perhaps as old as thirty at Athens, and marrying a girl of eighteen or even perhaps of fifteen years of age. Marriages between close relatives, the practice of endogamy, was not forbidden (unlike at Rome) for the purposes of keeping property within the extended family. Marriages between uncle and nieces, while not common, are attested, and led to complicated family relationships.

The major role of women was to produce and care for children. Alcestis grieves that she will not be present when her daughter gives birth, when a mother's presence is so comforting. Medea comments that she'd rather stand 'in battle with a shield three times than bear a child once' (Euripides, *Medea*, 250–1). Wealthy women could afford wet-nurses and servants to care for the baby, but most women looked after their own children and babies in addition to attending to their household duties.

In a society that did not have taps and plumbing, a major task for women was to collect water, which they did in jars, carrying these on their heads (see illustration 2.2). Women whose households had slaves would not have had to undertake this duty, but most women probably did. But in a very real sense, collecting water was also a social event, a chance for women to meet each other and to chat. Few women avoided household duties of any kind. Shopping was usually carried out, however, by the men, and so restricting women's access to money. Women, though, were able to enter the storeroom. Household tasks, such as cooking and cleaning, belonged to them, and most women would have weaved.

A man who accused his wife of adultery had, without exception, to divorce her. This disgraced her but more importantly was meant as a warning to other wives. Few men would want to marry a divorced woman who had been accused of adultery, and guilty wives might not even be accepted back into their father's family because of the dishonour involved.

Adulterous citizen women were not allowed to attend festivals, as their presence was considered to be polluting, and at Athens the secret agricultural ceremonies conducted for the fertility of the soil could only be attended by chaste Athenian wives. Adultery was feared because it could introduce illegitimate children into the *oikos*, with a stranger's child (or children) inheriting the family property. Even in the classical period, as can be seen from the lawsuit involving Eratosthenes, a husband could legitimately kill an adulterer if he caught him in bed with his wife. But the usual arrangement was the payment of financial compensation. Divorce itself was an informal process. The Greek word for 'to divorce' was *ekballo*, literally, 'to throw out'. A husband divorced his wife by making her leave his home, from which she would return to that of her own parents: but if she had not committed adultery, he would have to return the dowry.

A woman with servants would have spent much of her time indoors, with no excuse such as fetching water to go outside. Festivals and various religious ceremonies, especially those for women only, provided women with most of their social life, and the need to perform household duties and care of children kept many women inside. In addition, the women's quarters were separate from the men's and in the most secluded part of the house, such as at the back, or in the case of two-storey houses, at the top.

PREPARING FOR MARRIAGE

Odysseus is shipwrecked near the city of the Phaeacians. But the goddess Athena, ever loyal to her favourite, organises assistance for him. She appears in a dream to Nausicaa, daughter of the king of the land, and puts it in her head to go and wash her clothes in preparation for her wedding. When she has finished this, she is seen by Odysseus, who approaches her for help. The description of the washing and the girls' playing is very evocative, but in particular gendered roles for king, wife and daughter are all apparent in this passage. Athena speaks to Nausicaa in a dream. Homer, *Odyssey*, 6.25–109:

> 'Nausicaa, how did your mother come to have such an idle
>   daughter?   25
> Your shining clothes are lying around uncared for,
> but your marriage day approaches, when you will have to wear fine
>   clothes yourself,
> and provide these for those who escort you.
> For from such things a good reputation spreads among men,
> giving joy to the father and honoured mother.   30

But let us go washing when the dawn appears:
and I will follow you at the same time as a helper so that you can
    prepare yourself
as soon as possible, since you will not be an unwedded virgin for
    much longer:
for already you are wooed by the best of all the Phaeacians
in the land, to which race you yourself belong.   35
But, come, before dawn persuade your renowned father
to make ready the mules and wagon, to carry
the girdles and dresses and glossy bed quilts.
And for you yourself it is preferable to go in this way than on foot,
as the washing places are some distance from the city.'   40

Having said this the bright-eyed goddess Athena departed to Mount
    Olympus,
where it is said the seat of the gods is eternally secure.
Neither is it buffeted by winds nor ever washed
with rain nor does snow ever fall there, but the sky
spreads out empty of cloud, and a bright radiance covers it.   45
In that place the blessed gods delight all their days.
And there went olive-eyed Athena, when she had spoken to the girl.

At once, finely throned Dawn came, and she aroused
Nausicaa of the beautiful dresses: and straightaway she was amazed
    at her dream,
and went through the house, so that she could tell her parents,   50
her dear father and mother: she found them inside.

The mother sat at the hearth with the women servants
spinning wool dyed with sea-purple: she met her father
going towards the door to join the glorious lords
at council, to which the lordly Phaeacians summoned him.   55
Standing quite close to her dear father she said:

'Dear papa, won't you get a wagon ready for me,
the high one with the sturdy wheels, so that I might take my lovely
    clothes
which are lying around dirty to the river for washing?
And for yourself it is best to have clean clothes for your body   60
as you go to council to deliberate with the first men of state.
And you have five beloved sons living in your halls,
two are married, but three are sturdy bachelors:
they are always wanting freshly laundered clothes
when they go dancing. All of these things weigh on my mind.'   65

She said this, for she was ashamed to mention her youthful marriage
to her beloved father. But he understood everything and replied:
'I begrudge you neither the mules, child, nor any other thing.
Off you go: the slaves will get ready the high wagon
with the sturdy wheels, fitted out with a body.'   70

Agreeing so, he called out to the slaves, and they obeyed.
Outside, they got ready the quick-running mule wagon
and led up the mules and yoked them to the wagon:
and Nausicaa carried out the bright clothing from her bedroom.
She put it into the smoothly planed wagon;   75
her mother packed all sorts of tempting food in a box,
and put in delicacies, and poured wine
into a flask of goat-skin: and the girl hopped into the wagon.
Her mother also gave her supple olive oil in a golden flask
for her and the women servants to rub on.   80
She took the whip and the glistening reins
and flicking it set out: the mules clattered off.
They pulled without stint, and carried the maiden and the clothes,
not alone, as the others, the servants, went with her at the same time.

When they came to the beautiful stream of the river,   85
where the washing pools were always full, and plenty of
beautiful water gurgled up from below to remove stains from clothes
    however dirty,
there they loosed the mules from under the wagon's yoke.
They drove them along the eddying river
to eat the honey-sweet grass: they took the clothes   90
from the wagon in their arms and carried them into the dark water,
stamping them down into the troughs, striving in haste to surpass
    each other.
When they had washed and cleaned off all the dirt,
they spread it out in lines along the sea shore, where
the sea washed the pebbles clean against the land.   95
They bathed and anointed themselves with the supple olive oil,
then they had their lunch on the banks of the river
and waited for the clothes to dry in the sunlight.

When they had eaten enough, Nausicaa and her servants
throwing off their veils played with a ball: 100
and white-armed Nausicaa was their leader in the song.
And as the goddess Artemis the shooter of arrows roams the
    mountains,

either along tall Taygetus or Erymanthus,
delighting in the wild boars and swift deer
and with her the wild nymphs, daughters of aegis-bearing Zeus,   105
accompanying her play, and the heart of her mother Leto rejoices:
over them all Artemis holds her head and brows,
and she is easily distinguished, though they are all beautiful:
just so the unwed girl Nausicaa stood out from her servants.

As they are about to yoke up the mules, Athena intervenes, and
Nausicaa throws the ball to one of her servants, who fails to catch it: it
falls into water, and they all cry out. Odysseus hears the noise and
wakes up, and comes out of the bushes where he has been asleep. He is
naked, having lost all his clothes at sea: he brandishes a bush in front of
his 'manhood'. The servants run away, and only brave Nausicaa stands
her ground. The scene is one that must have delighted Homer's readers,
and it is depicted on vases. He entreats – and flatters – her. Homer,
Odyssey, 6.149–59:

Lady, I entreat you – but are you some god or mortal?
If you are one of the gods, who dwell in the broad sky,   150
it is Artemis, the daughter of great Zeus,
to whom I liken you most in appearance, size and stature.
But if you are one of the mortals who live on the earth,
thrice blessed are your father and lady mother
and thrice blessed your brothers; their hearts   155
must glow with pleasure for your sake
when they see such a relative joining the dance.
But he will be by far the most blessed of all
who prevails with his wedding gifts and leads you to his home.

Odysseus bathes and Nausicaa ponders how to bring him into the city. She
decides that he can follow the wagon back to the city for most of the way,
but must then leave her and make his own way to the palace, and gives him
directions. Homer, *Odyssey*, 6.251–88:

But white-armed Nausicaa considered what to do next.
Folding the clothes she put them in the fine wagon,
and yoked the mules with their sturdy hooves, got into the wagon,
and encouraged Odysseus, talking to him and addressing him:

'Rouse yourself now, stranger, to go to the city, so that I can send
    you to   255
the house of my wise father, where I tell you

you will get to know the best of all the Phaeacians.
Only do it this way, as you don't seem stupid:
while we go through the countryside and the fields ploughed by
   men,
during that time go quickly with the maid servants behind the
   mules   260
and wagon, and I will lead the way.
But when we come to the city there runs around it
a high wall, and a fine harbour on either side of the city,
and a narrow causeway: the ships rowed with oars on each side
are drawn up along the road, all have a mooring place, each one,   265
and there too is an assembly place, built of quarried stone
dug deep from the earth, around the fine temple of Poseidon.
There they busy themselves with looking after the tackle of the
   black ships,
the cables and sails, and plane the oars to a thin edge.
For the Phaeacians don't care for the bow and arrow   270
but sails and ship's oars and even-keeled ships,
delighting in which they traverse the grey sea.
It is their coarse speech I avoid, in case later one of them
makes fun of me: for there are insolent men in town,
and one of the baser sort might say if he comes upon us: 275

"Who is this handsome, tall stranger that follows
Nausicaa? Where did she find him? He'll now be her husband.
Surely he's someone she's brought from a ship,
a wanderer of men from a far off country, since none dwell near us.
Or some god much entreated by her praying came down   280
from heaven, and she will have him all her days.
Better so, if she has done the rounds and found a husband from
   somewhere else:
for here she despises the men of the race of Phaeacians,
where truly she has suitors, many and noble!"

That's how they'll gossip, and this would be a reproach to me.   285
I too would disapprove of another girl, who would do such things,
going against the wishes of her beloved father and mother, while
   they still lived,
consorting with men before the day of her public marriage.'

Nausicaa is like many young girls, not yet married and ignorant of
Aphrodite. The cold north wind, Boreas, chills the old man, but not the
young virgin. Hesiod, *Works and Days*, 519–24:

The north wind does not blow through the soft skin of the virgin
who stays at home inside with her beloved mother,   520
not yet acquainted with the works of much-golden Aphrodite:
and washing her delicate skin well, and richly anointing herself
with olive oil, she lies down in an inner room of the house
on a winter's day.

THE WEDDING

The toast at the marriage feast united the two families. The dew of the vine
is, of course, wine (line 3). Pindar, *Olympian Victory Ode*, 7.1–6:

A man takes from his wealthy hand a drinking bowl –
solid gold, most prized of his possessions –
with the dew of the vine frothing inside, and hands it to his young
    son-in-law
one house drinking to the health of another
honouring the joy of the feast and the marriage alliance,   5
and in the company of his friends makes him envied for the
    harmonious marriage.

Cleisthenes, tyrant of Sicyon (from about 600 to 570 BC, with his
daughter's marriage taking place in about 575 BC), not far from Corinth,
had a daughter for whom he thought only the best man would do. The
qualities that a father might seek in a son-in-law make interesting reading
and shed light on the aristocratic world of this period. Cleisthenes'
grandson (also named Cleisthenes), an Athenian born of this daughter's
marriage, became an important Athenian political reformer, introducing
democracy to Athens in 508 BC (the two Cleisthenes, the grandfather
tyrant from Sicyon and the grandson democrat of Athens, are sometimes
confused with each other). Individuals did not have surnames, but were
identified by their father's name, and if they and their ancestors were
important enough, a longer lineage might be given, as in the case of
Cleisthenes himself. The extent of the Greek world at this time is made
clear by the list of the suitors. The city of Sybaris was noted for its
luxurious way of life, hence our term 'sybaritic' (6.127.1). The disgrace of
Hippocleides is not so much dancing, though Cleisthenes disapproved of
this, but in dancing on his head, on a table: underpants had not yet been
invented. One can imagine the scene, perhaps acceptable among the
young bucks at the pre-wedding party, but hardly with the father-in-law-
to-be present. Cleisthenes, instead of Hippocleides, chose the other
Athenian, Megacles, to marry Agariste. The great Perikles himself was the

great-great-grandson of this Megacles and Agariste. Herodotus, 6.126.1–130.1:

(6.126.1) Cleisthenes, the son of Aristonymus, son of Myron, son of Andreas, had a daughter called Agariste. He wanted to find the best man of all the Greeks and to give his daughter's hand in marriage to that man. (6.126.2) So during the Olympic games, in which he was victorious in the four-horse chariot race, Cleisthenes made an announcement that whoever of the Greeks considered himself good enough to be the son-in-law of Cleisthenes was to come to Sicyon within sixty days or sooner, as Cleisthenes would preside over the marriage in one year from the end of that sixty-day period. (6.126.3) All of the Greeks who were proud of themselves and their native land came as suitors. For these Cleisthenes constructed, just for this purpose, a running track and a palaestra [wrestling building].

(6.127.1) From Italy came Smindyrides son of Hippocrates from Sybaris, who of all men had reached the peak of luxurious living (for Sybaris was especially prosperous at this time), and Damasus, son of Amyris who was known as 'the wise', from Siris. (6.127.2) These came from Italy, and from the Ionian Gulf came Amphimnestus son of Epistrophus of Epidamnus. From Aetolia came Males, brother of that Titormus who surpassed all the Greeks in strength and had fled from human company to the remotest parts of Aetolia.

(6.127.3) From the Peloponnese came Leocedes, son of Pheidon, tyrant of the Argives. Pheidon invented weights and measures for the Peloponnesians and committed the greatest outrage of all Greeks, for he expelled the Elean judges and ran the games at Olympia himself. There was also Amiantus, son of Lycurgus, an Arcadian from Trapezus, and Laphanes, from the city of Paeus in Azania, son of Euphorion who is said in Arcadia to have received the Dioscuri [Castor and Pollux] in his house and after this welcomed all men as his guests, and Onomastus son of Agaeus from Elis. (6.127.4) These came from the Peloponnese. From Athens arrived Megacles son of that Alcmeon who had visited the Lydian king Croesus, and also Hippocleides son of Teisander, who excelled all other Athenians in wealth and good looks. From Eretria, which at that time was prosperous, came Lysanias; he was the only one from Euboea. From Thessaly came Diactorides, one of the Scopadae from Crannon, and from Molossia came Alcon.

(6.128.1) These men were the suitors. When they had arrived on the appointed day, Cleisthenes first questioned each of them regarding their country and their family background, and then kept them for a year, testing their manliness and temper and upbringing and way of life, consorting with them as individuals and as a group. Those of them who were younger he would take to the gymnasiums, but the most important test was their table manners: for as long as he kept them with him, he did this all the time, and at the same time entertained them sumptuously.

(6.128.2) He was particularly pleased with the suitors who came from Athens, and of these two especially Hippocleides son of Teisander, leaning towards him because of his manliness and his long-standing family connection with the Cypselid tyrants of Corinth. (6.129.1) On the day decreed for the celebration of the marriage, and for the declaration by Cleisthenes himself as to whom he would choose out of them all, he sacrificed a hundred oxen and gave an enormous banquet for the suitors themselves and all the people of Sicyon.

(6.129.2) When dinner was over, the suitors held a competition in music and speaking in company. As the drinking progressed Hippocleides, who was winning easily, ordered the flautist to play him a tune, and when the flautist obeyed he danced. Doubtless he was pleased with his dancing, but Cleisthenes who was watching the whole affair looked on with suspicion. (6.129.3) After a while Hippocleides ordered a table to be brought, and when the table arrived first danced Spartan dance figures on it and then Athenian ones, and thirdly supported his head on the table and gestured in the air with his legs. (6.129.4) During the first and second dances Cleisthenes abhorred the thought of Hippocleides becoming his son-in-law because of his dancing and his lack of self-respect, but restrained himself, not wishing to lose his temper with him; but when he saw him waving his legs in the air he was no longer able to restrain himself and said, 'Son of Teisander, you have danced away your marriage.' (6.129.5) Hippocleides said in reply, 'It doesn't worry Hippocleides' – (6.130.1) a byword to this day.

Helen, who eloped with Paris of Troy, abandoning her husband Menelaus, might seem the unlikely beneficiary of a cult at Sparta. But she was the daughter of Zeus, and married Menelaus, second only to his brother Agamemnon in the Trojan War. After the Trojan War, as Book 4 of the *Odyssey* makes clear, Menelaus and Helen resumed a happy married life. Young girls on the verge of marriage at Sparta accorded Helen divine honours and worshipped her, to have her assistance in winning a handsome husband. Here a group of a dozen maidens, themselves nearing the time for marriage, sing, as was customary, the bridal song before the bed-chamber of a newly married couple: it is a hymn of Menelaus' marriage to Helen.

The girls will anoint themselves with oil and race each other (line 22). Girls at Sparta were encouraged to race (see illustration 2.3) and throw javelins and generally to be out of doors to keep them fit and healthy for child-rearing, while Athenian girls led a fairly sheltered life. A sneeze, at an appropriate moment, was considered to be a good omen (line 16). 'Helen's tree' did actually exist at Sparta (line 49). Hymen, in the very last line, is the god of marriage, and Hymenaeus, the personified marriage hymn. Theocritus, *Idyll 18, The Bridal Song for Helen*:

In Sparta, once, at the home of blond Menelaus
twelve maidens with hyacinth blooms in their hair
before a freshly painted bridal chamber lined up for the dance:
the finest girls in the town, the cream of Spartan girlhood,
when Atreus' younger son Menelaus had shut its doors   5
on his beloved Helen, whom he'd courted.
All in harmony they sang beating time to the tune with feet
intertwining, the house shaking to the sound of the wedding song.

'What, so early, dear bridegroom, have you gone to sleep?
Are your limbs so weary? Or are you in love with sleep?   10
Or had you drunk too much, when you threw yourself onto the
   bed?
If you were so keen to go to sleep so early then you should have
   done so by yourself,
and let the maiden-bride with the maidens at her loving mother's side
play late until dawn, since tomorrow, and its tomorrow,
and year upon year, Menelaus, she is your bride.   15

Blessed bridegroom, some good man sneezed, so that you might
be successful, when to Sparta you came as did the other lords, and
   alone
among the demi-gods you have Zeus, son of Cronus, as a
   father-in-law.
The daughter of Zeus, of whom among the Achaean maidens there is
no equal walking upon the earth, lies under the same bed-spread
   as you: 20
and great will be the child she bears, if she bears one like its mother.
And we, all her peers, race together
anointing ourselves like men at the bathing spots by the Eurotas
   river,
four groups of sixty maidens, a band of youthful girls, and there isn't
a single one who when measured beside Helen is not without defect.   25

Rising Dawn shines out her wondrous face,
Queenly Night, as does sparkling spring when winter draws to a close:
like this did golden Helen glow radiant among us
as a cypress adorns the rich field
or garden where it sprang up, or a horse from Thessaly a chariot,   30
so Helen of rosy-skin is an adornment for Sparta:
no one from her basket winds off such works as she,
nor on the cunningly wrought loom weaves closer warp with her
   shuttle,
cutting it from the great beams of the upright loom.
Nor is anyone so skilful at plucking the lyre   35
and singing to Artemis and Athena of the broad breasts
as Helen, in whose eyes all desires dwell.
Beautiful, gracious maiden, now indeed the mistress of a house.

But we at dawn will go to the running track and the flowering
   meadows
plucking sweet smelling garlands.   40
We will think of you often, Helen, as suckling
lambs long for the teat of their mother.
We first a wreath will weave for you of prostrate growing clover
and we'll hang it on the shady plane tree:
we first taking smooth oil from the silver flask   45
will let it drip under the shady plane tree.
And on its bark will be carved letters, that those who pass by
may read in Dorian, 'Reverence me, I am Helen's tree.'

Farewell, bride, farewell groom, with a god as a father-in-law;
Leto, Leto the nourisher of children, grant to you fair offspring   50
and Cypris [Aphrodite], the goddess Cypris, that you love each other
equally, and Zeus, Zeus the son of Cronus, no end of prosperity,
which can descend again and again from well-born parents
to well-born children. Sleep, breathing on each other's breast
   passion
and desire. Do not forget to wake up at dawn.   55
We at dawn will come, when the first song bird
from his bed is raising his well-plumed neck in song.
Hymen, oh Hymenaeus, rejoice in this marriage.

LOVE AND HATE IN MARRIAGE

Euripides' *Alcestis* features a wife that loves her husband to the point where
she will sacrifice her life to save his; Euripides' *Medea* has a wife betrayed

by her husband and revenging herself by killing their children. Two more different marriages could not be imagined. In *Alcestis*, Admetus of Thessaly in northern Greece has aided the god Apollo, who rewards him with a reprieve from death – if he can find someone to take his place. His own aged parents refuse to die for him, but his selfless wife agrees. As Alcestis lies dying she asks her husband not to remarry and bring a step-mother into the house for their two children.

There is a great deal of irony in the play: Alcestis could not live without her husband, but he is quite prepared to live without her, and her repeated request that he not remarry presumably indicates a lack of trust in his marital fidelity. First produced in 438 BC, this is a classic example of noble self-sacrifice for someone who is loved, someone who clearly in Admetus' case is not worthy of the honour. But there is a happy ending: Alcestis will be saved from Hades and untimely death by Heracles. Charon ferried the souls of the dead from the land of the living to Hades on his small skiff, and is referred to here as Charon with his oar (line 361). Orpheus was a mythical singer (line 357). Alcestis lies dying at the beginning of these lines. Euripides, *Alcestis*, 280–356, 416–44, 463–4:

Alcestis: Admetus, you see how things are with me: 280
I'd like to tell you, before I die, of my wishes.
I have given you precedence over my own soul,
ordaining that you behold the light of day
while I die. I didn't have to die instead of you,
but could have had any man of Thessaly I chose   285
and lived in the wealthy house of a king.
But I couldn't stand to live separated from you
with orphaned children, and I didn't spare
my youthfulness, though having much in which I revelled.
And yet your father and your mother betrayed you,   290
for whom it was fitting to die, having come to the end of their lives
    anyway,
a beautiful act to save their son and die gloriously.
For you were their only son, and there was no chance
once you were dead that they would raise others.
Then I could have lived, and you, for the rest of our lives,   295
and you wouldn't be mourning the loss of your wife or
raising orphaned children. But these things
one of the gods has brought about to be so.

Well then. Bear in mind what you owe me for this.
For I will not ask you for what the deed is worth –   300

for there is nothing more valuable than a human life –
but for a fair exchange, as you'll agree, for you love
these children no less than I do, if you have any sense.
Keep the children as lords of my house
and do not marry another and install a step-mother over these
    children,   305
a woman baser than I, who will lay a hand on
your children and mine out of jealousy.
Don't do this, I beg you.
For a step-mother comes in as an enemy
of the previous children, no gentler than a viper.   310

And a son has in his father a great tower of defence,
who he can talk to and receive advice from,
but you, my daughter, how will you grow up to be a fine young
    woman?
What sort of a step-mother will you get?
May she not cast shameful aspersions against you,   315
and in the prime of your womanhood destroy your chances of
    marriage.
For your mother will not see you married
nor be present and give you courage while giving birth,
daughter, where nothing is more welcome than a mother.
For I've got to die: and not tomorrow   320
or the day after does this evil come for me,
but now today I will be numbered among the no-longer living.
Farewell, cheer up. And you husband
can boast that you took the best wife,
and you, children, that you were born of the best mother.   325

Chorus: Take heart! For I don't shrink from speaking for him:
he'll do these things, if his judgement isn't muddled.

Admetus: Don't worry, I'll do this, I will.
While you were living you were my wife, and dead
you alone will be called such, and no bride of Thessaly   330
will ever address me as husband in your place.
There is no one of such good parentage,
no woman as distinguished enough in beauty for that.
And I have enough children. I pray to the gods
that I have the enjoyment of them, as I have not had of you.   335
I won't mourn for you for just a year
but my grief will endure for as long as I live, wife,

detesting the mother who bore me, hating my father,
for they loved me only in word, not in deed.
But you gave what was most precious to you, 340
saving my life. So why shouldn't I lament,
deprived of such a companion as you?

I'll put an end to revels and the company of fellow drinkers,
of festive garlands, and the music that once flowed through the
  house.
For not ever again will I either touch 345
the lyre or lift up my heart to sing
to the Libyan flute: for you have taken the delight from my life.
A likeness to your living body, shaped by the hand of craftsmen,
will be laid out on our marriage-bed.
I'll fall upon it and embracing it with my arms, 350
calling your name, I'll imagine that I hold my dear wife
in my embrace, although I do not:
a chill comfort, alas, but nevertheless in this way
I'll lighten a heavy heart. And haunting my dreams
you might make me happy. For it's pleasant to see 355
our loved ones in our sleep in the night, for however long it's
  allowed.

Chorus: Admetus, you have to bear this disaster. 416
For you aren't the first, or the last, of mortal men
to lose a noble wife. And realise that
death is the destiny of all of us.

Admetus: I know it, this sorrow did not fall on me unexpectedly: 420
I've been worn down for some time knowing this.
But as I will preside over the funeral procession,
remain, and while waiting you will sing
a hymn to the god below, without pouring libations.
I command all the people of Thessaly I rule over 425
to join in the mourning for my wife,
cutting their hair and wearing black clothes,
and those who yoke up four-horse chariots and those
who ride a single horse to cut the manes of their necks with iron.
There shall be no sound of flutes or lyres 430
throughout the city until twelve months have passed.
For I will never bury a dead person more beloved
or one kinder to me. She is worthy to be honoured
by me, since she alone died for my sake.

Chorus: Daughter of Pelias, Alcestis, 435
farewell from me as you dwell
in the sunless house of Hades.
Let Hades the black-haired god
know, and also the old man
who sits at his oar and tiller 440
and escorts the dead
that it is by far and away
the best woman that he conveys across
the lake of Acheron in his two-oared skiff.

May the earth lay light above you, woman. 463–4

Probably the greatest of Greek tragedies, first produced in 431 BC, *Medea* has been performed in numerous languages and has had several adaptations. It is a brilliant tragedy of a mother who kills her own children in order to have revenge on their father, her husband. Medea learns that her husband, for whom she has killed her brother and abandoned her parents, is to set her aside and marry the daughter of the King of Corinth. Jason will seek to justify his actions as providing a safe haven for the children, but for Medea his action is unpardonable. Medea complains that a husband can go out and seek the company of friends while his wife cannot (lines 244–6), and a timid wife going to let her husband in at night is shown on an Athenian vase; the wife holds a small lamp in her hand to light the way (see illustration 2.4). Medea here addresses the chorus of Corinthian women (sympathetic to her) and compares their lot with hers: she is a barbarian woman with no ties but to her husband, who now abandons her. Euripides, *Medea*, 225–65:

Medea: This unexpected blow, falling on me, 225
has destroyed my soul. I'm desolate, and the joy has gone
from my life, and dear friends I want to die.
For he who was everything to me as I well know,
my husband, has turned out to be the most vile of men.
Of all the living things that have soul and reason 230
we women are the most wretched,
who first by necessity with an extravagant sum
purchase a husband, and take a master of our body.
There is an even more painful evil than this one,
and in this the greatest risk, whether we gain 235
a bad or good husband. For divorce gives a woman
a bad reputation; it's not possible for us to reject a husband.
She needs to be a prophet, coming to a house with different usages
 and ways,

about which her home did not teach her,
and how she might be best useful to her bed-fellow.   240
And if we carry out these hard duties,
and our husband lives with us, not wearing the yoke unwillingly,
our life is enviable. But if not, we ought to die.
But a man, whenever being with those inside the house becomes
      intolerable,
can go out, putting a stop to his vexatious restlessness   245
turning either to some friend or companion.
But by necessity we can look to only one soul – his.
They say that we live a life without danger
at home, while they wage war with the spear:
they reason unsoundly: I'd rather stand in battle with a shield   250
three times than bear a child once.

But the same story does not hold true for me as for you:
this is your city and ancestral home,
you enjoy life and the companionship of friends.
But I am alone, without a city, and outrageously treated   255
by my husband who carried me off from a barbarian land.
I have no mother, nor brother, no relative
with whom I could find a refuge from these disasters.
So I would ask only this of you,
if I might find some way or means   260
to exact vengeance on my husband for these wrongs,
be silent! For a woman is full of fear at everything else,
tremulous at the sight of battle and of iron.
But when she is wronged in bed
there is no other spirit more bloodthirsty.   265

Jason and Medea confront each other in a bitter argument, and he takes up
this theme of a woman crossed in bed. Euripides, *Medea*, 569–75:

Jason: But women have come to such a state that if everything is
      going all right in bed
you think that you have everything,   570
but if something goes wrong in bed,
you make a fierce battleground of your best and finest interests.
Mortals ought to produce their children from somewhere else,
and there should be no race of women.
In such a way, no evil would befall men!   575

Medea sends the princess, whom Jason is about to marry, a poisoned robe which kills her, and also her father who attempts to take it off his daughter; but it sticks to him as well, bringing them both a hideous death. Medea resolves to kill her own children by Jason as the ultimate revenge against him; she vacillates and the decision is not an easy one, but she takes it. Yet Medea remains a loving mother, as her tender farewell to her children indicates. As another poet put it (Sophocles, *Phaedra*, Fragment 685), 'Children are the anchors of a mother's life.' Euripides, *Medea*, 1070–80:

> *Medea:* Give your right hand to your mother to kiss   1070
> Dearest hand, mouth and face so dear to me,
> and beautiful countenance of my children.
> May the pair of you prosper, but in that other place, Hades. Your father
> has taken away what was here. How sweet the embrace,
> how soft the skin, how sweet the children's breath.   1075
> Go, go into the house. I can no longer look at you
> but am overcome with troubles.
> I know the extent of the evils I am about to perpetrate
> but my wrath is stronger than any considered deliberations,
> wrath which is the greatest cause of evils for mortals.   1080

The leader of the chorus of Corinthian women, which has been present while Medea has spoken, now makes some observations on the grief involved in bringing up children. Euripides, *Medea*, 1090–1115:

> *Chorus:* I say that those mortals   1090
> who are completely inexperienced about children
> and have never borne them are closer to happiness
> than those who have raised children.
> For the childless, because of their inexperience
> as to whether children are a pleasure or a trouble to mortals,   1095
> not having children
> distance themselves from many griefs.
> But those who have the sweet offspring of children
> in their houses, I see them worn out
> with cares throughout their life,   1100
> firstly, how they will bring their children up well,
> and how they might bequeath them a livelihood.
> And after all this it isn't clear whether for good children
> they have undergone their troubles, or for bad.

From out of all these   1105
I'll mention the last grief for mortals:
suppose indeed they have found a sufficient livelihood for them
and the children's bodies have reached maturity
and they have turned out good: but if
their destiny so turns out, death carries off the bodies   1110
of the children to Hades, and they are clean gone.
So how does it bring us any benefit
that the gods add for mortals
this yet more grievous one
for the sake of heirs?   1115

Medea again addresses the chorus. Euripides intends to show how difficult a decision it is for Medea to kill her children, even for revenge against the man who betrayed her. In this way he sets up a moral dilemma for the audience, which can sympathise with her desire for revenge, but views the slaying of the children as abhorrent. Medea is cast in a sympathetic light, rather than simply being a murderer. Euripides, *Medea*, 1236–50:

Medea: Friends, I'm determined on this deed, to kill
my children as soon as possible, and to flee this land,
and not through tarrying to give the children
to another hand, less loving, to kill.
It is absolutely necessary for them to die. And since   1240
it must be done, it is I who gave them birth who will slay them.
But arm yourself, heart: why do I hesitate to carry out
the terrible deed that must be done?
Come, wretched hand of mine, seize the sword,
seize it, and arrive at the wretched goal of your life.   1245
Don't play the coward, don't remember your children
as your loved ones, as the ones you bore, but
for this brief day forget that they are yours,
and mourn them afterwards. For even if you slay them,
yet they were your loved ones. I am a desolate woman!   1250

Medea kills her two children, who cry out to the chorus for help. Jason arrives on the scene; his grief is genuine. Medea is suspended above the stage in a chariot given to her by her grandfather the sun, Helios; she has the corpses of the children and will bury them herself, without Jason's assistance, and then flee to Athens. In this way Euripides' greatest tragedy closes, with its themes of marriage and revenge, and the children who are the pawns in many marital disputes. The dialogue at the end of the play is one of the best-known exchanges of two estranged lovers in western literature. The *Argo* was the ship Jason and the Argonauts set out in to find the Golden Fleece, as a result of which he met Medea (line 1335). Euripides, *Medea*, 1323–85, 1415–19:

> *Jason:* Hateful one, woman most absolutely hated by the gods,
> by me, by the whole race of mortals,
> who dared to take a sword to your own children,   1325
> doing this to the ones you bore, and destroying me with this
>   childlessness!
> How can you look upon the sun and earth having done this,
> having committed such an impious act?
> Damn you! Now I am sane, but then I was crazy,
> when I took you from your home and barbarian land   1330
> and brought you to a Greek home, a great evil,
> a traitor to your father and the homeland that raised you.
> The gods have brought upon me the avenging spirit destined for
>   you,
> for you slew your own brother at the hearth
> and then went on board the *Argo* with its beautiful prow.   1335
>
> That's how you started. But married to me
> and bearing these children to me
> you murdered them because of bed and sex.
> There isn't a Greek woman who would ever have
> dared to commit such a deed, and yet I preferred you   1340
> in marriage, and what a hateful and destructive
> marriage it has turned out for me, married to a lioness, not a
>   woman,
> having a nature wilder than Scylla the Tuscan sea-monster.
> But since I could not sting you with ten-thousand insults –
> such is your impudent nature –   1345
> go, perpetrator of shameless deeds, stained with the blood of your
>   children.
> For me, there is my fate to lament,
> with no joy from the new bride of my marriage-bed,
> nor will I speak to alive the children
> I have raised but whom I have lost.   1350
>
> *Medea:* Long would I stretch out my speech to counter these words,
> if father Zeus was not acquainted with
> the benefits you had from me, and what you have done:

you were not going to slight my marriage-bed
happily spending your life laughing at me,   1355
nor was the princess, nor was Creon who bestowed her in marriage
on you going to throw me out of this land with impunity.
Say these things, and call me a lioness if you wish,
or Scylla who lives on a Tuscan rock.
For I had to pierce your heart.   1360

Jason: And you suffer just the same, and you are a partner in these
sorrows.

Medea: That's obvious. But the grief is less, if you can't laugh at me.

Jason: Children, what a wicked mother you gained!

Medea: Children, how you have been destroyed by your father's
wickedness!

Jason: They weren't killed by my hand!   1365

Medea: But it was your hybris and new marriage!

Jason: And did you think it proper to kill them because of marriage?

Medea: Do you think this is a small disaster for a woman?

Jason: Yes, for a sensible woman. But for you everything's a
disaster!

Medea: The children are no longer living: this will pierce you!   1370

Jason: Alas, they are alive as bloody avengers on your head!

Medea: The gods know who it was who began this misery!

Jason: They know indeed your abomination of a heart!

Medea: Abhor me! I hate the sound of your bitter voice!

Jason: And I yours! To be released from you will come easy.   1375

Medea: How so? What will I do? For I wish the same.

Jason: Permit me to bury their corpses and to mourn for them.

Medea: Indeed no, since I will bury them with my own hands,
taking them to the sanctuary of Hera Akraea at the cape,
so that none of my enemies might desecrate them,   1380
ripping open their tombs. And I will establish
a holy festival and rite in this land
for eternity, in recompense for this unholy murder.

Myself, I will travel to the land of Erechtheus, Athens,
to live with Aegeus, son of Pandion.   1385

Chorus: Zeus on Olympus has many things in his treasury   1415
and the gods bring about many unexpected things.
The anticipated is not accomplished,
but the gods find a way to accomplish the unlooked for.
So has this affair turned out.

THE WIFE'S RESIGNATION TO HER FATE

A female character here notes that women have no identity apart from their
relationship to their male relatives and husbands. Sophocles, *Tereus*,
Fragment 583:

But now on my own I am nothing. Many times
I have considered the nature of women to be this:
that we are nothing. As young girls in our father's home
we have the happiest existence, I think, of all people,
for careless ease always rears children happily.
But when we have good sense and have arrived at maturity
we are thrust out and sold
away from our ancestral gods and those who bore us –
some to husbands who are strangers, others to barbarians,
some to homes empty of joy, others to ones full of fault-finding.
And this, when a single night has yoked us,
we have to praise, and consider ourselves fortunate.

THE HUSBAND'S REVENGE

Penelope was the model for the loyal wife, waiting for Odysseus not just
for the ten years in which he fought with the Greeks outside Troy but
for the subsequent nine full years of his wanderings. Most assumed
Odysseus was dead and would never return, hence the presence of the
suitors for Penelope's hand in the house; they came to seek her in
marriage several years after the sack of Troy, when Odysseus had failed
to return. But she kept aloof from them, and would not agree to remarry.
Her behaviour is justified by Odysseus' return in the tenth year of his
wanderings. In the first years when the suitors were in the house she had
put them off with the ruse of weaving a funeral shroud. Helen, an
aristocratic woman like Penelope, also wove, and in wealthy households
there would also be women slaves put to this task, with cloth-making
being like a cottage industry (see illustration 2.5). Amphimedon, one of

the suitors, his soul now in Hades, speaks to Agamemnon. Laertes is Odysseus' father, who in fact lives to see his son's homecoming. Homer, *Odyssey*, 24.125–50:

We courted Penelope, the wife of Odysseus who was long gone; 125
she would not refuse the despised marriage, nor would she make a
   decision about it,
intending death and a dark fate for us,
but this other cunning scheme she plotted in her heart:
setting up a huge web in the palace, she commenced weaving
a fine, immense piece of cloth. Then she said to us: 130

'Young men, my suitors, since god-like Odysseus is dead,
wait awhile, though you are keen to marry me, until I complete
this robe, so that not in vain the threads be wasted.
This is a burial shroud for the hero Laertes, for the time when
the destructive fate of death that lays one low will seize him, 135
in case any of the Achaean women say it against me that
without a shroud he would lie, who had procured many
   possessions.'

So she said, and then the proud heart in us was persuaded.
Then daily she wove at the huge web, but at night,
when she would have torches set before it, unravelled her work. 140
So for three years she was successful with her ruse and deceived
   the Achaeans.
But when the fourth year came and the seasons did their rounds,
as the months waned, and many days had come and gone,
then one of her women, who was in the secret, told,
and we caught Penelope in the act of unravelling the shimmering
   web. 145
So she completed the shroud against her will, compelled to do so.

Now when she had shown us the robe – after weaving
and washing the great web – and it shone as the sun or moon,
a cruel god then led Odysseus from somewhere
to a lonely corner of his estate, where his swineherd dwelt. 150

Odysseus returns and slays the suitors who have wooed his wife for several years, and also eaten him out of house and home. This was the 'death and dark fate' Penelope had hoped for the suitors. Homer, *Odyssey*, 22.1–25:

But Odysseus of many schemes stripping off his beggar's rags
leapt onto the great threshold, with the bow and the quiver

replete with arrows, and emptied out the swift arrows
in front of his feet, and said among the suitors:

'Here is a perilous contest that has come to its conclusion:　　　　5
now for the next target, which not yet has a man ever hit,
but I will, if luck is with me and Apollo grants my prayer.'

He said this and aimed a bitter arrow at Antinous
who was about to raise a beautiful goblet to his lips,
a two-handled golden one that even now was in his hands　　　　10
so that he might drink the wine: and the thought of death was far
from his heart. Who might think that among men dining,
a single man among so many, even if he might be very strong,
would prepare for him an evil death and black fate?
But Odysseus taking aim at him struck him in the throat with an
　　　arrow　　　　15
and straight through the tender neck went its point.
He fell to one side and the goblet fell from his hand
as he was hit and straightaway up through his nostrils spurted a
　　　thick jet
of mortal blood: quickly he kicked the table away from him
with his foot, from it the food scattered falling to the earth　　　　20
and the bread and roasted meats were ruined. The suitors broke
into an uproar in the house when they saw the fallen man
and sprang from their seats, agitated, throughout the room, looking
　　　everywhere along the well-built walls:
but there was no shield or sturdy spear to seize.　　　　25

Odysseus addresses the suitors, reveals his identity, and refuses to be
bought off: he will fight the suitors to the death. Homer, *Odyssey*,
22.65–98:

'Now before you is placed the choice, either to fight　　　　65
or to flee, whoever might escape death and the fates:
but many of you I think will not escape total annihilation.'

So he spoke, and their knees and hearts dear to them quailed.
But Eurymachus spoke to the suitors for a second time:

'Friends, this man will not restrain his invincible hands,　　　　70
but since he has the polished bow and the quiver,
he will shoot from the smooth threshold, until he has slain
all of us. But remember our lust for battle.
Unsheath your swords and hold the tables before you against

the arrows of certain death. Let's all have a go 75
at rushing him, to see if we might drive him away from the
   threshold and the doors,
and go through the town so the shout for help might be raised
   quickly.
Then this man will soon have shot for the last time.'

When he'd finished speaking, he drew his sharp bronze sword,
sharpened on both sides, and rushed at Odysseus 80
with a murderous cry. At the same moment god-like Odysseus
loosed an arrow and struck him on the chest next to the nipple,
and anchored the swift arrow in his liver: and from his hand
Eurymachus let his sword fall earthwards, and prostrate over the
   table
he thrashed around and fell, and from it the food fell to the earth 85
and the two-handled goblet: he struck the ground with his forehead,
his soul writhing in agony, and kicking both his feet
wobbled the chair: and over his eyes the mist of death descended.

Amphinomus went for glorious Odysseus,
rushing against him, and had drawn his sharp sword 90
hoping somehow to force him from the doors. But Telemachus
anticipated him, hitting him with his bronze spear from behind
in the middle of his shoulders, and drove it through the chest:
he fell with a thump and struck the earth full on his forehead.
Telemachus sprang aside, leaving his long spear 95
in Amphinomus: for he feared that one of the Achaeans
would rush him as he drew out the long spear,
stabbing him with a sword or smiting him with its edge.

The suitors gain access to the weapons in the storeroom, and the battle
rages on. The goddess Athena appears in the guise of Mentor to encourage
Odysseus and then watches the battle as a swallow, intervening to assist
Odysseus, but not doing everything, making trial of his prowess. Ctesippus,
son of Polytherses, had kicked Odysseus when he came in disguise as a
beggar to his own home, and the herdsman of the oxen revels in his death
(lines 285–6). Homer, *Odyssey*, 22.241–309:

The suitors were spurred on by Agelaus son of Damastor,
with Eurynomus and Amphimedon and Demoptolemus,
and Peisander, son of Polyctor, and wise Polybus:
for of the suitors they were beyond compare the best in valour

of those still living and battling for their lives: 245
but the others the bow and the thick-flying arrows had laid to rest.
But Agelaus spoke among the suitors, addressing his words to all:

'Friends, now this man will restrain his invincible hands,
since Mentor has gone, vaunting empty boasts,
and they are left by themselves at the front doors.   250
Now do not all at once cast your long spears,
but come you six, hurl first, if ever Zeus
allows that Odysseus be struck and we win the kudos.
The others are of no account once this man has fallen.'

He said this, and they all hurled their spears as he had urged,   255
eagerly, but the goddess Athena caused them all to be futile:
one of them struck the door post of the well-built hall,
another the close-fitting door:
the ash spear heavy with bronze of another struck upon the wall.
But when they had escaped the spears of the suitors   260
much-enduring god-like Odysseus began speaking:

'Friends, now I would say that we cast
our spears into the crowd of the suitors, who are intent
on slaying us, adding this to their existing crimes.'

He said this, and they all hurled their sharp spears   265
shooting straight ahead. Odysseus slew Demoptolemus,
Telemachus slew Euryades, the swineherd slew Elatus,
and the herdsman of the oxen slew Peisander.
All of these fell at the same time, biting the vast floor with their
    teeth,
and the suitors retreated to the far corner of the hall.   270
The others sprang forward and pulled their spears free of the
    corpses.
Again the suitors all hurled their sharp spears
eagerly but the goddess Athena caused them all to be futile:
one of them hit the door post of the well-built hall
another the close-fitting door,   275
the ash spear of another, tipped with bronze, struck upon the
    wall.
Amphimedon nicked Telemachus on the hand at the wrist,
and the bronze ruptured the top layer of the skin.
Ctesippus with his long spear grazed the shoulder of Eumaeus
above the shield: but the spear glided over and fell on the ground.   280

Then once more wise and wily Odysseus and those with him
cast their sharp spears into the crowd of the suitors.
This time Odysseus, the sacker of cities, slew Eurydamas,
Telemachus slew Amphimedon and the swineherd slew Polybus.
Then the herdsman of the oxen struck Ctesippus   285
in the chest, vaunting boastfully,

'Son of Polytherses, revelling in sarcasm, never ever again
will you give yourself over to recklessness, talking big, but to the
   gods
leave speech, since they are indeed much stronger.
This is your guest-gift to equal the boot you gave   290
to divine Odysseus when he came begging through the house.'

So said the herdsmen of the curved-horned oxen: then Odysseus
with his long spear from up close stabbed the son of Damastor.
Telemachus hit Leiocritus, son of Evenor, with a spear
in the middle of the guts, driving the bronze clean through: 295
he fell headlong and struck the earth full on his forehead.
Then the goddess Athena held up her aegis, the curse of mortals,
from high up in the ceiling rafters: and the suitors' wits were
   frenzied.
They fled through the hall like a herd of cattle
which the darting gad-fly rouses and drives   300
in the season of spring when the days grow longer.
Just as vultures with curved talons and hooked beaks
glide out of the mountains to pounce on smaller birds:
the birds of the plain go flying from the clouds,
but the vultures swoop and destroy them, and there is neither   305
defence nor escape, and men marvel at the hunting:
so these men swooping on the suitors throughout the hall
struck them down on every side; their groaning rose hideous,
as heads were struck, and all the floor ran with blood.

Leiodes begs Odysseus for mercy, clasping Odysseus' knees; this was a
traditional supplicating position. But Odysseus refuses, and then tells
Telemachus to inform Eurycleia, many years before Telemachus' nurse and
now Penelope's aged housekeeper in charge of the women servants, about
what has happened. Eurycleia starts to raise the ceremonial cry shouted by
the women when the axe came down on the sacrificial victim, but Odysseus
forbids this. He asks her which of the women slaves have been faithful to
Penelope, and which had consorted with the suitors: the unfaithful will go
to their deaths. Homer, *Odyssey*, 22.399–418:

Eurycleia opened the doors of the well-built hall,
and in she went: Telemachus led the way before her.　　　400
There she found Odysseus, among the corpses of the
　　slaughtered,
splattered with blood and gore as if he were a lion
which comes from devouring an ox in the field:
all his chest and both sides of his face
stained with blood, hideous to look at, face to face:　　　405
so Odysseus' feet and hands above were splattered.
But Eurycleia when she saw the corpses and the blood without
　　end
started to raise the ritual sacrificial cry, looking on the great
　　work of slaughter.
But Odysseus restrained her and checked her enthusiasm,
and addressed her speaking winged words:　　　410

'Exult in your own heart, old one, but restrain yourself and don't
　　raise the sacrificial cry:
it is not holy to boast over slain men. The fate decreed
by the gods and their own vile deeds overcame these men here:
for they honoured not a single man on earth,
either base or noble, of whoever came among them:　　　415
and by this arrogance they fell to a shameful death.
But come, name for me the women in the house,
which ones show me no honour, and which are innocent.'

Penelope and Odysseus are now reunited. The emphasis here on mutual
conjugal love can be set against the misogynistic writings of ancient Greece.
Homer, *Odyssey*, 23.289–301:

Meanwhile Eurynome and the nurse made up the bed
of soft bedclothes, by the light of blazing torches.　　　290
But when they had busily spread the strongly-built bed,
the old servant went back to her room to lie down,
and Eurynome the bedroom servant led them
on their way to the marriage-bed, with a torch in her hands.
Leading them to the bedroom, she went back again. Odysseus　　　295
and Penelope then joyously came to their old, habitual
　　marriage-bed.
Then Telemachus and the ox-herder and the swineherd
stilled their feet from the dance, and stopped the women,
and themselves lay down to sleep in the shadowy halls.

But when Odysseus and Penelope were satiated with the passion of
  love,   300
they found joy in swapping stories, each telling their story.

A WIFE'S ADULTERY

Adultery was a chief source of fear for Athenian husbands. The speaker of
the following defence speech, Euphiletus, has killed Eratosthenes, a charge
that he does not deny. He claims that he found Eratosthenes in bed with his
wife and slew him there, in front of witnesses. This was technically allowed
by Athenian law, but by the time of this speech, at the very close of the fifth
or beginning of the fourth century BC, this was an unusual course of action,
and most husbands accepted monetary compensation from adulterers.
Eratosthenes' relatives accuse Euphiletus of luring Eratosthenes into his
house, fabricating the charge of adultery against him, and murdering him
unjustly. As with most cases the ultimate verdict is unknown. Euphiletus in
the early sections of the speech claims to have been a happily married man,
whose union is destroyed by a seducer, who deserved his fate. This speech
by Lysias is arguably his best, and is one of the finest pieces of litigation to
have survived from classical Greece.

Like many dwellings with two storeys, Euphiletus' house had no stairs
(an expensive item) but rather a ladder. Many Athenian vases show a bride
at the foot of a ladder that led to the upstairs quarters of the house, where
the women had their separate rooms, away from the gaze of any men who
came to the house. This family is moderately prosperous, having a double-
storey house and one maid. But the mother cannot afford a wet-nurse, and
the husband seems to work hard for his living. However, there is a slave-girl
who helps with the baby. More than one Athenian vase shows a slave-girl
who has been looking after a child bringing it to its mother (see illustration
2.6). The Thesmophoria was a women-only fertility festival (20). Lysias 1
(*Against Eratosthenes*), 9–20, 22–7, 30–1:

(1.9) When a child was born to us, its mother herself gave it her own
breast. In order that she did not face the danger of falling down the
ladder when the baby needed bathing, I lived above, and the women
below. (1.10) This had become such a normal state of affairs that my
wife would often leave me and go below to sleep with the child, to give it
the breast and so that it wouldn't cry. Things went on like this for a long
time, and I wasn't any the wiser, but was so foolishly inclined that I
thought my wife was the most respectable of all the wives in the city.
(1.11) Time went by, jurors, and I unexpectedly returned from the
country, and after the evening meal the child was crying and

troublesome, for the nurse was intentionally annoying it, so that it would behave like this, for the man was in the house. For later I found out all about this. (1.12) And so I told my wife to go and give the child her breast, so that it might stop howling. She didn't want to go at first, as if it rather pleased her to have me home at this time. When I grew angry with her and ordered her to go, she said, 'So that you can try your luck with the little slave. Once, when you'd been drinking, you made a pass at her.' (1.13) I laughed, and she got up; leaving she closed the door, and turned the key as if in jest. And I giving no thought to the matter and not in the least suspicious went to sleep, content after coming from the country.

(1.14) When it was nearly day she came and opened the door. When I asked her why the doors had slammed during the night, she answered that the light kept next to the child had gone out, so she had relit it at the neighbours. I kept quiet and believed what she'd said. But it did strike me, men of the jury, that she had make-up on her face, though her brother was not yet thirty days' dead. Despite this I didn't say anything about the matter, but going out I left the house in silence.

(1.15) After this, men of the jury, time meanwhile passed by, and I was quite ignorant of my woes; then an old woman approached me, sent by a woman with whom that man was having an adulterous affair, as later I heard: this woman was angry and thought that she was being misused, because he no longer visited her as had been his custom, so she kept an eye on him until she found out the reason why. (1.16) So the old woman, waiting near my house, approached me, 'Euphiletus,' she said, 'in no way consider me meddlesome in approaching you: for the man who is dishonouring both you and your wife happens to be our enemy. So if you would take your servant girl who walks to the market-place and serves you, and torture her, you will discover everything. It is,' she said, 'Eratosthenes of the *deme* Oe, he has not only seduced your wife but many others as well. (1.17) For he has this skill.' Saying this, she made off, men of the jury, and I was immediately agitated, and everything crowded into my mind, and I lacked nothing in suspicion, calling to mind how I was locked in my room, and remembering that on that night the door of the inner court and the house door had slammed, which hadn't previously happened, and it had seemed to me that my wife was wearing make-up. All of this came to my attention, and I lacked nothing in suspicion.

(1.18) Going home, I commanded the slave-woman to follow me to the market-place, and led her to the house of a good friend and informed her that I knew everything about the goings on in my house: 'So you,' I said, 'can take a choice of either of two possibilities: either to be whipped and sent to a mill, and never cease from being oppressed by evils of such a sort, or by speaking the truth not to suffer anything bad, but to have pardon from me for all your wrong-doings. No lies now: speak nothing but the whole truth.'

(1.19) She denied it at first, and told me to carry out my wishes, as she knew nothing. But when I mentioned Eratosthenes to her, and said that he was the visitor to my wife, she was terrified, assuming that I had accurate knowledge of the whole affair. So then she threw herself at my knees, and extracted an oath from me that she would not come to any harm. (1.20) She accused him first of coming up to her after the funeral, then how she finally acted as his messenger, and how my wife was persuaded over time, and the ways in which she organised his entries to the house, and how at the Thesmophoria, when I was in the country, my wife went to the shrine with his mother, and she gave a full and detailed account of everything else that had taken place.

(1.22) Sostratus was a close friend of mine. At sunset I met him coming from the country. Knowing that arriving at that time he would find none of his close friends at home, I invited him to dinner. Coming to my house we went to the upper floor of the house and dined. (1.23) When he'd dined well, he left me and went on his way, and I fell asleep. Eratosthenes, men of the jury, entered the house, and the maid-servant woke me up at once and told me that he was inside. Telling her to watch the door, going down I silently went outside, and called at the houses of one friend and then another; and I found some of them at home, but others were not in town. (1.24) So taking as many of those who were at home, I walked on. Taking torches from the nearest shop we entered the house; the door was open, as the maid-servant had it ready. Pushing the door of the bedroom open the first of those who entered saw him still lying next to my wife, and those who came in next saw him standing on the bed, stark naked.

(1.25) And I, men of the jury, struck him, knocking him down, and pulling his two hands behind his back tied them and asked him why he had the audacity to come into my house. That man openly admitted his guilt, then he entreated and begged me not to slay him but to exact money instead. (1.26) I said, 'It isn't me that slays you, but the law of the city, which you are flouting, and have regarded as less important than your own pleasures, choosing instead to commit this offence against my wife and my children rather than obeying the laws and behaving decently.'

(1.27) So, men of the jury, that man enjoyed the fate which the laws command for those who do such things. He was not hauled off the street into the house, nor had he taken refuge at the hearth, as his relatives claim.

(1.30) You have heard, men of the jury, how the court of the Areopagus itself, to which both in our fathers' time and that of our own trials for homicide have been allocated, says of this quite categorically that whoever will exact this penalty, catching a man in adultery with his wife, will not be convicted of murder. (1.31) And so firmly was the law-giver Solon convinced that this was just in the case of wedded wives, that he established the same penalty in the case of concubines, who are worthy of less consideration. And yet it is clear that if he had access to a greater penalty in the case of wives, he would have imposed it.

Adultery could not be kept a secret. Pindar, *Pythian Victory Ode*, 11.25–8:

Adultery in young wives
is a most hateful fault and impossible to hide
from other people's tongues
for one's fellow citizens gossip wickedly.

Hesiod also had something to say about gossip. Hesiod, *Works and Days*, 760–4:

Keep away from the cunning talk of men. 760
Talk is wicked, light and very easily aroused,
heavy to bear, and difficult to get rid of.
Talk is never completely put to rest when many people
spread it. Talk herself is rather like a goddess.

MALE ATTITUDES TOWARD WOMEN

The women of Athens met once a year to celebrate the festival of the Thesmophoria, honouring Demeter and Persephone, invoking their good-will for the fertility of the field and of women's bodies. Men were excluded. Aristophanes' play (produced in 411 BC) set at this festival has a meeting of women discussing Euripides and accusing him of slandering women in his plays. While Aristophanes often refers to Euripides' mother as a vegetable seller, she was in fact an aristocrat and the joke here is unclear. The 'Two Goddesses' are Demeter and Persephone (line 383). The brother of the young girl does not like the colour of his sister's complexion, suspecting it is brought on by love (line 406). One of the women, Mica, presents the case against Euripides. Aristophanes, *Women at the Festival of the Thesmophoria*, 383–432:

Mica: By the Two Goddesses it is not because I am in any way ambitious
that I have risen to speak, women, but
because for a long time I have taken it badly,   385
seeing you trampled in the mud by Euripides –
son of that mother who sold vegetables in the market –
and hearing all sorts of numerous slanders.
For what slurs hasn't Euripides mocked us with?
Where has he not hurled these, wherever at all   390
there is an audience, and tragic actors and choruses,
labelling us as adulteresses, as lusting after men,
as drunks, cheats, gossips,
as unhealthy, an evil in men's lives?
So as soon as the men return from the theatre   395
they suspiciously look us up and down straightaway, searching
inside the house in case there is a hidden lover.
It's no longer possible for us to do the sorts of things we used to:
so shocking are the things that this Euripides has taught
husbands about us.   400

If a wife so much as arranges a bunch of flowers, her husband thinks she's in love:
and if she drops one of the household utensils as she goes about the house,
her husband asks: 'Who was she day-dreaming about when she dropped that pot?
Surely about our guest from Corinth!'
A girl is sick; straightaway her brother remarks: 405
'I don't like the look of this girl's complexion.'
Well then. A childless wife who wants to pass off a child
as her own isn't able to get away with it,
because our husbands park themselves close by.
He's slandered us to the old men too, who used to marry   410
young girls, so that none of the grey-beards
wants to get married because of this line in one of Euripides' plays:
'The old man marries a tyrant as a wife'.

Then, because of Euripides, they have placed
seals and bars on the women's rooms 415
to guard us, and not only that they breed
Molossian hounds to frighten off lovers.
All of this is understandable. But the tasks that used to be ours,
managing the stores and choosing what food to take out,
the grain, olive oil, wine, we aren't allowed to do any more. 420
For our husbands carry the keys around,
hidden, devilishly tricky ones
from Sparta, the ones with three teeth.
Before that we could secretly open the door
with a locking seal specially made for just three obols. 425
Now this Euripides, this household slave,
has instructed them to wear tiny locking seals made of worm-eaten
   wood.
So now it seems to me that in some way or another
we should cook up some form of destruction,
either with drugs or by some other means, 430
so that he is destroyed. I've argued these points clearly:
the other issues I'll write up with the secretary.

Euripides has sent a male relative ('Kinsman') along to the
Thesmophoria festival, disguised as a woman. He (or rather 'she') speaks
in Euripides' defence, much to the chagrin of the women. Women's
exaggerated sexual appetites as mocked here obviously raised a laugh
with the male audience in the theatre. The woman pours water over the
door socket so that it will not creak as she goes out (line 487). It was a
standing joke that women would chew garlic after illicit sex to lull their
husband's suspicions: no one would want to have sex with a woman
reeking of garlic (lines 494–6). Melanippe and Phaedra were tragic
characters, especially Phaedra, who fell in love with her step-son
Hippolytus and committed suicide, and caused Hippolytus' father to
curse him (line 547). Aristophanes, *Women at the Festival of the
Thesmophoria*, 466–519, 531–67:

Kinsman: Women, it's not surprising that you are absolutely furious
with Euripides, hearing such slanders,
nor that your blood is boiling.
For I myself – may I have joy from my children –
hate that man, and I'd be a lunatic not to! 470
Nevertheless, it's important that we have a discussion among
   ourselves,

for we are by ourselves here, and nothing that we say will be divulged
   outside.
Why do we keep on blaming him for these things,
taking it so badly just because he knows about two or three
of the thousand wicked things we get up to?   475
For I myself, to start with, speaking for myself and not anybody
   else,
have a lot on my conscience. I'll tell you the worst of them:
when I had been married for just three days,
my husband was sleeping next to me. But I had a lover,
who had seduced me when I was seven.   480
He came to scratch at the door, passionate for me;
I realised straightaway it was him. I was sneaking downstairs
but my husband asked, 'Where are you going downstairs?'
   'Where?
I've got a cramp and a pain in my stomach:
I'm going to the loo.' 'Go then.'   485

And he grinds up juniper pine, aniseed and sage,
while I poured water into the door socket
and went out to my lover. Then I leant up against
the pillar of Apollo, hanging onto the laurel tree.
Euripides, you see, never mentioned that.   490
Nor does he tell how we go hell for leather with
the slaves and mule drivers if we can't get anyone else,
nor how whenever we've been totally whored
by someone all night, we chew garlic at sunrise,
so that when our husband returns home from the city walls and
   smells it   495
he doesn't suspect that we've done anything wrong.
Euripides has never, you see,
mentioned these things. If he reviles Phaedra,
what does that matter to us? He's never told how
the wife showing her husband her robe by holding it up to the
   light   500
got the lover out of the house; he's never told that one.

And I know of another wife who pretended to be giving birth
for ten days until she could buy a baby.
Her husband rushed around buying drugs to bring on childbirth.
An old crone brought the baby in a pot, its mouth bunged up   505
with honeycomb so that it wouldn't cry out.
Then the old crone gave the signal, and the wife cried out,

'Go away, go away, husband, for I think I'm going to have the
  baby.'
For the baby kicked the belly of the pot!
He ran outside, delirious with joy, and she unblocked   510
the baby's mouth, and it cried out.
Then the wretched crone, who'd brought the baby,
runs grinning to the husband and announces:
'A lion, a lion you've sired, your spitting image,
in absolutely every way, and his dicky   515
just like yours, taut as a beam.'
Don't we do these wretched deeds? By Artemis, we do!
And why then do we get infuriated with Euripides,
who doesn't do anything worse to us than what we've done?   519

Chorus leader: For there is nothing born more shameless than
  women,
                                                                         531
nothing worse, if not all women.

Mica: By the goddess Aglaurus, women, you're not thinking right,
but you're drugged, or you're suffering chronically from some other
  great affliction,
to allow this cursed woman to insult us all so completely.   535
Perhaps there is someone in the audience who will help out, but
  if not,
we ourselves and our slave-girls – getting a hot coal from
  somewhere – will singe her fanny,
to teach the woman not to speak badly of women ever again.

Kinsman: Surely not my fanny, women! For if   540
there is free speech here, and as many of us here who are citizens
  are eligible to speak,
then if I say on Euripides' behalf what I know to be just,
do you have because of this to punish me by plucking out my hairs?

Mica: Why shouldn't you pay the penalty? You are the only woman
  who has dared
to speak on behalf of that man who has done us so much harm,   545
who has made an art-form of finding stories in which a woman
  becomes bad,
creating Melanippes and Phaedras; but he's never written
about Penelope, because she was considered to be respectable.

Kinsman: Well, I know the reason for that! You couldn't name
a single Penelope alive today. All of them are Phaedras.   550

Mica: Do you hear that, women, what the wretch
again says about all of us?

Kinsman: By Zeus, I haven't yet mentioned all I know. Do you want me
to say more?

Mica: But you don't have anything left to say. You've poured out
everything you know like water.

Kinsman: By Zeus, not even a thousandth part of what we get up to.   555
I haven't pointed out, you see, how we use our kitchen pots to
siphon off the wine –

Mica: You should be annihilated!

Kinsman: And how we give the meat from the Apatouria festival to
our go-betweens
and say that the weasel got it –

Mica: Wretched me, you're blabbering!

Kinsman: And I haven't told the one about how another woman
made her husband bite the dust   560
with an axe blow, nor how another woman drove her husband
insane with drugs,
or how the woman in the countryside buried her father . . .

Mica: May you die!

Kinsman: . . . under the bath-tub.

Mica: Do we have to listen to this?

Kinsman: Or how your slave gave birth to a son, and you took it
as your own, giving your baby girl to the slave.   565

Mica: By the Two Goddesses you won't say these things
with impunity, but I'll pluck out your hairs.

The magistrate who comes to challenge the women on the acropolis in
Aristophanes' *Lysistrata* (produced in 411 BC), which they have seized as
part of their sex strike to end the Peloponnesian War, complains that it is
men's fault for spoiling their women. Aristophanes, *Lysistrata*, 403–30:

Magistrate: By briny Poseidon, we've got our just deserts.
For we ourselves go along with our wives' dreadful behaviour
and teach them a decadent lifestyle;   405
these are the sorts of plots they bring to fruition!

We go to the craftsmen and say such things as:
'Goldsmith, about that necklace which you made:
when my wife was dancing around in the evening
the bolt fell out of the hole. 410
As for me, I have to sail over to Salamis:
so if you can spare the time, drop by in the evening
and with all your skill fix a bolt into her hole.'

Another husband has this conversation with the shoemaker,
a young man, but not with a little boy's dicky: 415
'Shoemaker, about my wife's foot: the little toe
is pressing against the thong of her sandal,
where it's tender: so drop by about lunch-time
and loosen it, so that you can make it a bit wider?'

It's these sorts of things that have led to this situation, 420
when I, an official of the state, have organised the oars
for the ships, and have come here to get the money to pay for them,
and am shut out of the gates by the women.
But I won't achieve anything standing here. Bring the crowbars,
so I can put an end to their hybris. 425
What are you gawking at, you wretched slave? Where are you
looking?
All you're doing is looking around for a wine shop.
Why don't you put the crowbars under the gates
and force them open there? I'll join you in forcing them,
over here. 430

ORPHANED AND DEAD CHILDREN

Priam, as Achilles abuses the body of his son Hector, wishes to go out of
the city to him, to beg for the corpse. Hecabe, his mother, grieves for him
too. But news has not yet reached Hector's wife, Andromache. She is
weaving at home, and has just called on the maid-servants to prepare a hot
bath for Hector, for when he returns from battle. Hearing the lamentations,
Andromache fears the worst. She briefly bewails Hector's lot – and her own
– but in this the moment of Hector's death, most of her thoughts are spared
for their son Astyanax and his destiny. The sad fate that Andromache
foresees for Astyanax would have been far better than the one that in fact
actually befalls him, for he is to be dashed against the city's walls at its fall.
Astyanax' name means 'lord of the city', and he is called this by the Trojans
due to his father, because 'it was Hector alone who protected the gates and
the long walls' (line 507). This passage brings *Iliad* Book 22 to a

conclusion, the author ending it on a high note of pathos. Andromache is speaking. Homer, *Iliad*, 22.482–515:

'Now you, Hector, are departing to the house of Hades in the depths
of the earth, but you leave me here in a bitter grief,
a widow in your house: and your boy is only a baby,
whom you and I, ill-fated, gave birth to: and you will not be　　　　485
of any assistance to him Hector, when you are dead, nor he to
　　you.
For even if he might escape the tearful war of the Achaeans,
he will always have toil and sorrows
hereafter, for others will take away his fields.

The day of orphanhood deprives a child of all the friends of his
　　youth:　　　　490
he always hangs down his head, and his cheeks are washed with
　　tears
and needy he goes, a child to his father's friends,
tugging at the cloak of one, the tunic of another:
and of the ones moved by pity one lets him drink from his cup
　　briefly,
he wets his lips but doesn't slake his thirst.　　　　495
And a child with both parents living drives him away from the
　　feast,
punching him with his fists and abusing him with insults:
'Get out of here! Your father isn't feasting with us.'
And the crying child goes back to his widowed mother.
Astyanax, who before on his father's knees　　　　500
would eat only marrow and the marbled fat of the sheep:
then when sleep overpowered him, and he finished with his
　　childish play,
he would sleep in a bed in the arms of a nurse,
on his soft couch, his heart full of good things.
But now he will suffer much, deprived of his beloved father,　　　　505
Astyanax, whom the Trojans have called by this name, 'lord of
　　the city',
for it was Hector alone who protected the gates and the long walls.
And now Hector by the curved ships far from your parents
the wriggling maggots will feast, when the dogs are glutted,
on your naked corpse: while in your house clothes are lying around
　　for you　　　　510
fine and pleasing, made by the hands of women.

But all of these I will reduce to ashes with blazing fire,
no use to you, since you won't rest in them,
but as an honour to you rendered by the Trojans and their wives.'
She wept as she said this, and the women began weeping.   515

The epigrams of Theocritus were carved as inscriptions. They combine his usual beauty of language with, in many cases, a genuine poignancy. Here the seven-year-old girl joins her little brother, whose loss she herself had been grieving, in Hades; perhaps they were both carried off by an illness. The parents took the trouble to commission Theocritus to write this epigram for their daughter, whom they clearly loved. 'Aiai' was a term of dismay, much greater in intensity than our 'alas' (line 5). It was particularly used in mourning. 'God' here is '*daimon*', used generically of divinity and not implying a monotheistic creed (line 6). Theocritus, *Epigram*, 16:

This girl, Peristere, untimely journeyed in her seventh year
to Hades before she had even begun to know of life;
child of misery, she grieved for her twenty-month brother,
an infant, tasting the heartlessness of death.
Aiai! Piteous, suffering Peristere, how close
has god placed dreadful tragedies for mortals.

Medeius built a tomb for his nurse when she died. He was probably a man when he did so, but describes himself as '*mikkus*', little one, which was probably his nurse's term of endearment for him. A Thracian, the nurse was presumably a slave. Theocritus, *Epigram*, 20:

The little one, Medeius, raised here by the road-side this monument
for his Thracian nurse, carving on it 'Cleita'.
The woman will have her reward for the boy she reared.
Well, how? She will always be called 'devoted'.

Achilles has withdrawn to his ships, bitterly aggrieved about Agamemnon's treatment of him in taking away his favourite slave woman, Brisis. Without his assistance, the war against the Trojans goes disastrously for the Greeks, until Agamemnon swallows his pride and sends an embassy to Achilles to win him back to battle, offering a tremendous inducement of wealth in addition to the return of the woman herself. But Achilles refuses. Old Phoenix 'burst into tears, for he feared for the ships of the Achaeans' (Homer, *Iliad*, 9.433). He had brought Achilles up, and offers him some fatherly advice. Homer, *Iliad*, 9.485–98:

And I raised you to be the man you are, Achilles like the gods,   485
loving you from my heart, for you wouldn't go with anyone else
either to the feast or to eat in the halls,
until I had sat you on my knees and given you the cooked meat
    cut up beforehand
to have your fill, and held out the wine.
Many times you have soaked the tunic on my chest,   490
spurting out the wine in your childish difficulties:
so I've suffered much because of you, and gone to a lot of trouble,
always bearing in mind that the gods wouldn't give me any offspring
of my own. But you, Achilles like the gods, I made my child
so that you might always ward off shameful ruin from me.   495
So, Achilles, be master of your proud spirit: you shouldn't have
a pitiless heart: even the gods themselves are also flexible,
they who have greater virtue and honour and strength.

TRUE LOVE

Creon has ordered that Antigone be put to death. But his own son,
Haemon, is in love with her. Creon has told him to put this love aside. But
Haemon joins her in death, without his father's knowledge. As often, love is
greater than filial devotion. 'Love' here translates the word *eros*. Sophocles,
Antigone, 781–800:

Chorus: Love unconquerable in war
Love that falls on men's property,
Love who passes the night
on the soft cheeks of the young maiden,
roaming over the seas   785
and into abodes out in the wilds;
there is no refuge from you
for any of the deathless gods
nor for man who lives but for a moment,
and whoever is under your influence is possessed.   790
The unjust minds of the just
you wrest into outrage,
and you have stirred up
this quarrel between related men.
The clear desire of the eyes of the beauteous bride   795
conquers,
Desire seated among the powers
of the great laws:

for Aphrodite goes unchallenged
as she plays. 800

True love endures a lifetime, and one carries the bite of love until death.
Plutarch, *On Love*, Fragment 137:

Love does not have its origin
in a sudden moment or immediately
as does anger,
nor does it fade away, fleet-footed
even though it is claimed to be winged.
But it takes fire gently and, so to speak,
almost seeps itself in molten,
and taking fast hold of the soul
it there abides, for a long time,
and in the twilight years of some men
it does not slumber
but is in its prime among the grey hairs –
ever fresh, ever youthful.

But if it ever does slacken and melt away
wasting away with the winds of time
or is extinguished through rational thought
it does not completely escape the soul
but leaves behind it a charred forest and a glowing mark
as do thunderbolts where they smoulder.

For when deliverance from sorrow comes
and sharp anger falls away
no trace of them remains dwelling in the soul,
the blazing of desire too shortens its sail
having furnished a savage upheaval:
and the teeth marks of love
even if the beast lets go
do not expel his poison
but the gashes inside the soul swell up
and one is ignorant
of what it is
how it originated and
from where it came
to fall upon the soul.

A romantic dinner for two. Achilles Tatius, 2.9.1–3:

(2.9.1) When it was time for dinner, again we drank with one another as before. Satyrus served the wine and he employed a lover's device. He exchanged the drinking cups, giving my cup to Leucippe, and hers to me, and mixing the wine he poured it into both cups. (2.9.2) I noticed which side of the cup her lips had touched when she drank, and I drank setting my lips to the same place, sending a kiss to her by long distance as I kissed the cup. (2.9.3) She saw this, and she realised at once that I was kissing the shadow of her lips. Satyrus took the cups away again and exchanged them for us. Then I saw her mimicking me and drinking from where I had drunk, and I was even more delighted. This happened a third and a fourth time, and so for the rest of the evening we pledged kisses to each other.

HOMOEROTICISM

Homosexual attractions to boys who had reached puberty and might have the first down on their cheeks were accepted in Greece, but the relationship between an older lover and the boy was not meant to be exploitative. In Athens, in fact, sodomy with citizen boys, even in these situations, was prohibited. Such relationships did not exclude heterosexuality, and men generally engaged in homoerotic affairs before getting married. Here Pindar describes those who chose only the heterosexual path as taking a 'totally frigid road', and sees lack of homoeroticism as unmanly, befitting a woman's character. He describes his own love, when he himself is past his prime, for Theoxenus, son of Hagesilas, from the Aegean island of Tenedos. Pindar, *Encomion*, 123:

One has to pluck out love, my heart, at the appropriate
season while one is still in one's prime,
but whoever looks upon the shafts flashing from the eyes of Theoxenus
and is not overwhelmed with waves of desire
has a black heart forged in a cold flame   5
from the adamant stone or iron, and is held in no honour
by Aphrodite of the darting glance, or labours
by necessity for money, or having a woman's spirit
journeys serving a totally frigid road.

But I thanks to Aphrodite melt like the wax   10
of sacred bees bitten by the sun
whenever I look at the youthful new limbs of boys.
So in truth in Tenedos
Persuasion and Charm abide
in Theoxenus son of Hagesilas.   15

Much graffiti (singular: grafitto) even today is love graffiti, for example, 'Alex and Sharon forever'. Similar graffiti survives from ancient Greece, but is largely homoerotic in nature, like the material often found in gentlemen's public toilets. This graffito is insulting; it dates from the sixth century BC and was scratched on a water jar, discovered in the Athenian market-place (*agora*). Titas' Olympic prowess might have matched his sexual. M. Lang, *Graffiti and Dipinti. The Athenian Agora XXI* (Princeton, 1976), p. 12, C5: 'Titas the Olympian victor is a poof.' This fifth-century BC graffito from Athens is also meant to be insulting. Lang, *Graffiti and Dipinti*, p. 13, C18: 'Sosias is a fag, so says the writer.'

From the island of Thera in the Aegean come several male homoerotic graffiti dating to the seventh century BC. In the graffito below, the word translated 'beautiful' is *kalos*. Coupled with a name, *kalos* is a typical homosexual phrase. Many graffiti scratched on vases and pots have the '*kalos* formula', a name followed by the word *kalos*, scratched by one man praising the good looks of another, often a youth. An example from a vase is: 'Leagros is beautiful'. Here, in a graffito from Thera, Laqydidas is a male's name. F.H. de Gaertringen (ed.), *Inscriptiones Graecae*, vol. XII.3 (Berlin, 1939), no. 540: 'Laqydidas is fantastic'. Crimon on Thera boasted of his homosexual conquest of Amotion. Another graffito by him, not given here, makes the same claim, but the name of his partner has worn off the rock. *Inscriptiones Graecae*, vol. XII.3, no. 538: 'In this spot here Crimon had it off with Amotion.'

A complex sexual ritual is perhaps hinted at by a series of graffiti inscribed together on a rock at Thera by different males; each line is in a different handwriting. In the first line, four males boast ('me', who does not identify himself, does the writing); Empylos scratches an addition, not wishing to be left off the record. A third line adds an insult, while a fourth writer appends his name, and states that he can dance as well (as have sex with men). *Inscriptiones Graecae*, vol. XII.3, no. 536:

Pheidippides screwed. Timagoras and Empheres and me – we screwed too.
So did Empylos.
Fag!
Empedocles wrote this bit. And by Apollo what a dancer he is too!

On the Aegean island of Lesbos in the sixth century BC Sappho was part of a circle of girl and women lovers. Here she calls on Aphrodite for assistance with an affair of the heart. She herself was not exclusively homosexual, but was married and had a daughter. The term 'lesbian' derives from Lesbos and was coined in the nineteenth century AD to denote female homoeroticism. Sappho, 1:

Aphrodite on your throne ornate never yielding to death,
daughter of Zeus, weaving your wiles, I implore you,
do not, mistress, yoke my soul
with heartaches and anguishes.   4

But hasten here if ever before
my voice you have given ear to from afar,
and leaving the house of your father came
harnessing the golden chariot.   8

Beautiful swift sparrows
have brought you over the black earth
whirring their feathered wings
from heaven through mid-air.   12

They arrived swiftly, and you blessed one
had a smile on your immortal face
when you asked what now I had suffered
and why now I called you,   16

and what I particularly desired to happen
in my maddened heart. 'Whom do I
persuade this time to be in love with you? Who,
O Sappho, is wronging you?   20

And if she flees, soon she will pursue you.
And if she does not accept gifts, she will.
And if she does not love you, she soon will –
willingly or not.'   24

Come to me Aphrodite and now remove
my painful care; accomplish all that
my heart desires to have accomplished.
Be you yourself my ally.   28

LOVE THY NEIGHBOUR, BUT NOT THY ENEMY

Good neighbours are so keen to help each other that they rush out of their homes to give assistance without stopping to arm themselves, while relatives live far off, and will arm themselves before coming. Hesiod, *Works and Days*, 342–51:

Invite your friend to a feast, but leave your enemy out of it,
and especially invite the one who lives near you:
for if you have some trouble at home,

neighbours come ungirt, while relatives arm themselves. 345
A bad neighbour is a curse, just as a good one is a great strength.
He has his portion of honour, who has a good neighbour.
No cow would die, were it not for a bad neighbour.
Borrow good measure from your neighbour, and pay it back well,
the same amount or more if you can 350
so that if you find yourself in need later on, you might find him
  reliable.

THREE

Farmers and Traders

The boorish man scrutinises a silver coin someone has paid him with and won't accept it because it looks too much like lead, and exchanges it for another. If he has loaned someone his plough, basket, sickle or a bag, he asks for these back in the middle of the night, when he has remembered them while lying awake.

Theophrastus, *Characters*, 4, *Boorishness*, 13–14.

Ancient Greece was above all an agrarian society, in which the production of food occupied most of the people, with crafts and trading conducted in the cities. Farming was carried out with the aid of ploughs drawn by oxen, and the majority of farmers would have worked a couple of hectares (about 5 acres) planted with a mix of cereals – barley and some wheat, as well as olives, figs and grapes. They would also have had some small stock animals, such as sheep and goats. The wealthy owned larger estates, but in Greece even these were not very large holdings, perhaps comprising 20 to 25 acres.

The main crop was grain and the ancient Greeks did not have a varied diet, which was based largely on cereals, legumes, oil and wine. Cereals, especially barley and wheat, were the staple food and principal source for carbohydrates, generally eaten as porridge and bread. Milk was used for making cheese. The most important drink was wine, usually heavily diluted with water, and even consumed by young children. The use of butter was the mark of barbarians, as was drinking beer and milk.

Meat was a luxury; in classical Athens it was generally eaten only at festivals, following sacrifices, as part of a cult celebration. For ordinary people, vegetables (onion, garlic, turnip, radish, lettuce, artichoke, cabbage, leek, celery and cucumber) were the most important addition to their diet; wild plants were also gathered and used as herbs. Fruits included figs, grapes, apples and pears.

Many of the chief elements of modern western diets, the ubiquitous potato, as well as corn, sugar cane, bananas and tomatoes, to name a few introduced from the New World (not to mention chocolate), were of course not available. Most people would have lived on bread, wine, olive oil, cabbages, fish (fresh or dried) and onions, though at places such as Athens delicacies were available – at a price.

In Athens, the retail trade in grain was clearly controlled by a small group of merchants, who greatly profited from it, especially in times of crisis. The state actually appointed officials to supervise the sale of grain in Athens to prevent price-rigging by the merchants, and these officials were sometimes executed for failing in their duties. Much Greek trade was carried on by sea, on the *penteconters*, or fifty-oared trading vessels (see illustration 3.1). These were small craft, and must have been cramped when they were loaded.

The main food staples that were traded in the Greek world were grain, olive oil and wine, and these were in many ways the culinary definition of Greek culture. Olive oil was needed for cooking and lighting, but also for anointing one's body prior to sports or after bathing. It was traded in large pottery jars, and the Athenians awarded jars of olive oil to the victors in the games held at Athens in honour of the goddess Athena at her festival the Panathenaea. Harvesting the olive was manual and back-breaking work, and carried out as it still is in many parts of Greece and Turkey: the olives would be knocked out of the tree with sticks and then collected (see illustration 3.2). On some farms, slaves would probably have been put to this task.

There were many other products that were traded, such as everything from livestock to wool. A very fine Spartan cup depicts the King of Cyrene, a Greek colony on the Libyan coast, supervising the weighing of a product, which could well be wool, for Cyrene was renowned for its flocks of sheep and their wool. But the medicinal herb silphium was also exported from Cyrene, and this may be what is depicted here.

Trade among the Greek cities became increasingly important during and because of the great colonisation movement of 750 to 550 BC, which saw the establishment of numerous cities along the shores of the Black Sea, in Sicily and southern Italy and even on the coast of France, while a large Greek trading colony grew up in Egypt. In return for Greek oil, wine and luxury goods (including Athenian pottery), Greek traders received Egyptian grain, metals and slaves.

In Athens, by the fourth century BC a system of maritime trading finance had developed, with insurance (and insurance fraud) for ships in face of the ever-present danger of shipwreck, which the Greeks tried to avoid by sailing only at the time of year when the sea was relatively calm. Bankers lent money to finance cargoes: a merchant or ship-owner borrowed money for the voyage; the loan and interest were repaid out of the proceeds of the sale of the cargo purchased with the borrowed money. There was only one condition, that the ship arrived safely at its destination, otherwise the loss was borne by the lender. High risks justified high interest ('maritime interest'), and in fourth century BC Athens this was anywhere from 12½ to 30 per cent.

Farmers and traders between them ensured that the ancient Greeks had the basics to live on, as well as luxury items. In Plato's discussion of those required to meet the needs of a city, farmers are essential as the ones who provide food, while merchants are the people who trade in goods not produced by the city (Plato, *Republic*, 369b–371e, see pp. 114–18).

FARMING AND WAR: THE SHIELD OF ACHILLES

Achilles decides to return to the battle outside Troy when his close friend Patroclus is slain by Hector. But his mother first goes to the god of metal-working, Hephaestus, for a new set of armour: Achilles had given his to Patroclus, which Hector has now taken as his own. Hephaestus proceeds to his task: 'first he made a strong, huge shield' (Homer, *Iliad*, 18.478) and decorated it with the sun, ocean, moon, sky and the constellations, and then with two cities. Linus was a mythological musician (line 570). For a couple getting married, holding each other's wrists was a standard matrimonial custom (line 594) and was often depicted on vases showing the newly married couple. Clothes were scented with perfumed oil (line 596); perfumed oil is mentioned on the Mycenaean tablets from Pylus in the Peloponnese. Homer, *Iliad*, 18.490–606:

> On the shield Hephaestus worked two beautiful cities of
>   mortal men.   490
> In one there were marriages and festivals,
> and they were leading brides from their chambers with the light of
>   torches
> through the city, and the bridal hymns rose noisily.
> Young men whirled in the dances, and among them
> flutes and lyres kept up their noisy music: and the women standing   495
> each before her own door looked on in admiration.
> But the people were gathered in the place of assembly: there a quarrel
> had occurred. Two men were arguing over blood-money in compensation
> for a murdered man. One swore that he had paid it in full,
> declaring so before the people, but the other denied anything of
>   the sort.   500
> Both went to a judge to make a decision.
> The people cheered on both men, advocates for each.
> But the heralds kept the people in order: and the old men
> sat on polished stones in the sacred circle,

holding in their hands the sceptres of the loud-voiced heralds: 505
there they would rise up and each in turn give judgement.
And there lay in their presence two talents of gold
to be awarded to whoever pronounced the truest judgement.

But around the other city lay two forces of armed men
resplendent in their battle-dress; and two different plans found
    favour with them: 510
either to sack the city or to share equally with its inhabitants
all the possessions the charming city had shut within it.
But those in the city were not yielding, and were arming for an
    ambush.
Their beloved wives and young children standing on the walls
kept guard, and with them the men possessed of old age. 515
The others marched out. Ares and Pallas Athena led them,
both fashioned by Hephaestus in gold, and wearing golden robes,
beautiful and magnificent in their armour, and since they were gods,
conspicuous from every direction: but the people beneath them
    were tiny in comparison.

But when at once they had come to a place where it seemed good
    to them to lay an ambush, 520
in the river where there was a watering hole for all the beasts,
there at once they sat down enwrapped in flashing bronze.
Then sitting apart from the main body were two spies,
waiting until they might see the sheep and the spiral horned cattle.
And these came along shortly, and with them two shepherds 525
playing on their pipes, who had no thought of treachery.
But the spies saw them coming along and rushed against them, then
    quickly
cut off the herds of cattle and the fine flocks
of white sheep, and slew the shepherds.
But when the besiegers sitting in debate 530
heard the great clamour from the cattle, at once they mounted
behind their brisk horses, and quickly reached them.

Getting into ranks they fought the battle by the river banks,
and struck each other with bronze-tipped spears.
Then among them both Strife and Uproar joined the battle, and
    murderous Fate 535
holding a living man freshly wounded, and another one unhurt,
another, dead, she dragged by his feet through the butchery:
the cloak around her shoulders soaked red with the blood of men.

So on the shield, like living men, they joined the battle and fought,
snatching away the corpses of the enemy's slain.   540

And on the shield Hephaestus also wrought freshly ploughed land,
rich and triple-ploughed: and on it many ploughmen,
turning, drove their yoke teams this way and that.
And whenever turning they would come to the boundary of the field,
then a man would come forth and place a cup of sweet wine in
    their hands,   545
and then they turned again in the furrows
hastening to come to the deep boundary of the fallow land.
And the field changed black behind them, and looked like ploughed
    earth,
despite it being gold: that was the marvel of what Hephaestus
    crafted.

And on the shield Hephaestus crafted a king's domain: in it hired
    servants   550
were reaping, holding sharp sickles in their hands.
Some handfuls of the reaped grain fell in rows along the furrow
    line,
while the sheaf-binders tied others up with bands.
Three sheaf-binders stood by the sheaves, while children
behind them picked up the sheaves, bearing them in their arms,   555
continuously bringing them to the binders. Among them the king
stood in silence grasping his sceptre, his heart rejoicing in the harvest.
Heralds, set apart, prepared a feast under an oak tree,
dressing a great ox they had sacrificed: and the women
sprinkled much white barley on the meat for the reapers' meal.   560

Hephaestus also fashioned a vineyard on the shield, beautiful and
    wrought in gold,
groaning with great clusters of grapes: black were the clusters of
    grapes upon it,
and the vines were set up throughout on silver poles.
And around it he incised a ditch, inlaid with dark blue metal, and
    about that he beat a fence of tin:
there was only a single path leading to it   565
on which the grape-bearers came and went when they picked the
    fruit from the vineyard.
And maidens and youths with light hearts
bore the sweet fruit in woven baskets.
And in their midst a boy played charming music

on his well-tuned lyre and sang the beautiful Linus song 570
with a delicate voice: and they followed him dancing together,
with singing and joyful shouting and skipping feet.

Hephaestus also fashioned on it a herd of straight-horned cattle:
he made the cows out of gold and tin,
bellowing, hastening out of the dung of their enclosure to the
    pasture 575
beside the roaring river, along the swaying reeds.
Four golden herdsmen went alongside the cattle
and nine dogs, fleet of foot, followed them.
But two awesome lions among the foremost cattle
held a bellowing bull, who lowing loudly 580
was dragged off, pursued by the dogs and young men.
The two lions ripping open the hide of the great bull
were greedily devouring the entrails and the black blood, while
the herdsmen vainly pursued them and encouraged the swift dogs.
But the dogs shrank back from sinking their teeth into the lions: 585
standing close by, barking, they shied away from them.

And on the shield the famous strong-armed god made a pasture
in a beautiful glen, a great pasture of white sheep,
and houses and covered huts and sheep pens.

On it also the famous strong-armed god made a dancing circle 590
similar to the one that once in spacious Cnossus
Daedalus crafted for Ariadne of the beautiful hair.
There were young men and virgins – requiring of would-be
    husbands gifts of numerous cattle –
dancing, holding their hands on the wrists of each other.
Of these the virgins wore fine linen clothes, and the youths 595
finely spun tunics glistening lightly with olive oil:
and the virgins had beautiful tiaras, the youths
golden daggers slung from silver belts.
And now they would run very lightly with skilful feet,
as when a potter sitting at his wheel tests 600
it, fitted in his hands, to see if it will run.
And now at another time they would run in lines toward each
    other.
A great throng stood around the lovely circle of dancers,
enraptured: and among the dancers two acrobats 604–5
whirled through the middle of them, leading them in song and
    dance.

The context for the following passage is Odysseus returning to his ship where his anxious men await news of his encounter with the sorceress Circe: they react like calves. Homer, *Odyssey*, 10.410–14:

As in the country, when the calves, around the herds of cows   410
returning from the fields with full stomachs to the dung of the farmyard,
all together frisk before them, and the pens no longer
hold them, but with unceasing lowing they run
about their mothers.

FARMING AND FOOD SUPPLY

The rising of the constellation Pleiades was the sign for farmers to commence ploughing. The wooden yoke worn by the oxen was attached to the wooden plough by a strap. As the oxen moved off, their yoke pulled on this strap, fixed by a wooden peg, and pulled the plough. Spring is 'grey' because the ears of grain, not yet ripened, retain their greyish husks (line 478). Hesiod, *Works and Days*, 458–82:

As soon as it appears to be the time for men to plough
then show haste, both you and your slaves alike,
whether wet or dry, ploughing in the season for ploughing,   460
exerting yourself very early in the morning, so that your fields
    might be full.
Plough in springtime, though land ploughed in summer will not
    disappoint you.
Sow the fallow land when the soil is still light:
fallow land is a protection against want and makes for children free
    of care.

Pray to Zeus of the earth and to pure Demeter,   465
to ripen Demeter's holy grain and make it heavy, when you first
begin the ploughing, when taking the point of the plough's handle
in your hand you bring down the goad on the backs of the oxen,
as they pull the yoke peg by the yoke strap. Let a slave a little behind
with a mattock make trouble for the birds   470
by hiding the seed. For good farming practices are best
for mortal men, as bad practices are the worst.

So the ears of corn weighed down with abundance will bow to the
    ground
if Olympian Zeus himself, at the end, gives a good yield,
and from the grain bins you'll sweep away the spider webs, and   475

I expect that you'll rejoice as you take hold of the food laid up inside.
Having plenty you will come to grey spring, and will not look
   longingly
at others, but another man will be in need of your assistance.

But if you plough the ground later, at the solstice's turning of the
   sun
you'll harvest sitting down, grasping a little in your hand,   480
covered in dust, binding the sheaves the wrong way, certainly not
   rejoicing,
you'll bear the whole crop in a single basket: few will admire you.

In a large city like Athens, the grain supply was a major concern. The main
reason that Athens lost the Peloponnesian War against Sparta and her allies
in 404 BC was because Lysander the Spartan admiral had in the previous
year blockaded the entrance to the Black Sea, cutting off Athens' grain
supply and causing a famine in the city; many people starved to death. In
this speech, from about 386 BC, speculation in the grain trade is dealt with.
Lysias, 22 (*Against the Grain-Dealers*), 11–16:

(22.11) But, gentlemen of the jury, I believe that they will say, perhaps as
they did before the city council, that it was as a benefit to the city that
they purchased the grain, so that they might sell it to you at the most
reasonable price. But I'll provide you with water-tight and transparent
evidence that they are lying. (22.12) If they had bought up the grain for
your benefit, they need to be shown to have sold the grain at the same
price for many days, until the grain they had bought up had all been sold.
But now, sometimes on the same day, they sold the grain for a *drachma*'s
profit, as if they were buying up the grain a measure at a time. And I
present you yourselves as witnesses to this fact. (22.13) I find it strange
that, whenever it is necessary to contribute to an emergency financial levy
fixed by the state, which everybody knows about, these men are not
willing to give any money, but plead that they are too poor to do so, but
in matters that are against the law, for which death is the penalty, and in
which it is important for them to escape detection, they say that they do
these for your benefit! Yet you all know that it is least appropriate for
these men to make such statements.

(22.14) For what is advantageous for them is the opposite for other
men: for they make the most profit whenever some disaster is announced
in the city and they sell grain at a higher price. In this way, they are so
excited to see your disasters that they hear of them before anyone else, or
they themselves act as rumour-mongers: either it is your ships destroyed

in the Black Sea, or captured by the Spartans as they sailed out, or your trading ports blockaded, or the imminent collapse of the peace treaty. And their hatred of you grows to such lengths (22.15) that they plot against you in the same timely circumstances in which your enemies do so. For whenever you are particularly in need of grain, these men grab it and refuse to sell it, so that we won't haggle about the price, but we are happy if we come away from them having bought it at any cost. So sometimes, even though it is a time of peace, we are besieged by these men.

(22.16) For such a long time has the city recognised the roguery and the maliciousness of these men that, while you have established market supervisors to watch generally over all the other goods on sale, for this grain trade you have specifically appointed grain superintendents by lot. Often you have exacted from those officials the extreme penalty (of death), although they were citizens, because they were not able to overcome the manipulations practised by these men. And yet, what then should the wrongdoers themselves suffer at your hands, when you condemn to death even those who are not able to guard against them?

TRADE AND CIVILISATION

Odysseus' description of the land in which the one-eyed Cyclopes (singular: Cyclops) lived makes very clear the contrast between the civilised world of the Greek city-state and the uncivilised. The Cyclopes do not practise agriculture or viticulture (bread and wine are the marks of the enlightened). They are lawless, and do not have political organisation, another mark of the civilised world of the Greek city-state. Each Cyclops' family unit is sufficient to itself, whereas a Greek city is an agglomeration of family units. Another factor in the backwardness of the Cyclopes is their lack of ships, which would bring them all the necessities of life. In fact, they choose to live in the mountains in caves, when right next door there is an island rich with agricultural possibilities, which could be settled and made prosperous. Here can be seen the outreaching of the Greek world at the time the *Odyssey* was written, just as the great age of colonisation, in which the Greeks sailed forth and settled new lands, is taking place. Homer, *Odyssey*, 9.106–39:

We came to the land of the arrogant and lawless Cyclopes
who placing their trust in the deathless gods
neither cultivate plants with their hands nor plough,
but everything grows without sowing and ploughing,
wheat and barley, and grapevines as well, which bear wine   110

fermented from fine grapes, and the rain of Zeus makes these grow.
They do not have assemblies for making decisions, or laws,
but they live on the peaks of high mountains
in hollow caverns, and each is lawgiver
for his wife and children, and they don't care about anyone else.   115

Now there is an overgrown island stretching outside the harbour,
neither close to the land of the Cyclopes nor far off,
wooded, and on it wild goats beyond reckoning live:
for there is no tread of men to scare them off,
nor do hunters travel to it, who in the forests   120
suffer toils trekking over the peaks of mountains.
Neither with flocks is it covered, nor by cultivated fields,
but unsown and unploughed all the days it is bereft
of the presence of man, but feeds the bleating goats.
For the Cyclopes don't have ships with cheeks painted vermillion,   125
nor are there ship-builders among them, who could construct
stout-benched ships, which could carry out their needs
voyaging to the cities of men, as men frequently
travel across the seas to one another in ships:
and these ship-builders could have made the island well-settled
   for them.   130

For the island is not at all a bad one, but would grow all things in
   season:
on it are meadows along the shore of the grey sea
well-watered and soft: there the vines could bear fruit all year long.
On it there is level plough land, and men could reap a heavy harvest
whatever the season, since the soil underneath is so rich.   135
On this island there is also good anchorage, so cables aren't needed,
nor anchor-weights thrown over the side nor fastened stern cables.
Beaching the ship you could simply wait for the time when the heart
of the sailors roused itself and the breezes blew.

THE SEA! THE SEA!

Many Greek cities were not on the coast, but others were, and the cities
founded in the great wave of colonisation from 750 to 550 BC all tended to
be on coastlines, so that the sea would make for easy contact with their
mother-city. The irrepressible excitement of the 10,000 Greek mercenaries,
who had fought their way through the interior of Asia Minor to the coast,
when they see the sea is indicative of its importance. Xenophon, *Anabasis*,
4.7.21–6:

(4.7.21) They arrived at the mountain on the fifth day; its name was Theches. When those who were in front reached the summit of the mountain, they let out a noisy shout. (4.7.22) When Xenophon and the guards in the rear heard it they thought that other enemies were attacking ahead. For enemies were following them, from the countryside that was on fire, and the rear guards had killed some of them and by setting an ambush taken others alive, and had also captured around twenty wicker shields covered with hairy, raw ox-hides. (4.7.23) The shout kept growing louder and nearer, as each rank in turn broke into a racing sprint towards those ahead who were joining in the shouting, and the shout grew louder in proportion to the number of men. So it seemed to be something greater than enemies to Xenophon, (4.7.24) and mounting a horse, taking with him Lycius and the cavalry, he went to the rescue. And soon they heard the soldiers shouting, 'The sea! The sea!', spreading the news. Then all the soldiers guarding the rear also started running, and even the baggage-beasts and the horses began forging ahead. (4.7.25) When they had all reached the summit, there they cried and hugged each other, including the generals and captains. Suddenly, someone passing on the word, the soldiers started carrying stones and building a great cairn. (4.7.26) On it they placed a number of raw ox-hides, staffs and the captured wicker shields.

A MARITIME FRAUD

It was common business practice for bankers to lend money for ship-owners to buy a cargo; the ship-owners sailed with their cargo and sold it, repaying the bankers with interest. In this speech, Zenothemis and Hegestratus borrowed money on the security of a cargo of grain that they pretended was theirs but which in fact belonged to Protus, who had travelled with the ship from Athens to buy this grain with money he had borrowed from Demo, the uncle of Demosthenes, who makes the speech. As with all such maritime loans, if the ship sank and the cargo was lost, the loan was annulled. The ship set out from Syracuse in Sicily where Hegestratus borrowed the money on false pretences and sent it to Massalia (modern Marseilles in France, a Greek colony), his home town. After landing at Cephallenia (west of the Corinthian gulf), the ship eventually arrived in Athens, where it had started out: this gives a good idea of the sailing voyages of the ancient Greeks. When the ship reached Athens, Demo went to the Piraeus to demand his share, but found Zenothemis claiming that the cargo of grain was his own as he had lent the money to the deceased Hegestratus to buy it, and that it did not belong to Protus! Demosthenes, 32 (*Against Zenothemis*), 4–9:

(32.4) This man Zenothemis here, in the employ of Hegestratus the ship-owner, who Zenothemis himself has written in his accusation was lost at sea (how, he has not added in writing, but I will tell you), thought up the following scam in league with him. He and Hegestratus borrowed money in Syracuse. Hegestratus agreed that he would say to those lending money to Zenothemis, if they asked, that there was a large quantity of grain on the ship belonging to Zenothemis, while Zenothemis here said to those lending money to Hegestratus that the ship's cargo belonged to Hegestratus. As one was the ship's owner and the other was a passenger, the two sets of creditors believed what each said about the other.

(32.5) Getting hold of the money, they sent it to the city of Massalia [Marseilles], and put nothing in the hold of the ship. The agreement with the creditors was, as is usual in all these cases, that the money would be paid back if the ship reached port safely, so in order to defraud the creditors they planned to sink the ship. So Hegestratus, when they were two or three day's sailing from land, went below down into the hold of the ship at night, and began to cut a hole through it. And this Zenothemis here, as if he knew nothing about it, remained above with the rest of the passengers. When the noise was heard, those on the ship realised that something wrong was going on in the hold of the ship, and they rushed below.

(32.6) Hegestratus, caught in the act, and realising he would have to pay the penalty, fled, and as he was pursued threw himself into the sea, but since it was dark he missed the ship's life-boat and drowned. So that wicked man met a bad end as he deserved, suffering for himself the fate which he had planned for others. (32.7) As for this man here, his partner and accomplice, on the ship after the crime, he immediately as if he knew nothing but pretending to be terrified himself, at first tried to persuade the officer in command and the sailors to embark on the life-boat and abandon the ship as quickly as possible, as their safety was beyond hope and the ship was going down fast, thinking that in this way their plans would be accomplished: the ship would be lost at sea and the lending agreements rendered void.

(32.8) He failed in this, because the banker's agent (Protus) who was sailing on the ship spoke against this course of action, and promised a lot of money to the sailors if they would save the ship, and the ship was brought safely to Cephallenia, mainly through the intervention of the gods, and next in importance through the bravery of the sailors. Again after this, with the Massaliots, Hegestratus' fellow citizens, Zenothemis sought to prevent the ship from sailing to Athens, saying that he himself was a Massiliot and that the money came from there, and that the ship-owner and the creditors were Massaliots. (32.9) But he also failed in this, and the officials in Cephallenia decided that the ship was to sail to Athens, from where it had set sail. He, whom no one would think would dare to come here, having fabricated and carried out such deeds, this man, Athenians, is so exceeding in shamelessness and daring, that not only has he come here, but also disputes about my grain and has brought legal proceedings against me!

SAILING AND SHIPWRECK

Works and Days is addressed to Hesiod's brother, Perses, who is mentioned in this section. Hesiod's distrust of the sea and his preference for agriculture is clear throughout his work. Hesiod, *Works and Days*, 618–34, 641–5, 663–77, 689–94:

But if yearning for rough and stormy sailing seizes you
when the constellation of Pleiades falling into
the misty sea flees Orion's mighty strength,   620
then indeed gales of all manner of winds storm.
Then no longer sail ships on the wine-dark sea
but mind you work the land, as I instruct you.
Drag your ship up on to the dry shore, and protect it with stones
all around, to keep at bay the force of strong winds blowing
    damp,   625
drawing out the plug in the bottom of the ship so that the rain
    of Zeus might not rot it.
Store up all the ship's gear and tackle in your house
and neatly fold the wings of the sea-going vessel.
Hang the well-worked rudder over the smoke.
Yourself, wait until the season of sailing has come: 630
and then drag the swift ship into the sea, and load it
with a marketable cargo so that homewards you bring a profit
even as your father and mine, Perses, you great fool,
used to sail on ships, in want of a better livelihood.   634

You, Perses, remember to do all things   641
in their proper season, and especially sailing.
Speak in praise of a small ship, but load your cargo in a big one.
The bigger the cargo, the greater the profit on top of profit
will be, if only the winds restrain their destructive storms.   645

For fifty days from the solstice's turning of the sun 663
when the season of exhausting heat has come to an end
the season for men to sail comes: not then will you wreck 665
the ships nor will the sea destroy the crew,
unless Poseidon the Earth-Shaker puts his mind to it
or Zeus, king of the deathless gods, wish to slay them.
For in the gods is the end of good and of bad alike.
At that time there are steady winds and the sea is propitious. 670
Then without anxiety trusting to the winds
drag your swift ship to the sea and put all the cargo aboard,
but hurry as quickly as you can to return home again.
Don't wait until the new wine, or the rain at the end of summer
and the onset of winter and the terrible storms of Notus, 675
the south wind, who travels with the heavy autumn rain of Zeus,
churning up the sea and making it dangerous.

Don't put all of your livelihood in hollow ships
but leave most of it behind; carry the lesser portion as cargo, 690
for it is terrible among the ocean waves to meet with calamity.
And terrible too, if by lifting an excessive weight onto the wagon
you shatter the axle and the cargo is reduced to pieces.
Keep to a modest scale: nothing to excess is best in all things.

Athens' control of the sea, and her possession of a great harbour, the Piraeus, made her a maritime power and trading mecca. *The Old Oligarch*, 2.7:

Whatever delicacy comes from Sicily or Italy or Cyprus or Egypt or Lydia or Pontus or the Peloponnese or anywhere else is brought into Athens because of its control of the sea.

Different parts of Greece were renowned for different products, and most of these would be transported by sea. Athens, for example, was well known for its beautiful pottery. Pindar lists some places and the commodities they were famous for. Pindar, *Hyporchema*, 106:

From Mount Taygetus in Sparta comes the Laconian hound,
the most cunning breed for running down wild beasts;
goats from the island of Scyros are most excellent to squeeze for
  milk,
weapons from Argos are best, and a chariot from Thebes,
but from Sicily, which produces delicious fruits, seek a well-crafted
  wagon.

Cleenorides, homesick for his country, put his life in the hands of the winter weather in his eagerness to return home. Anacreon, *Epigram*, 102d:

> You also, Cleenorides, were laid waste by yearning for your ancestral
>   home
> putting your confidence in the south wind's wintry blast,
> for the fickle weather put its shackles on you,
> your lovely youth washed away by the wet waves.

JUSTICE AND PROSPERITY

Justice, or judgement, was Dike, a personified concept that the Greeks placed great stress on. Hybris, another important idea, meant violence, arrogance and overweening pride; it is embodied here (line 217). An oath is also a personified concept. The bribe-taking men are, literally, 'gift-eating' (line 221). The rulers are the local nobles (line 248). Hesiod, *Works and Days*, 213–64:

> O Perses, listen to Justice, and don't encourage violence,
> for hybris is evil for wretched mortal man: and even the noble
>   man
> cannot easily endure it, but is weighed down under it,   215
> having fallen into rash behaviour: the better road is the other one,
> to arrive at what is just. Justice prevails over Hybris
> when she comes to the final reckoning: but the fool learns this only
>   through suffering.
> For Oath immediately runs alongside crooked judgements.
> There is a clamour when Justice is dragged about, wherever bribe-   220
> devouring men, handing down the law with crooked verdicts,
>   take her.
> And Justice weeping follows to the city and the haunts of people,
> clothed in mist, bringing evil for men
> who have driven her out and have not dealt with her
>   straightforwardly.
> Those who to strangers and locals give judgements   225
> that are straight and do not deviate from what is just,
> their city prospers, and the people in it flourish:
> Peace, who rears children, is throughout the land, nor does
> far-seeing Zeus ordain for them cruel war.
> Famine does not accompany men who give right judgement   230
> nor destruction, but festively they reap the fruit of the work that
>   is their care.

For them the earth bears much subsistence, and on the mountains the
oak bears acorns at its peak and in its midst bees,
their woolly sheep are weighed down with fleeces,
their wives bear children like their parents,   235
they flourish continually with good things, nor do they go
on ships for the life-giving land bears them fruit.
For those who care for evil violence and cruel deeds,
for them far-seeing Zeus, son of Cronus, ordains a punishment.
Many times even a whole city suffers because of one wicked
    man   240
who sins and contrives outrages.
For them down from heaven the son of Cronus devises great
    calamity,
famine and pestilence alike, so that the men perish,
their wives become barren, and their households decrease
through the plotting of Olympian Zeus. Again, at another time   245
the son of Cronus destroys their broad-fronted army
or their walls or he destroys their ships on the sea.

You rulers, you yourselves too ponder this punishment:
for the immortal gods are near among men and watch
those that grind down others with crooked judgements   250
not heeding the vengeance of the gods.
For Zeus has placed on the prosperous earth
three times ten thousand deathless guards of mortal men:
and these keep watch over judgements and cruel deeds
as they wander, clothed in mist, all over the earth.   255

And there is virgin Justice, born from Zeus,
majestic and honoured by the gods who dwell on Olympus.
And whenever someone harms her, slandering her crookedly,
she immediately sitting by her father Zeus, son of Cronus,
speaks of the wicked mind of man so that the people   260
might pay for the arrogance of the rulers, who thinking evil
turn Justice from her path, speaking crookedly.
Be on your guard against this rulers, judge straightly
you bribe-devourers, and completely forget about giving crooked
    judgements.

THE NEED TO WORK

Two characters talk to the god of wealth, Plutus, and his important role in
stimulating crafts and inventions. Aristophanes, *Wealth*, 160–8:

Chremylus: Every skill and device among men   160
was invented because of you.
For your sake, Wealth, one of us sits and makes shoes.

Carion: Another one is a blacksmith, another a carpenter.

Chremylus: One works gold, gold that comes from you.

Carion: One, by Zeus, is a thief, another a burglar.   165

Chremylus: Another is a fuller.

Carion: Another washes sheep fleeces.

Chremylus: Another is a tanner.

Carion: Another sells onions.

Chremylus: And it's through money that an adulterer caught in the
act gets off being killed, and only has his hairs plucked out!

Two translations are given of a line from a play of Sophocles that
survives only in quotations, the first more literal than the other. Sophocles,
The Prophets, Fragment 397:

You'll never reach the top without hard work.

Nothing ventured, nothing gained.

FARMERS, TRADERS AND THE RISE OF THE CITY

Slaves were essential to Greek society. But the vital building block of Greek
culture, the city-state (*polis*), came about as a conglomerate of free workers
exchanging their products and skills. Socrates ('I' throughout) is discussing
with Adeimantus the formation of a city-state (Adeimantus' role in the
dialogue is largely confined to brief agreements with what Socrates is
arguing). The city arises through the provision of goods and services for
each other by its inhabitants, and producers and workers 'co-operate' to
make a city a reality. Note the aristocratic bias against traders and
merchants. Plato, *Republic*, 369b–371e:

(369b) 'So the city comes into being,' I said, 'as far as I'm concerned,
because each of us is not self-sufficient but requires many things. Or can
you think of any other principle that establishes the city?'
'No other,' Adeimantus replied.

(369c) 'So, what with one man calling in another for one service, and
another man another for some other service, we, being in need of many

things, gather together in one dwelling place many partners and helpers, and to this gathering together we give the name, 'city'. Don't we?'

'That's certainly the case.'

'And there is an exchange between one man and another, and if one gives or receives something, it is because each man thinks that he will be better off for it.'

'Yes, indeed.'

'Come then,' I said, 'let us, in theory, make our city from the beginning. It will come about, so it seems, from our needs.'

'Why not?'

(369d) 'But the first and the greatest of our needs is the provision of foodstuffs, necessary both to exist and to live.'

'Absolutely.'

'Our second need is housing, and the third clothing and that sort of thing.'

'That's true.'

'Tell me,' I said, 'how will our city be sufficient to provide for such things? There will be a farmer for one need, a house-builder for one, a weaver for the other. And will we add a shoe-maker to these, and anyone else needed for the needs of the body?'

'Certainly.'

'The smallest possible size of the city would be four or five men.'

'It appears so'.

(369e) 'So what next? Should each of these men contribute his work for the good of all? Should the farmer, who is one man, provide food for all four men and spend four-fold time and toil to provide food, and share it with the others? Or should he care only about himself (370a) and produce only a quarter of the food in a quarter of the time, and spend the rest of the three-quarters of his time in the provision of a house, a cloak and shoes, and not have interests in common with the others, but himself for himself, have an interest only in his own affairs?'

Adeimantus replied, 'But, Socrates, perhaps the first alternative is easier.'

'It wouldn't, by Zeus, be odd,' I said. 'For as you said it I myself thought that, firstly, each of us is not born like the other, (370b) but differ in nature, each from the other for carrying out work. Don't you think so?'

'I do.'

'Would one man be better off working at many skills, or one man at one skill?'

'One man,' he said, 'at one skill.'

'Moreover I think that it is clear that if someone misses the right moment, the work is ruined.'

'That's obvious.'

'For I think that the performance of the task is not willing to wait upon the leisure of the worker, but it's necessary for the worker (370c) to attend to the task straight away, and not as part of some subsidiary concern.'

'That's essential.'

'As a result, more of each thing is made, and better and easier, when one man makes them, according to his nature and at the proper time, free from all other tasks.'

'That's absolutely true.'

'Then we need more than four citizens for the provision of the needs we've been talking about, Adeimantus. For the farmer, it is apparent, will not make his plough himself, if it is going to be a good one, (370d) nor his hoe nor any of the other implements he needs for farming. The same applies to the house-builder, who also needs many things, and similarly with the weaver and the shoe-maker.'

'You're right.'

'Carpenters, and blacksmiths, and many other such craftsmen, joining us in our very small city, will make it larger.'

'Certainly.'

'But our city would still not be very big if we were to add to them cowherds and shepherds and other herdsmen, (370e) so that the farmers might have cattle for ploughing with, and yoke animals for both the house-builders and the farmers to use for transport, and the weavers and shoe-makers hides and fleeces.'

'And yet it wouldn't be a small city,' he said, 'if it had all these things.'

'But,' I said, 'it is hardly possible to establish this same city in such a place where it will not require imported goods.'

'It would be impossible.'

'So there will be a further need for other men, who will bring what is required from another city to our own.'

'It will be necessary.'

'But if our agent were to go abroad empty-handed, not taking any of the things that those men require (371a) from whom he is to purchase such necessities as are needed by us, he will return empty-handed. Won't he?'

'It seems to me so.'

'So it is necessary that what they produce at home should not only be sufficient for themselves, but be in quality and quantity such as those men require.'

'That would be necessary.'

'So it's vital that our city have both more farmers and other craftsmen.'

'Many more.'

'And also more agents who are to export and import all these goods? These men are called traders, aren't they?'

'Yes.'

'So we will also require traders.'

'Certainly.'

'And if the trading occurs by sea, (371b) we will need many others skilled in maritime matters.'

'Many more.'

'But within the city itself, how will they exchange with one another the fruits of their labour? For it was on account of this that we made our association and established the city.'

'Obviously by buying and selling,' he said.

'And from this there will come about for us a market-place and a currency as a mode of exchange.'

'Of course.'

(371c) 'And if a farmer or some other craftsman, arriving at the market with his produce, does not come at the same time as those requiring the items that he has for exchange, will he neglect his craft and sit in the market-place?'

'Not at all,' Adeimantus said, 'but there are those who see to this, appointing themselves to this task, and in a well-run city they are usually those who have the weakest bodies and are useless for carrying out any other task. They must stay there (371d) in the market-place and exchange money for the goods of those who need to sell, and exchange goods for money for as many who need to buy.'

'This need,' I said, 'creates the origin of shopkeepers in our city. Don't we call shopkeepers those who are established in the market-place, serving us by buying and selling, while those who travel to the cities are merchants?'

'That is the case.'

'And there are also others who serve, so I think; these are those whose (371e) intellectual accomplishments are not a worthy contribution, but who have a strong body fit for hard work. They sell the employment of this strength to those who need it, and call the price for it a 'wage', while they are called, I think, 'wage-earners', aren't they?'

'Certainly,' he said.

'Then wage-earners, it appears, have made up the full number of our citizens?'
'I think so.'
'So Adeimantus, our city has indeed grown, but is it complete?'
'Perhaps.'

DEBTORS AND CREDITORS

An old man, Strepsiades, cannot sleep at night worrying about the debts he has incurred on behalf of his horse-mad son. He isn't bitten in bed by the usual bed-lice, but by thoughts of the money he owes. He is frightened to punish his slaves because of the Peloponnesian War, fearing they will run away to the enemy (line 7). The interest on his loans is due at the end of the month (line 17). Aristophanes, *Clouds*, 1–40:

Strepsiades: Oh dear, oh hell!
Lord Zeus, what a long night.
Without end. Will day never come?
A while ago I did hear a rooster.
But the slaves are snoring. They wouldn't have done that in the
   old days.   5
Curse you war, for reasons beyond number,
since I can't even punish my own slaves.
But this fine young man here
won't get up while it's still night, but farts away
rugged up in five cloaks.   10
Right then, let's get wrapped up and snore.
But wretched me, I can't sleep, bitten
by expenses and feed bills and debts,
all because of this son of mine here. He has long hair
and rides horses, and also drives a pair of horses,   15
and even dreams about horses. But I'm on the point of death
seeing the moon draw close to the end of the month,
for the interest on my loans is nearly due. Slave, light a lamp
and bring out the accounts book, so that I can find out
to whom I owe money, and can calculate the interest.   20
Let's see, what do I owe? Twelve *minas* to Pasias.
Twelve *minas* for Pasias? What did I borrow them for?
When I bought that pedigree horse! Wretched me,
if only I'd had my eye knocked out with a stone first!

Pheidippides: [Talking in his sleep.] Philon, you're a cheat! Drive in
   your own lane.   25

Strepsiades: That's it, that's the curse that's ruined me:
even when he's sleeping he dreams of horses.

Pheidippides: How many laps will the war chariots drive?

Strepsiades: You're driving your father many laps.
But what debt got hold of me after Pasias?   30
Three *minas* to Amynias for a small board to stand on, for the
   chariot, and a pair of wheels.

Pheidippides: [Still talking in his sleep.] Give the horse a roll and take
   him home.

Strepsiades: Dear boy, it's me you've been rolling – rolling me right
   out of my money, and I've incurred lawsuits,
and other creditors say they'll seize my goods for the interest.

Pheidippides: [Awake.] Really, Dad,   35
why do you grumble and toss and turn all night?

Strepsiades: There's a debt collector in the bedclothes biting me.

Pheidippides: In the name of Heaven, let me get some sleep!

Strepsiades: So you go to sleep. But just you realise
that one day you'll inherit all these debts!   40

VIEWS ABOUT MONEY

As Strepsiades realises, money – or rather indebtedness in his case – can
be a major problem. The Greeks admired wealth and the hard work
needed to accumulate it. They realised that careful management was
needed to maintain inherited wealth, and squandering it was viewed
negatively and could be a point of attack against an opponent in a
lawsuit. But riches dishonestly gained were not approved of. Solon,
Fragment 15:

Many bad men are wealthy, many good ones poor,
   but we will not swap our virtue
for their wealth, for virtue is a solid possession for ever,
   but as for money, now one man has it, then another.

Pindar echoes a similar sentiment. Pindar, Fragment 158:

Wretched, ephemeral creature, you talk like a child
bragging about your money to me.

But elsewhere Pindar is aware of the value of 'solid cash'. Pindar, Fragment 222:

> Gold is the child of Zeus,
> consumed by neither moth nor weevil.

Pindar quotes a common saying. Pindar, *Isthmian Victory Ode*, 2.11:

> 'Money, money makes a man.'

In a fragmentary play of Sophocles, the materialistic truth about humankind is revealed some 2,400 years ago. Sophocles, *Creusa*, Fragment 354:

> For even mortal men who have great wealth nevertheless hold tight
> to gain more profit, and everything else for mortals
> takes second place after money.

Money exchangers were crucial to a Greek world that used dozens of different currencies. Theocritus, *Epigram*, 14:

> This bank dispenses to citizens and foreigners alike:
> deposit and withdraw according to the amount calculated in the
>   reckoning.
> Let others think of an excuse, but Caicus calculates
> foreign monetary transactions after dark for those who want them.

Artemon has somehow gone from rags to riches. Anacreon, 388:

> Before, he owned a shabby cloak, a tightly fastened hood,
> wooden dice as earrings and a plucked ox-hide
> around his ribs, the unwashed covering
> of an ill-fated shield: the vagabond Artemon
> who kept company with bread women and easy whores,   5
> contriving a fraudulent means of livelihood;
> many times his neck was in the stocks, often was he on the torture
>   wheel,
> frequently his back was whipped with the leather scourge,
> his hair and beard rooted out;
> but now, with gold earrings he rides in a carriage,   10
> the son of Cyce, and carries an ivory handled parasol
> just like the ladies.

STINGINESS

Greek culture was in many senses communal at various levels. Men could belong to dining groups and eat in rotation at each other's houses; the rich were expected to make financial contributions to the state, and at Athens had to perform various compulsory financial duties. In the world of Homer's *Iliad* and *Odyssey* individuals exchanged gifts regularly. There were hereditary links of guest-friendship and one could travel around expecting and receiving hospitality from friends in other cities. While in classical Athens conspicuous consumption was not the norm, the ungenerous man could be parodied. 'Love of honour', *philotimia*, was an important concept, motivating individuals to deeds for personal reputation and the common good (1). Stinginess reveals itself in a mean thanksgiving offering to a god (2), and in carrying home your own shopping, even though boys could be hired very cheaply for this task (7). The stingy man has only one cloak, so when it is being cleaned he stays at home (8), and hitching up his only garment when he sits down to save his cloak from wear and tear means that he will have to sit on his naked buttocks (13). He's so stingy he plucks the fleas off the couches himself, rather than own a slave to do this (12)! Theophrastus, *Characters*, 22, *Stinginess*:

(22.1) Stinginess is an absence of love of honour when this involves financial expenditure, and the stingy man is the type (22.2) who if he wins the prize for the best tragedy dedicates to the god of drama, Dionysus, just a strip of wood with only his own name written on it.

(22.3) When emergency financial levies are being decreed by the political assembly, he either keeps quiet or leaves in the middle of the proceedings. (22.4) When he gives away his daughter in marriage, he sells the meat from the sacrifice, except for the priest's share, and hires waiters for the wedding feast who have to bring their own food from home. (22.5) When he is responsible for the expenses for the maintenance of a war ship he spreads the captain's bedding on the deck for his own use, and puts his own away.

(22.6) He is likely not to send his children to the teacher for the Muses' festival, but says that they are sick, so that they will not have to make a contribution towards it. (22.7) When he shops he carries the meat from the market himself, in his hands, and the vegetables in a fold of his cloak. (22.8) He stays indoors whenever he takes off his cloak for laundering. (22.9) If a friend is seeking an interest-free loan and has talked it over with him, when he sees him coming he veers off and goes home in a roundabout way. (22.10) Despite the fact that his wife brought a dowry of her own into the marriage, he won't buy her a maid but hires a slave-boy from the women's market to accompany her when she goes out. (22.11) He wears shoes mended with patches and maintains that, 'They are as strong as horn.' (22.12) Waking up, he cleans the house, and plucks the fleas from the couches. (22.13) When he sits down he hitches up his threadbare cloak, the only thing he wears.

THE PICNIC WHEN THE WORK IS DONE

The heat and toil of summer serve as a foil to this beautiful rustic scene: tender meats, good wine, special cakes and a shady spot, all rounded off with a libation in thanks to the gods. The wine is from Biblis in Thrace, indicating trade in wine, this particular one having travelled several hundred kilometres by sea and land from Thrace to central Greece (line 589). Hesiod, *Works and Days*, 582–96:

> But when the artichoke flowers and the noisy cicada
> sitting in a tree monotonously pours forth his shrill song
> from beneath his wings in the season of exhausting heat,
> then the goats are fattest and wine the best,   585
> and women at their most lusty, but the men most feeble,
> their heads and knees Sirius scorches,
> and skin is also parched by the heat. But then, indeed,
> let me have a shaded rock and wine from Biblis,
> also a barley-cake made with milk, and the milk of goats who've
>   nearly dried up,   590
> with the flesh of a heifer fed in the woods, which has not yet
>   calved,
> and also of first-born kids. Let me drink sparkling wine
> sitting in the shade, my heart satisfied with food,
> turning my face to the refreshing west wind Zephyr,
> and from the ever-flowing, running, clear spring,   595
> let me pour out three libations of water but the fourth of wine.

WINE AND THE FEAST

Grain, olive oil and wine were the main items of trade. Wine was the essential complement to any meal or feast; it was mixed with water in large clay jars and served in cups. To drink undiluted wine was the mark of the barbarian (the Scythians drank undiluted wine). Many of the vases from Athens are beautifully decorated drinking cups, with a painted

1.1. A lowing heifer is led in procession during the Panathenaic Festival at Athens in honour of the goddess Athena. Athens, Parthenon frieze (south), marble, *c.* 447–432 BC, slab 54, figures 133–6. (© *British Museum*)

1.2. A deceased young boy bidding farewell to his mother while Charon waits in his boat to ferry him to Hades. The boy takes his go-cart with him. Athenian funerary vase, *c.* 450–425 BC. ()

1.3. Preparations for the sacrifice of a ram. The main officiant washes his hands in a vessel of water while the ram is restrained at a low altar. Athenian vase, *c.* 450–420 BC. (*Catharine Page Perkins Fund. Courtesy, Museum of Fine Arts, Boston. Reproduced with permission. © 2002 Museum of Fine Arts, Boston. All rights reserved*)

1.4. Statue of a youth praying, with arms outstretched. Athenian, bronze, 128 cm high, end of the fourth century BC. (*Bildarchiv Preussischer Kulturbesitz, Berlin, 2002, Erich Lessing*)

1.5. A woman mourning over the corpse; the male at the top of the funerary bier is much less emotional. Athenian funerary vase, *c.* 450–425 BC. (© *British Museum*)

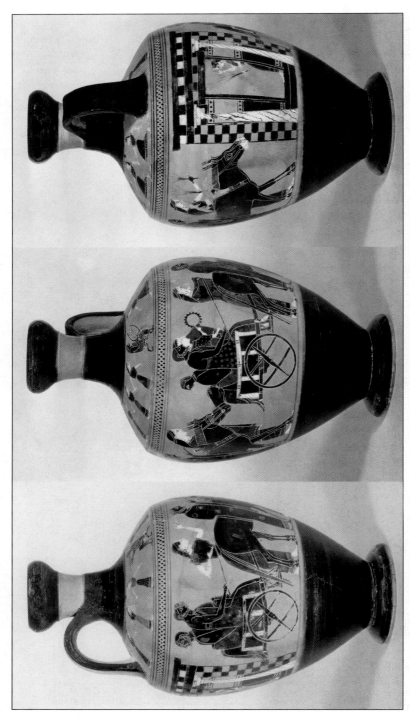

2.1. The wedding procession: the bride and groom travel by cart and arrive at his mother's house, who holds a wedding torch. Athenian vase, c. 550–530 BC. (All rights reserved, The Metropolitan Museum of Art, Purchase, 1956, Walter C. Baker Gift)

2.2. Women collecting water at the fountain house, and exchanging gossip. Athenian vase (actually a hydria such as the women are carrying on their heads), c. 530–500 BC. (© *British Museum*)

2.3. Girl running, with exposed breast and short tunic. Spartan bronze statuette, archaic period, c. 560 BC. (© *British Museum*)

2.4. A timid wife answers the door at the return of her husband, probably from a drinking party; he bangs on the door with his staff rather than using the knocker. Athenian vase, *c.* 425 BC.

2.5. Women weaving, perhaps the slaves of the household. Athenian vase, *c.* 550–530 BC.

2.6. A slave hands a child to its seated mother. The object in the middle is a basket for holding wool, and indicates the domestic context of the scene. Athenian vase, *c.* 450 BC. (© *British Museum*)

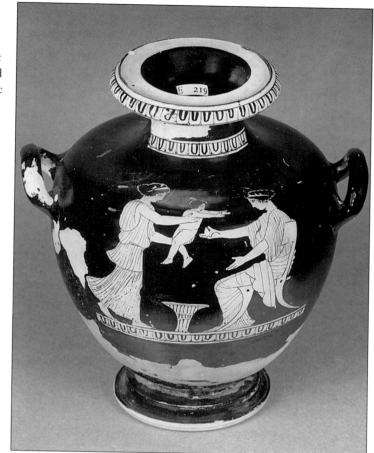

3.1. A *penteconter* (fifty-oared ship), trading vessel, being rowed and under sail. Athenian vase, *c.* 530–480 BC. (*Photo RMN, Chuzeville*)

3.2. Knocking olives out of a tree with sticks, and collecting them. The naked figures may well be slaves. Athenian vase, *c.* 530–500 BC. (© *British Museum*)

interior at the bottom of the cup which the drinker only saw when he had consumed most of the contents (respectable wives and daughters did not, of course, join in the drinking parties). There were clearly various types of wine from different parts of the Greek world, but those from the Greek islands were the most prized. Wherever the Greeks went, they took the vine, which surpassed even the olive tree in its geographical range (olives could not be grown in the very cold regions of the Black Sea). Dionysus was the god of wine; drinkers of wine were possessed by him. Women involved in women-only rites worshipping Dionysus clearly drank wine as part of the process, but away from the eyes of men. All-male drinking parties could be accompanied by the music of flute girls. A selection of passages about wine and drinking follows. Hesiod, *Works and Days*, 369–70:

> When the wine jar is first broached, and when it's nearly empty, stop drinking only when you've had your fill,
> be sparing of the middle, but there's no point going easy on the dregs.

Anacreon, 356 a, b:

> Boy, come and bring me a wine cup
> so I can drink without coming up for air
> and fill it up with ten measures of water
> and five of wine so I can
> once again be a follower of Dionysus
> doing it the right way.

> Come now, no longer let us in this way
> with pandemonium and clamour
> over the wine drink Scythian-style,
> but drink in moderation
> to the sound of beautiful hymns.

Anacreon, *Elegy*, 2:

> I have no time for someone who drinks his wine beside the full mixing bowl,
> talking of quarrels and of tearful battle
> but for he who by blending together the beautiful gifts of both the Muses
> and of Aphrodite is mindful of the charm of the banquet.

Anacreon, 373:

> I dined, breaking off a small bit of thin sesame honey cake,
> but a flagon of wine I drank down. Now delicately
> I pluck my lovely harp, serenading my beloved girl.

Often a drinker knows when to stop but a companion will urge him on.
Anacreon, 412:

> I say it again, won't you let me, drunk, depart homewards?

FOUR

Workers and Entertainers

Far-sighted Zeus deprives a man of half his virtue
on the day when slavery seizes him.

Homer, *Odyssey*, 17.322–3.

Slavery was an integral part of Greek society, and those who could afford slaves bought them, as noted by Xenophon, *Memorabilia*, 2.3.3: 'Those who are able to do so buy slaves so as to have fellow-workers.' Often slaves did not relieve a master of all his work but were rather used to supplement his own labour, in the same way as a small businessperson will nowadays hire help. In this way slaves worked in numerous occupations, and there were no exclusively slave tasks, except perhaps at the silver mines near Athens, where the work was dangerous.

Slaves were a heterogeneous group; many came from the barbarian lands around Greece, but the enslavement of fellow Greeks in warfare also meant that there were many Greek slaves. The lack of slave revolts in ancient Greece is due to the characteristics and nature of the Greek slave system. Slaves did not come from simply one place; they spoke many different languages and in being brought to Greece individual slaves were uprooted from home, family and kin. Many households owned only one or a few slaves, so there were few large groups of slaves who could meet. The Greeks were aware that there was potential danger from slaves, as indicated by Xenophon, *Hieron*, 4.3: 'For citizens without pay protect each other against slaves and wrongdoers so that none of the citizens may die a violent death.'

Rather than revolt, the major problem faced by slave-owners was runaway slaves. This was the main way in which slaves expressed their discontentment with their enslavement. But there had to be somewhere to flee to, and so it was usually in war situations, when the enemy encouraged slave desertions, that there were large numbers of absconding slaves.

Greek attitudes to slavery were complex. At the individual level there were clearly good relationships between some masters and slaves. But much would depend on the value of the slave, the temperament of their master, and the nature of the work: slaves in the mines never saw their masters and had no opportunity to forge links with them, whereas slaves in a household situation could easily become valued members of the family.

The Greeks viewed their slaves ambivalently: they might be loyal and hard-working, and expected to share in their master's joys and sorrows, but there was also the popular conception of them as lazy, gluttonous and untrustworthy. Philosophical attitudes as articulated by Aristotle were probably a little more theoretical than was the practice. But his point that the slave was a living tool is indicative of a wider morality of slavery: that slaves were human beings who were property to be used as tools to assist production, either agricultural or manufacturing.

Among the slaves were prostitutes, and after domestic slaves they formed the second biggest category of women slaves. They could also be free, if they were 'skilled' enough to earn their freedom. In addition to the ordinary prostitute, there was also the category of the *hetaera*, into which Pericles' lover Aspasia fell. They were usually free (or freed) women with social skills, or 'better' at their occupation than the average call-girl (a *porne*, hence our word pornography). Prostitutes were so important that the price of hiring flute girls was fixed at Athens, where a social ideology of prostitution was well articulated: men's access to call-girls was thought to reduce the chances of adultery. Sexual intercourse with a prostitute, even by a married man, was not considered immoral, and there was no 'moral' dimension to the act.

Prostitutes as well as gaming and cock-fighting, as will be seen in the extracts from Aeschines' speech *Against Timarchus*, provided avenues of entertainment. Festivals were also a key diversion for the Greeks from their work. And it was at these events that the great athletic, musical and equestrian contests took place. There were four main festivals, the Olympic, Pythian (at Delphi), Nemean (at Nemea) and the Isthmian (held at the Isthmus of Corinth). These were the crown games, at which the victors only received a crown of vegetation as a prize; at Olympia it was a wreath of olive. Only first-place winners were presented with an award at the crown games. This was a very competitive culture, and there were no prizes for second best at the most important festivals. However, at the contests held at the less-prestigious Panathenaea at Athens prizes were distributed to those who did not gain first place.

Pindar wrote victory odes (*epinicia*) to celebrate the winners, and a victory at one of the crown games was the highpoint of an athlete's career. While some writers such as Euripides might criticise athletes and athleticism, contests were intrinsic to Greek culture, and there was hardly a festival without these. There were numerous events, and wrestling and boxing in particular were popular with the Greeks. There were umpires and referees, who could punish the competitors if necessary. The *pancration* was an 'all-in' wrestling match, and biting and eye-gouging were permitted. However, the precise etiquette of these matches is uncertain, and several vases show umpires raising their sticks to strike competitors who have obviously broken some rule (see illustration 4.1).

'BOTH GODS AND MEN RESENT A MAN WHO LIVES IDLE'

There was no place for the idle in the Greek world. The shame of poverty harms a man, of course, but it also profits, 'for shame or fear of poverty induces men to work' (line 318). Hesiod, *Works and Days*, 302–20:

> Famine is a fitting companion for the man who does not work.
> Both gods and men resent a man who lives idle,
> he is by nature like the sting-less drones
> who consume the work of the bees, feasting without toiling: 305
> but let your work be dear to you and organise it properly
> so that your barns are full of provisions in the right season.
> Through hard work men become rich in flocks and wealth,
> and working they are more loved by the deathless gods.
> Work is not a reproach, but indolence is a scandal. 310
> But if you work, the lazy man will soon envy you
> as you become wealthy:
> for virtue and kudos accompany riches.
> Whatever your lot in life, working is the best thing to do,
> so turn your witless soul from other men's possessions 315
> toward your own work, taking care of your livelihood, as I bid you.
> A shame that is not good accompanies the man who is in need,
> shame, which greatly harms, but also profits.
> Shame goes with poverty, but confidence is coupled with prosperity.
> Wealth should not be stolen; wealth given by the gods is much
>   better. 320

THE TREATMENT AND MANAGEMENT OF SLAVES

Farmers might have slaves to help them. Socrates speaks to Critobulus on the need for rewards, even for slaves. Xenophon, *Oeconomicus*, 5.15–16:

(5.15) If anyone is going to make a success of farming it's necessary that he ensure that the labourers are eager and willing to obey. Someone who is a leader in war must achieve these same ends by rewarding those who behave as brave men should, and punish those who are disobedient. (5.16) For the farmer it is no less necessary to encourage his workers often, than for a general to encourage his soldiers. Slaves also require no less encouragement through good expectations than do free men, and in fact need more, so that they stay with you – willingly.

The discussion on the treatment of slaves continues, and Ischomachus offers this advice. Xenophon, *Oeconomicus*, 13.9–12:

(13.9) It is possible to make men more obedient by pointing out how it is advantageous for them to obey, but with slaves the training thought sufficient for wild animals is also a very useful way of teaching obedience. For you will get them to do many tasks by filling their stomachs with the food that they desire. Those who are ambitious by nature are also encouraged by praise. For some by nature hunger for praise no less than others do for food and drink.

(13.10) Now these are the very things which I myself do to make men more obedient, teaching this to those I want to appoint as managers, and I give the managers the following assistance. I don't make all the clothes and the shoes which I have to provide for my slaves identical, but some are better than others, some of inferior quality, so that I can reward the better slave with the better items, and I give the inferior items to the worse slave. (13.11) For it seems to me the case, Socrates, that it's very discouraging for the good slaves when they see that they are the ones doing the work, and the others, who are not willing to toil or take risks when necessary, receive the same that they do.

(13.12) So I myself don't think that the better slaves should be on an equal footing with the worse ones, and whenever I see that my managers have distributed the best things to those who most deserve them, I praise them, but if I see that by flattery or some other useless favour some slave is given special treatment, I don't ignore it, but rebuke the manager, and try to teach him, Socrates, that it is not in his interests to do this.

In the fourth century BC work entitled *Oeconomicus*, attributed to Aristotle but certainly not by him, some ideas on handling slaves and rewarding them are provided and give an insight into how slaves were viewed and treated. *Oeconomicus*, 1344a23–1344b21:

(1344a23–1344a29) The principal and most necessary part of property is that which is best and most profitable in the running of the household: and this is man. Because of this it is first necessary to acquire worthy slaves. There are two kinds of slaves: the overseer, and the worker. Since we observe that it is their education which moulds the character of the young, it is also necessary to train the purchased slaves who are to undertake work fit for a free person.

(1344a29–1344a34) The relationship with slaves should not be such that they are allowed to be insolent or to relax. To those who are nearer in position to that of free men, a share of honour should be given, and to those who are labourers, more food. Since the drinking of wine makes even free men insolent, and in many cultures the free men also abstain from wine, such as the Carthaginians when they are at war, it is obvious that wine should never be given, or only in small amounts, to slaves.

(1344a35–1344b6) There are three areas of importance in dealing with slaves: work, punishment and food. Not being punished and not being worked but having food makes slaves insolent. Yet being worked and punished but not having food is an act of violence and makes the slave unable to work. So it remains to give him work and sufficient food. It is not possible to manage slaves without payment, and the payment for slaves is food. As with others who also, when they get nothing better by behaving better, and when there are no rewards for goodness or punishments for badness, become worse, so it is also the case with slaves.

(1344b7–1344b11) So it is necessary to maintain surveillance and to distribute and withhold everything according to worth, food as well as clothing, and leisure and punishment, and in both word and deed imitate the power of the doctors in writing prescriptions, observing besides that food, unlike medicine, must be eaten regularly.

(1344b12–1344b14) The races that are best for work are those that are neither excessively cowardly nor excessively brave, for both do wrong. For those that are excessively cowardly do not stick to their work, and the high-spirited are not easy to manage.

(1344b15–1344b21) It is also necessary to fix an end to everything. For it is both just and advantageous to offer freedom as a reward. The slaves will be willing to labour when a reward, and the time-frame for it, are set. It is also necessary to let them have children, to serve as hostages. Also, do not acquire many slaves of the same race, as they do in the cities. In addition, celebrate sacrifices and holidays for the slaves' sake rather than for the free men, as free men have more of such things, and it is on their account that these things were established.

Ischomachus reports to Socrates what he told his young bride about her duties in training unskilled slaves. Xenophon, *Oeconomicus*, 7.41:

There are other duties that are specifically yours, my wife, and pleasant for you, as when you take an unskilled slave girl and train her, and she becomes worth twice as much, and when you take a slave girl ignorant of housekeeping and her duties, making her skilled and trustworthy and mindful of her duties, so that she is worth any amount of money at all, and when you are able to reward both the self-controlled and useful slaves in your household, and punish anyone who seems bad.

The details of the following lawsuit at Athens are complicated, but it is apparent that slaves could only give evidence under torture, and that it was clearly not in everyone's interest for this to happen. Isocrates, 17 (*Trapeziticus*), 13–14:

(13) Men of the jury, you have heard from the witnesses. I had already lost money and had to answer the most fraudulent accusations, and myself left home for the Peloponnese to enquire into matters. Menexenus discovered the slave here, and seizing him demanded that he be tortured both about the deposit and also about the accusations his master had brought against us. (14) But Pasion rose to such a degree of audacity that he had the slave released on the grounds that he was a free man. Bereft of shame and lacking in fear, he asserted that the slave – whom he alleged had been kidnapped by us from him and had given to us that money – was a free man, and he prevented his torture.

While there were laws to prevent slaves being struck by people other than their owners, as was the case at Athens where slaves, foreigners and citizens often wore the same clothes and were similar in appearance, clearly in certain circumstances strangers did strike slaves that did not belong to them. The speaker in this lawsuit was the object of an attempted entrapment. Demosthenes, 53 (*Against Nicostratus*), 16:

Being neighbours and having a farm adjacent to mine, they sent a young citizen lad into my farm during the day, and ordered him to pluck the roses that were growing, so that if I caught him and clapped him in irons or beat him up thinking that he was a slave, they might bring a legal case for assault against me. But they failed in their scheme.

Desertions by slaves in wartime could be expected and were encouraged by the enemy to weaken their opponents. In 413 BC when the Spartans fortified Decelea near Athens, 20,000 slaves absconded. Slave revolts did not occur in the classical period, but the *helots*, the enserfed peasants ruled over by the Spartans, did rebel. Two examples of slave desertions follow. In the civil war in Corcyra in 427 BC, the slaves defected to the democrats, and on the island of Chios in 412 BC, the desertion of slaves was clearly a result of mistreatment. Thucydides, 3.73, 8.40.2:

(3.73) Each side sent into the country calling upon the slaves and promising them their freedom: the majority of the slaves joined forces with the common people.

(8.40.2) The Chians had many slaves and possessed more of them than any other single city except the Spartans, and at the same time on account of their number their wrongs were punished more severely, so that when the Athenian army seemed firmly established with fortifications, the majority of the slaves immediately deserted to the Athenians, and because of their knowledge of the country they caused great damage.

The kindness of the speaker (his name is unknown) to his old slave indicates the bonds that could grow between free and slave. Demosthenes, 47 (*Against Evergus and Mnesibulus*), 55–6:

(47.55) My wife happened to be having lunch with the children in the courtyard, and with her was an elderly woman, who had been my slave-nurse, a kind and faithful person, who had been manumitted [released from slavery] by my father. She lived with her husband after she had been freed. But when he died and she herself was an old woman, there was no one to look after her, so she returned to me. (47.56) I couldn't bear to see my nurse, or the slave who was my boyhood attendant, in want.

Manumitted slaves might not always be grateful, as the former master was a constant reminder of their previous slavery. Demosthenes, 24 (*Against Timocrates*), 124:

Slaves who have been freed, men of the jury, have no gratitude towards their masters for their freedom, but hate them more than any other men, since they share the knowledge of their enslavement.

The following passage suggests that at Athens the murder of a master in a house by a slave, if the guilty slave was not known, would lead to all of the slaves in the house being put to death. Why the boy stabbed his master is unfortunately not stated, but some form of maltreatment must be assumed. Antiphon, 5 (*On the Murder of Herodes*), 69:

Not long ago a slave-boy, not yet twelve years old, sought to murder his master. If he had not panicked and fled when his master screamed, leaving the knife in the wound, but dared to stay, all of the slaves in the house would have been put to death, as no one would have thought that the boy would ever have dared to do such a thing. But he was caught and confessed that it was him.

The Greeks realised that some masters could be overly harsh, and at Athens slaves were allowed to take refuge from such masters at the altars of the gods, especially at the temple of Theseus. But as this passage and the one from Andania make clear (see below), the slave was not allowed to go free. If she or he was found to have been the victim of gross abuse, someone else was entitled to buy the slave. Aristophanes, *The Seasons*, Fragment 577:

In my view the best option is to make a dash for the temple of Theseus, and wait there until we find someone to buy us.

Euripides also refers to the practice. Euripides, *Suppliant Women*, 267–9:

The wild beast has the rocks as a place of refuge,
the slave the altars of the gods, and a city when it is beset with
    difficulties
takes cover with another city.

The cult regulations for a festival in the Peloponnese include rules about what was to happen in the case of fleeing slaves. The priest judges only the cases of run-away slaves from Andania, the city hosting the festival. It is not stated who, if anyone, judged the cases of run-away slaves not belonging to masters from Andania. F. Sokolowski, *Lois sacrées des Cités grecques* (Paris, 1969), no. 65, lines 80–4:

There is to be refuge for slaves. Let the shrine be a refuge, in the area marked out by the priests. No one is to receive run-away slaves or give them food or any assistance. Anyone who acts contrary to what is written down may be prosecuted by the master of the slave for twice the slave's worth and for a penalty of 50 *drachmas*. The priest is to make a judgement about the run-away slaves from our own city [Andania], and all those he condemns are to be given back to their masters. But if the priest does not give back a run-away to his master, the slave may leave the master who has him.

Slaves do not speak to us directly, but there were slave characters in comedies. Common charges against slaves were laziness, gluttony and drunkenness. Epicrates, *Hard to Sell*, Fragment 5:

> *Slave:* What is more hateful than to be called to the place where they are
>   drinking with 'Slave, slave!',
> and by some mere lad who hasn't got a beard yet,
> or to have to get him the chamber pot, and to see
> half-eaten milk-cakes and birds lying around,
> which even though they're left-overs a slave mustn't eat,
> as the women tell us. But what makes us mad
> is when they call us 'greedy-guts' when one of us does eat
> any of these things!

The productivity and skills of slaves and their importance in manufacturing is made clear in this passage where Demosthenes relates his father's income. For the monetary values, see the glossary. Demosthenes, 27 (*Against Aphobus* 1), 9:

> My father left me two workshops, neither small: one made swords, with thirty-two or thirty-three slaves, most of them worth five or six *minas*, and none of them worth less than three. From these he received a clear profit of thirty *minas* annually. The other workshop, with twenty slaves, made couches . . . and yielded a clear profit of twelve *minas*.

An economic relationship could exist between master and slave that was beneficial to both. The skilled slaves worked in their own shop with a slave manager. They kept the profits and paid the owner a fixed rate, retaining the rest of the money. Such slaves could save up and pay their master for their freedom, if he agreed. Aeschines, 1 (*Against Timarchus*), 97:

> Timarchus' father left him property with which any other man would have been able to carry out financial services for the state, but Timarchus was not able even to make it do for himself. There was a house behind the acropolis, a boundary estate at Sphettus, another piece of land at Alopeke, not to mention nine or ten slaves skilled in making shoes, each of whom paid to him two *obols* a day as a fee, and the manager of the workshop paid him three *obols*. In addition to these there was a slave-woman skilled in working flax, who made fine goods for sale in the market, and a slave man skilled in the art of embroidering.

It is often said that the Greeks accepted slavery as an everyday fact of life and could not conceive of a society without slaves, but Aristotle's own arguments and the ideas of others to which he refers indicate that while there was never any move to abolish slavery, there was nevertheless serious discussion about it and its legality, if only among the educated elite. Aristotle argued that some by nature were free and others slaves: the slaves were physically built as slaves and did not have the intellectual talents of the free. The reality of course, which in fact Aristotle (and other Greeks) recognised, was that many became slaves who were born free, and that being a slave was often a matter of chance and not of physical or mental attributes. The practice of manumission indicates that many saw slaves as human beings who could be free. Aristotle may well have been thinking primarily in terms of non-Greek, barbarian slaves, who made up a large if not the main proportion of slaves in Greece. Aristotle, *Politics*, 1253b14–1254a17:

(1253b14–1253b23) Firstly, let's discuss master and slave, so that we might see how these relate to the provision of necessary services, and whether we are able to arrive at a better understanding of them than the assumptions that are currently put forward. For some think, as I discussed previously, that to be a master is a skill, and that the management of the household, and being a master, and politics, and royal rule, require the same skill. Others say that mastery over slaves is contrary to nature, and that the distinction between slave and free is made by law, but that nature does not have this distinction, and so slavery is unjust, for it is based on force.

(1253b23–1253b33) So since property is part of the household and acquiring property is part of household management (for without necessities it is impossible to live or to live well), so for the practice of crafts it is necessary for there to be the proper tools, if one is going to complete the task, and this is also the case for the management of the household. Some tools are inanimate and some are living: for the captain of a ship uses an inanimate rudder, but uses a living man as the officer of the bow. For the slave is classed as a tool of his particular craft. So a piece of property is a tool that enables one to live, and property is a collection of tools, and the slave is a possession that is alive, and so like all slaves is a tool in charge of other tools.

(1253b33–1253b39) For consider that if each tool could complete its work if it were ordered to do so or as it realised that its work needed to be done, just as they say the statues of Daedalus did, or the tripods made by Hephaestus which Homer says 'automatically enter the assembly of the gods', so shuttles would weave themselves and harps play music automatically, and then master craftsmen would not need assistants and masters would not need slaves.

(1254a1–1254a8) The tools that I have mentioned are producing tools, as distinct from possessions useful in their own right. That is to say, a shuttle produces something other than simply the use of it, while from clothes or a bed there is only the actual use of them. Moreover, since producing something is different from being useful in its own right, and since both of these require tools, there must be the same similar difference between these two categories of tools. Now life is action, and not production, so the slave is a tool used for action.

(1254a8–1254a13) A 'possession' is spoken of in the same way a 'part' is. For a 'part' is not simply a 'part' of something else but completely belongs to that something. It's the same with a possession. So a master is simply the master of a slave, and does not belong to the slave, but the slave is not simply the slave of the master but completely belongs to him.

(1254a13–1254a17) Therefore the nature and functions of a slave are clear from the above considerations: a human being who by nature does not belong to himself but to another is a slave by nature, and a human being belongs to another when he is a man but also a possession, and a possession is defined here as a tool used for action and having a separate existence.

Aristotle points to physical differences between free and slave which probably did exist in the case of barbarian slaves used for hard work, but that in reality could not have applied to many skilled slaves, especially those of Greek origin. But here we see the Aristotelian ideal of the citizen freed by slaves from hard work and able to engage in political life. This was his ideal and not the reality: the overwhelming majority of the 30,000 citizens of Athens, even those with slaves, worked hard for a living and also attended meetings of the assembly and served on juries. Aristotle, *Politics*, 1254b24–1254b34, 1255a1–1255a12:

(1254b24–1254b34) The use made of slaves does not differ much from that of our animals: both of them help with their bodies to furnish our essential needs. Nature chooses to make the bodies of free men and slaves different, those of slaves strong for use in necessary work, but those of free men upright and useless for the performance of hard work, but useful for political life (a life divided between the demands of war and peace). But the opposite frequently happens: some have the bodies of free men and not the souls, and some the souls but not the bodies.

(1255a1–1255a12) Some by nature are clearly free and some are slave, and for the slaves slavery is expedient and just. But it's not difficult to see the point of view of those who argue the opposite. The expressions 'slavery' and 'slave' are two-fold in meaning. For there is a slave and slavery by nature and by law. For the law is a provision that the things which are captured in war are said to belong to the conquerors. But many of those who are versed in law treat this right in the same way as a politician who makes an unconstitutional proposal and argue that it is horrible that one will become a slave through force because someone has the ability to do violence and is more powerful. Among the experts some hold this opinion, but some do not.

Aristotle's ideal is that the wealthy will have slaves to do their work, and an overseer to organise the slaves (usually the supervisor was a slave purchased specifically for this purpose: in the fifth-century BC Nicias, the general, paid the enormous sum of one talent for an overseer of his mine slaves). The slave-owner is then totally a man of leisure, able to devote himself to the finer things of life: running the city or philosophising. Aristotle, *Politics*, 1255b31–1255b37:

The master's knowledge is in how to use slaves. For he is master not in acquiring the slaves but in using them. But this knowledge itself is not important or highly regarded: for of the things that it is necessary for the slave to know how to do, it is necessary for the master to instruct the slave how to do them. So those who have the financial means don't undertake this task, but have an overseer for this function, and devote themselves to politics or philosophy.

Eutherus, once wealthy but ruined by Athens' defeat in the Peloponnesian War of 431–404 BC, would rather hire out his labour than beg, but views working as someone's overseer as a form of slavery. Xenophon, *Memorabilia*, 2.8.1–4:

(2.8.1) When Socrates met an old friend after some time he said, 'From where have you come, Eutherus?'

'When the war ended I came home from abroad, Socrates, and now am living here,' he replied. 'For since we were deprived of our foreign property, and my father did not bequeath me any property in Attica, I am forced to live here now and provide for my wants by physical labour. It seems to me better to do this than to beg from other men, especially as I possess nothing that I could use as security to borrow money.'

(2.8.2) 'And how long do you think,' Socrates enquired, 'your body will be strong enough to earn money for your daily needs?'

'By Zeus, not long,' Eutherus said.

'And moreover,' Socrates commented, 'when you grow old, it's clear that you will need spending money, but nobody will be willing to give you money for your physical labour.'

(2.8.3) 'You speak the truth,' he said.

'Well then, Socrates said, 'it would be better for you to at once lay hold of some kind of work that will be sufficient for you when you grow old, and to go to someone possessing lots of money and who needs an assistant, and to receive a profit in return for your labour, in your employment as his overseer, bringing in his crops and guarding his property.

(2.8.4) 'Socrates, it would be difficult for me to submit myself to slavery.'

While a few places had large numbers of farm slaves, and Sparta had *helots*, most slaves were found in the towns and cities of Greece. Plato provides important advice on handling slaves, especially that they should not all be from the same country. This dialogue is between an Athenian 'stranger' and two individuals named Megillus of Sparta and Clinias of Crete. The quotation from Homer (777a) is from *Odyssey*, 17.322–3, but instead of 'virtue', Plato has 'mind'. Plato, *Laws*, 776b–778a:

(776b) *Athenian:* The next thing to consider is possessions and what a man should possess to be provided with a reasonable amount of property. For most possessions it is not difficult either to suppose what they should be or to acquire them, but slaves present all sorts of problems. The reason is this: the way we speak about them is not entirely correct but in some ways is correct, (776c) for the language we employ about slaves is both contradictory to our actual experience and partly in agreement with it.

Megillus: But what do you mean by this? For we don't yet understand, stranger, what you are saying.

Athenian: That's quite understandable, Megillus. For the Spartan system of the *helots* presents nearly the most difficult controversy in all of Greece, which some contend is good, but which for others is bad. There is less controversy about the enslavement (776d) of the Mariandyni in the slave system of the Heracleotes, and that of the class of serfs in Thessaly. Considering these and all other such cases, what should we do about the possession of slaves? The case that I happened to mention during my discourse, and which you naturally asked me what I meant by, is this: we know that we'd all agree that it is necessary to own slaves who are as docile and well behaved as possible. For in the past many slaves have exceeded brothers or sons in every virtue, and have saved their masters, their possessions, and their entire house. (776e) Surely we know that such things are said about slaves?

Megillus: Certainly.

Athenian: And isn't the opposite also said: that the soul of a slave is unsound, not to be trusted, and that a man in possession of his faculties should never put any faith in such a class? And the most knowledgeable of our poets, Homer, actually declares, in speaking of Zeus, that, (777a)

> Far-sighted Zeus deprives a man of half his mind,
> on the day when slavery seizes him.

Each takes a different opinion about this. There are those who put no trust in the class of slaves, treating them as if they had the nature of beasts, and with goads and whips not only three times, but many times over enslave the souls of the slaves. Others act, on the other hand, completely contrary to this.

Megillus: That's the case.

Clinias: (777b) So what are we to do about slavery in our own state, stranger, since there is such a difference of opinion about both the ownership of slaves and their punishment?

Athenian: What indeed, Clinias? It is obvious that since man is a difficult creature, he is not likely to make the necessary distinction easy, either now or in the future, between the slave and the free master in actual practice.

Clinias: That appears to be the case.

Athenian: The slave is a difficult possession. For history frequently shows – (777c) as in the many revolts customarily arising in Messenia, and in the cities where many of the slaves owned speak the same language – that such evils arise, as also with those called the 'Marauders' who go round Italy committing all sorts of deeds and suffering reprisals. Bearing in mind all of these factors one is at a loss as to how one should act concerning all such matters. There are only two options left: (777d) not to allow the slaves, if at all possible, to be from the same country if the slaves are to bear the yoke of slavery easily, and the other is to treat them properly, not just for their sake, but more for our own sake. The proper training of the slaves should not involve hybristic ill-treatment of the slaves, but to punish them less, if possible, than our own equals. For when he can do harm against those whom it is easy for him to wrong, this shows whether a man is natural and not counterfeit in his honouring of justice and hatred of wrongs.

(777e) He who in his attitude and his actions towards slaves is undefiled by what is impious and unjust can most successfully sow a crop of virtue. The very same can also be rightly said of the way in which a master and tyrant and all those wielding power treat someone weaker than themselves. It is necessary to punish slaves according to the dictates of justice, and not to let them give themselves airs by simply admonishing them as if they were free men. Almost every address to a slave ought to be an order; there shouldn't be jesting of any sort with slaves, (778a) neither the female ones nor the males. Many are foolishly and excessively indulgent toward their slaves, making life more difficult, for the slaves to be ruled, and for themselves to rule.

Clinias: That's certainly the case.

THE FATE OF THE CONQUERED

Homer describes one of the most poignant scenes bringing out the horror of war: a young son recoiling from the sight of his own father, dressed to kill. Hector has come back to the city but does not find his wife Andromache at home. The housekeeper tells him that she has gone to the walls of Troy. The threat of slavery looms over Andromache if the city is defeated. Homer, *Iliad*, 6.390–493:

So spoke the housekeeper, and Hector hurried from the house	390
back along the same way through the well-built streets.	
When he had come to the gate as he passed through the great city,	
the Scaean Gate, through which he intended to go out into the plain,	
there at last his richly dowered wife came running to meet him,	
Andromache, daughter of great-hearted Eetion,	395
Eetion who lived under wooded Mount Placus,	
in Thebe below Placus, lord over the men of Cilicia:	
for it was his daughter that bronze-armoured Hector had as wife.	
She met him there, together with a maid-servant	
carrying the tender boy in the fold of her breast, a mere baby,	400
the beloved son of Hector, like a beautiful star,	
called by Hector Scamandrius, but by everyone else	

Astyanax [lord of the city], for only Hector preserved Ilion.
Then Hector smiled, looking silently at the child:
but Andromache stood close to him, crying,   405
took his hand and spoke to him, calling him by name,

'Husband, your own strength will be your destruction, and you
   have no pity
for your little son or for wretched me, who soon will be
your widow: for soon the Achaeans will all set upon you
slaughtering you. And for me it would be better   410
having lost you to sink into the earth: for there is no other
comfort when you have met your destiny,
nothing but woes: I don't have a father or honoured mother.
In truth, god-like Achilles slew my father,
when he sacked the finely situated city of the Cilicians,   415
high-gated Thebe. He slew Eetion,
but did not strip him of his armour, for he respected him in his
   heart,
but burned him with his cunningly wrought armour
and heaped up a grave mound. The mountain nymphs, daughters
   of Zeus
who bears the aegis, planted elm trees around it.   420
And they who were my seven brothers in our halls,
all of them in a single day went into the hall of Hades:
for all of them were slain by god-like swift-footed Achilles,
among the shuffling oxen and the white sheep they tended.
And my mother, who was queen under wooded Placus,   425
when he had led her here with the rest of the plunder,
released her again for a huge ransom,
but Artemis, shooter of arrows, struck her in the halls of her father.
So, Hector, you are a father to me and a queenly mother
and brother, and you are my vigorous husband: 430
but come now, take pity, and stay here on this tower,
and do not make your child an orphan and your wife a widow,
but draw up the army by the wild fig tree, where the city
is vulnerable and the wall may be scaled.
Three times coming to that spot the best Achaeans have made an
   attempt on it   435
with the two Ajaxes and famous Idomeneus
and the sons of Atreus and the stout son of Tydeus [Diomedes]:
whether this is because someone well versed in oracles told them,
or whether their own heart urges them on and compels them.'

Then great Hector with his shining helm spoke to her: 440
'All these things are on my mind too, wife, but I have dread shame
of the Trojans and the Trojan wives with their trailing dresses,
if I stood aside like a coward, avoiding battle.
My heart won't let me do this, since I have learned to be always
    valiant
and to fight in the front ranks of the Trojans,   445
striving for great glory for my father and myself.
For this I know well in my heart and soul,
the day will come when sacred Ilion will be destroyed
and Priam and his people armed with the strong ash spear.
But I do not feel so much concern for the grief of the Trojans
    hereafter
                                                                         450
nor for Hecabe herself nor for lord Priam
nor for my brothers, who many and brave
will fall in the dust at the hands of hostile men, but
for you, when one of the bronze-armoured Achaeans
leads you away, weeping, robbing you of your day of freedom.   455
And in Argos you will weave the loom of another woman,
and carry water from the spring Messeis or Hypereia,
much against your will, but strong compulsion will be on you.
And at some time a man seeing you weeping will say:
"Here is the wife of Hector, who was the best warrior of the   460
horse-taming Trojans, when they fought around Ilion."
So will one then speak of you: and to you it will be a fresh grief
from want of such a man as me to ward off from you the day of
    slavery.
But may I have perished and may the piled-up earth hide me
before I hear your cries as you are dragged away.'   465

So saying glorious Hector stretched out his arms to his son:
but the boy snuggled back into the breasts of his fair-girdled nurse
crying, terrified at the sight of his dear father,
fearful as he saw the bronze and the crest of horse's hair,
thinking that it waved terribly from the top of the helmet.   470
At this both his dear father and queenly mother laughed:
and glorious Hector immediately took the helmet off his head
and laid it gleaming brightly on the ground:
he kissed his beloved son and tossed him in his hands,
and spoke in prayer to Zeus and the rest of the gods: 475

'Zeus, and you other gods, grant that this my child
be distinguished among the Trojans, just as I am,

and valiant in strength, and be a mighty ruler over Ilion:
and some day let someone say, "He is a better man than his
    father",
as he comes back from battle; and may he carry home blood-
    stained armour,   480
having slain his enemy, and bring joy to his mother's heart.'

So saying he put his child in the arms of his beloved wife
and she took him to her fragrant bosom
smiling through her tears: and her husband was moved to pity,
and stroked her with his hand and spoke to her, calling her
    by name,   485

'Wife, do not grieve too much in your heart for me:
for which man, contrary to Fate, will cast me into Hades?
I think that no man has ever fled his fate,
neither a coward nor a brave warrior, when he has once been born,
but going to the house carry out your tasks,   490
both the loom and the distaff, and order your maid-servants
to ply their work: war shall be for the men,
for all of them living in Ilion, but particularly for me.'

GREECE'S 'LADIES OF THE NIGHT'

The gods were thanked for success in all fields of endeavour. In Corinth,
when the goddess Aphrodite answered people's prayers, they dedicated
slave-prostitutes to her, sending them to her temple on the Corinthian
acropolis. The monies these women subsequently earned in their trade
belonged to Aphrodite. Xenophon of Corinth vowed that if he won his
event at the Olympics he would pledge 100 prostitutes to her. Pindar seems
a little embarrassed at the task before him in singing of Xenophon's gift to
Aphrodite. Persuasion was a deity associated with Aphrodite. The verb 'to
graze' had sexual overtones for the Greeks. Pindar, *Encomion*, 122:

O queen of Cyprus, Aphrodite, here into your precinct
Xenophon has brought a herd of one-hundred girls
to graze, glorying in the fulfilment of his vows.

Young women who welcome many strangers,
attendants of Persuasion in wealthy Corinth
who burn yellow tears of fresh incense,
often flying in your thoughts
to the mother of loves heavenly Aphrodite.

To you, young ones, she has allowed
without criticism in charming beds
to pluck the fruit from soft youth.
When there is the need, all is fair . . .

But I wonder what the lords of the Isthmus of Corinth
will say about me for devising such a beginning
for the honey-sounding song?

Athenaeus also refers to this practice of dedication, and quotes an epigram composed by Simonides to accompany the list of prostitutes on a painting of them standing praying to the goddess. Athenaeus, *The Wise Men at Dinner*, 573c–e:

(573c) It is an ancient custom in Corinth . . . whenever the city prays to Aphrodite about important matters, to take along numerous prostitutes to her temple, to join in the supplication of the goddess, and these prostitutes join in the prayers to the goddess, and later are present at the sacrifice. When, in fact, the Persian forces invaded Greece . . . (573d) the Corinthian prostitutes going to the temple of Aphrodite prayed on behalf of the safety of Greece. When the Corinthians dedicated to the goddess the plaque on which they separately recorded the names of the prostitutes who had made supplication to the goddess, and who were later present at the sacrifice, Simonides composed this epigram:

These women stand praying with heaven's favour to Aphrodite
for Greece and its battle-brave citizens,
(573e) for the divine Aphrodite was not minded to hand over
the citadel of Greece to the bow-carrying Persians.

Even private individuals make vows to the goddess that if what they pray for is accomplished they will even dedicate prostitutes to her. So, this being the custom, when Xenophon of Corinth went to the Olympic games he vowed that he would dedicate prostitutes to the goddess if he was victorious.

Prostitutes could become very wealthy and famous. In the closing decades of the fourth century BC, Phryne had an exceptional career, though at one stage she was nearly executed for dabbling in exotic religious practices. A wealthy, free prostitute in fact was considerably more emancipated (and had greater economic power) than the average Athenian housewife. The jurors considered Phryne to be the priestess and temple servant of Aphrodite, the goddess of love, because Phryne was so beautiful (590e). The statue of Knidian Aphrodite was named after its home, Knidus, in Asia Minor (591a). Philip, son of Amyntas, was Alexander the Great's father (591c). Athenaeus, *The Wise Men at Dinner*, 590d–591d:

(590d) Phryne came from the town of Thespiae. When she was prosecuted by Euthias for a capital offence, she was acquitted. This so angered Euthias that he never spoke at another trial, so Hermippus says. (590e) Hyperides, the Athenian orator, when he was speaking in court in Phryne's defence and was arguing to no avail and it was probable that the jurors were going to convict her, brought her in to where she could be seen and ripping open her garments exposed her breasts, and at the sight of her began lamenting as he summed up his speech, and he made the jurors feel superstitious fear about this priestess and temple servant of Aphrodite, and choosing to be compassionate the jurors did not condemn her to death. After she was acquitted a decree was passed that no one was to lament in court while speaking on someone's behalf, nor should the man or woman being prosecuted in the trial be shown naked.

(590f) Phryne was beautiful in the parts not exposed to view. On account of this it was not easy to see her naked, for she a wore a tunic that clung to her body, and she did not make use of the public baths. At the festivals of the Eleusinia and Poseidonia in the sight of all the Greeks she took off her outer cloak, and letting down her hair stepped into the sea. Apelles painted his 'Aphrodite Rising from the Sea' with her as the model.

(591a) Praxiteles the sculptor, loving her, used her as his model for his Knidian Aphrodite, and on the base of his statue of Eros, below the stage of the theatre, he inscribed:

Praxiteles has carved to perfection the Eros that he suffered,
drawing the pattern from his own heart,
and giving me [Eros] to Phryne as the price of me [Eros]. The love-spell
    I throw
no longer comes from my arrows, but from looking at me.

(591b) He gave her a choice of his statues, whether she would wish to choose his Eros, or his Satyr, which stood in the street of the tripods. Choosing the Eros, she dedicated it in Thespiae. Of Phryne herself her neighbours had a golden statue made and dedicated on a pillar of Pentelic marble at Delphi; Praxiteles made the statue. When the cynic philosopher Crates saw it he said that it was an offering to Greek incontinence. The statue of Phryne was set up between that of

Archidamus the Spartan king (591c) and Philip, son of Amyntas, with the inscription, 'Phryne, daughter of Epicles, of Thespiae'; so Alcetas writes in the second volume of his work *Concerning the Dedications at Delphi*.

(591d) Phryne was excessively rich and promised that she would build a wall around the city of Thebes if the Thebans would inscribe on it, 'While Alexander destroyed the wall, Phryne the prostitute rebuilt it'; so Callistratus writes in his book, *About Prostitutes*.

Many prostitutes were slaves, and manumission was the ultimate reward for them, as with other slaves. Neaera was a prostitute (*hetaera*) at Corinth who had particularly pleased her clients and was able to get them to make contributions towards her freedom. Not all men, unlike in this passage, gave up prostitutes and mistresses after marriage. The passage opens with Neaera being owned by the woman Nicarete, her pimp. Demosthenes, 59 (*Against Neaera*), 29–32:

(59.29) Neaera had two lovers, Timanoridas the Corinthian and Eucrates from Leucas, who since Nicarete was excessive in the amount she exacted from them (for Neaera's services), demanding that they meet all the daily expenses of the household, paid out thirty *minas* to Nicarete as the price for Neaera's body, and purchased Neaera outright from her, according to the law of the city, to be their slave.

(59.30) They had her and made use of her for as much time as they wished. When they were about to marry, they told her that they did not wish to see their own *hetaera* working in Corinth, or under the control of a brothel-keeper, but that they would be happy to take less money from her than they had paid for her, and to see her having some benefit for herself. So they said they were willing to forego one-thousand *drachmas* from the purchase price of her freedom, five-hundred *drachmas* each, and they told her to pay them the twenty *minas* when she had found it. When she heard of this arrangement of Eucrates and Timanoridas, she summoned to Corinth, among others who had been her lovers, Phrynion of the *deme* Paeania in Attica, the son of Demon and the brother of Demochares, who was leading a wanton and extravagant lifestyle, as the older ones among you will recall.

(59.31) When Phrynion came to her she spoke to him about the arrangement that Eucrates and Timanoridas had made with her, and gave him the money that she had collected from her other lovers as a contribution she had got together towards her freedom, together with whatever she had saved up herself, and begged him to provide the balance needed to make up the twenty *minas*, and to give it to Eucrates and Timanoridas so that she could be free.

(59.32) He happily listened to what she had to say, and taking the money that had been paid to her by the other lovers, and himself adding what was wanting, gave the twenty *minas* to Eucrates and Timanoridas for her freedom, with the proviso that she was not to work as a prostitute in Corinth.

At Athens there were regulations concerning prices for hiring flute-girls, harp-girls and lyre-girls, most of whom would have been slaves. These entertainers would have performed at a symposium, a drinking party for men (though it could also be the setting for intellectual conversation). The girls often finished their evening's musical work with sexual intercourse with the men they were entertaining. Aristotle, *Constitution of the Athenians*, 50.1–2:

(50.1) Ten citizens are elected by lot as city superintendents. (50.2) Five of them hold office in the Piraeus and five in the city of Athens itself. They supervise the flute-girls and harp-girls and lyre-girls so that these don't receive more than two *drachmas* in payment, and if several men are eager to take the same girl, the city superintendents cast lots and hire the girl out to the winner. And they ensure that the excrement collectors don't dispose of the excrement within ten stades of the city walls . . . and they remove the corpses of those who die on the roads: they have public slaves to do this.

TIMARCHUS: 'A KEPT MAN'

An adult citizen at Athens who acted as a male prostitute was deprived of many citizen rights: he could not speak in the assembly, hold political office or be a herald, ambassador or priest. Strict laws prevented the sexual abuse of children. Relationships between older men and boys began only with the onset of puberty, and at Athens these liaisons were not to involve sodomy. At Sparta, however, intercourse in pederastic relationships between older men and youths approaching adulthood was socially sanctioned as part of the system of military training.

In 345 BC the Athenian orator Aeschines prosecuted a citizen, Timarchus, for having been an infamous male prostitute. The disgrace of anal intercourse for a citizen related to the submission of oneself to another man's sexual power, and the adoption of a submissive passive sexual position in a society in which male sexual power was meant to be dominating. The male prostitute added to this disgrace by accepting money for his services. Aeschines, 1 (*Against Timarchus*), 40-2, 51-2, 58-9:

(1.40) Timarchus, once he was no longer a boy, went to live in the Piraeus at the surgery of Euthydicus, allegedly as a student of this skill, but actually because he wanted to sell his body, as what happened shows. The names of the merchants or other foreigners or those of our own citizens who made use of Timarchus' body at that time I willingly omit, so that it might not be said that I am excessively attentive concerning all the details. But I will speak about whose houses he has lived in, disgracing his own body – and the city – earning wages by the very activity that the law prohibits to be undertaken on pain of not being allowed to speak in the assembly.

(1.41) Fellow Athenians, there is one Misgolas, son of Naucrates, of the *deme* Collytus, a man who in other respects is fine and upright, and in no other way would he be blameworthy, but for this thing he goes beserk, like a man possessed, and he is accustomed always to have around him some singers or lyre-players. I say this, not to be vulgar, but so that you might know what type of man Misgolas is. Misgolas, realising why Timarchus here was spending his time at the doctor's house, gave him some money in advance and had him change his place of residence and brought him to his own house. For Timarchus was nicely built and young and not averse to disgusting behaviour, and suitable for what Misgolas wanted to do, and Timarchus wanted to submit to.

(1.42) And he didn't shrink from these things but rather this Timarchus here consented, though he wasn't lacking for money for moderate needs. For his father had bequeathed to him a substantial property, which he has squandered, as I will prove as I develop my argument. But he acted in this way because he was enslaved to the most shameful pleasures, to gluttony and extravagant dining, to flute-girls, prostitutes, dice and all the other things, none of which should have power over someone well born and free. This wretch felt no shame in leaving his father's home, living with Misgolas, who was not a friend of his father's, or his own age, but was a stranger who was older than himself, someone who was licentious in these things, Timarchus being in the prime of life.

(1.51) Well then, fellow Athenians, if Timarchus here had stayed at Misgolas' house and never come to another man's house, what he has done would have seemed more decent, if indeed any of such things is decent, and I at least would not have had the audacity to accuse him of anything other than what the lawgiver states clearly: simply, that he is a kept man! For the man who does this with one man, and does this act for money, seems to me liable to this very accusation.

(1.52) But if I state the names of those in whose houses he has lived, I will remind you and demonstrate that he has sold his body not only in the house of Misgolas, but also in the house of another man, and again in another's, and from this one he went to another, no longer indeed does he appear to be simply a kept man, but – by Dionysus, I don't know how I can keep this under wraps all day – as a common whore! For the man who does this at random and with many men, and for pay, seems to me liable to this very accusation.

(1.53) Well then, after Misgolas renounced Timarchus because of his expensiveness and sent him away from him, Anticles, son of Callias, of the *deme* Euonymon, took Timarchus on. Anticles is away in Samos at a new colony, so I'll talk about what happened after this. For when this Timarchus here had left the house of Anticles and Misgolas, he didn't admonish himself, or fasten on to a better way of life, but spent his days in the gambling den, where the gaming table is set up and cock-fighting and dice-throwing take place. I think that some of you have seen the place or if not have at least heard about it.

(1.54) Among those who while away their time in this place is one Pittalacus, a public slave owned by the city. This man has plenty of money, and seeing Timarchus spending his time here, took him and kept him in his own house. This wretch Timarchus here was not disgusted that he was about to disgrace himself with a man who was a public slave owned by the city. But he had only one consideration: if he could gain this man as a defrayer of the costs of his own licentiousness; he never gave a thought to what was good or what was shameful.

An individual called Hegesandrus while gambling in Pittalacus' house sees Timarchus and persuades him to move into his house. After the incident described in this next paragraph, events move on to the point where Aeschines prosecutes Timarchus.

(1.58) When he had removed from the house of Pittalacus and been taken on by Hegesandrus, Pittalacus was furious, I suppose because he thought that he had spent so much money in vain, and he was jealous about what was happening. So he would visit the house. Since he was annoying them, Hegesandrus and Timarchus hatched a great plot. They and certain others, whose names I don't want to mention, were drunk (1.59) and at night burst into the house where Pittalacus was living. First they broke up his gaming equipment and threw it into the street, his often-used dice, dice boxes and other gambling apparatus, and they killed the quails and the cocks, which the miserable wretch loved, and finally binding Pittalacus himself to a pillar they whipped him; the blows were inhuman and went on for such a long time that the neighbours heard his cries.

PRAISE AND BLAME FOR ATHLETES

Slaves assisted many owners in their work, but it was only the very wealthy who need not do any work at all, employing slave managers to supervise their slaves. But the ancient Greeks did have leisure time, and the most celebrated leisure activity was watching athletic contests. In the classical period athletes tended to come from the wealthy class, which had time for exercise and training. In the following ode Pindar celebrates the victory of Hagesidamus of the Greek city of Locris in Italy for his victory in the boy's boxing category in the Olympic Games of 476 BC. Pindar, *Olympian Victory Ode*, 11.1–19:

There is a time when for men the greatest need
is for winds, and there is a time for the rivers
of heaven, the wet children of the cloud:
and if someone does well by stint of hard work
honey-throated hymns foreshadow words   5
to be voiced later, and a faithful promise for great exploits.

This praise dedicated to victors
in the Olympics is unstinted.
My tongue wishes to shepherd these praises,
but a man blossoms just as well in wise   10
understanding, the gift of a god.
Now know, Hagesidamus, son of Archestratus,
that because of your boxing
I will sing a sweet refrain embellishing your crown of golden olive,
honouring the race of western Locris.   15

Join in the celebration there: I will swear, Muses,
that you will not come to a people hostile to guests
nor without experience of beautiful things: they are the summit
of wisdom, and warriors as well.

This encomion was addressed to Thrasybulus of the Greek city of Acragas in Sicily, now Agrigento, famous for its well-preserved temples. Here, the drinkers at the feast use Athenian pottery drinking cups, the finest in the Greek world. The fruit of Dionysus is wine, the 'sea of golden wealth', and Pindar's songs will enhance the enjoyment of this. Pindar, *Encomion*, 124b.1–8:

> Thrasybulus, I send you this chariot of lovely songs
> for after the feast. In the general company may it be
> sweet incentive for your fellow drinkers,
> for the fruit of Dionysus and for the drinking cups from Athens.
> When the wearisome anxieties of men depart from their breasts   5
> on a sea of golden wealth, we all alike set sail to an imagined shore.
> Whoever is poor becomes rich there . . .
> seduced by the arrows of the vine.

Greek society as a whole worshipped its athletic heroes, but Euripides raised his voice in protest. Euripides, *Autolycus*, Fragment 284:

> Of the thousands of things that are wrong with Greece
> nothing is worse than the tribe of athletes:
> first, they don't learn how to live properly
> nor are they able to do so. For how could any man who is
> both a slave to his jaw and ruled by his stomach   5
> acquire wealth to exceed that of his father's?
> Such men are not able to endure poverty and adapt to the winds of
>   fortune:
> for they are not accustomed to good habits
> and they change with difficulty in the face of hardships.
> In their youth they are famous and bestow glory on their city.   10
> But when they arrive at bitter old age,
> they disappear, like cloaks worn to threads.
> I put the blame on the custom of the Greeks,
> who convene a grateful assembly on account of these useless men
> honouring them with the useless pleasures of a feast.   15
> For how does a man benefit his ancestral city
> by winning a crown for wrestling well or sprinting
> or throwing the discus or punching a jaw skilfully?
> Will they fight against the enemy with a discus
> in their hands or smash through the shields by throwing
>   punches   20
> and so expel the enemy from their country?

No man standing face to face with cold iron
would be stupid enough to do such things.
We ought, I think, to crown wise and good men with leaves, and
    the man
who guides the city best: a man wise and just, 25
who also averts evil deeds with words,
preventing battles and civil dissension. For such things
are good for the whole city and all of Greece.

Despite Euripides' condemnation of athletes, he wrote a poem praising Alcibiades' victory in 416 BC at Olympia, in which he had entered several chariot teams and won the first three places. Euripides, 755:

But you Alcibiades, son of Cleinias,
I admire: victory is a wondrous thing
but most wonderful of all to accomplish what no other Greek has:
to come first, second and third in the chariot race,
and finish without effort, and crowned with the olive of Zeus
to be the one whose name is announced by the herald.

Thucydides also refers to Alcibiades' victory in 416 BC but gives Alcibiades first, second and fourth places. The discrepancy cannot be resolved. Despite Euripides' criticism of athletics and its uselessness to the city, Alcibiades' speech, made in 415 BC before thousands of Athenians in their assembly, that he should lead the Sicilian Expedition mentioned these victories. The other Greeks thought that Athens was finished off by the long Peloponnesian War that had commenced in 431 BC, but Alcibiades proved them wrong. Thucydides, 6.16.1–3:

(6.16.1) It is more fitting for me than for any of the others, Athenians, to be in command of the expedition against Sicily . . . and at the same time I also think that I'm worthy of this. For concerning the things for which I am criticised, these bring fame to my ancestors and me, and are also a benefit to the country. (6.16.2) The Greeks who formerly expected the city to be exhausted by war considered the strength of the city to be greater than it was because of the magnificence of my delegation to Olympia, since I entered seven chariot teams, which no individual had previously yet done, and I was victorious, coming first, second and fourth, and I prepared everything else so as to be worthy of my victory. Custom honours such displays, and also at the same time from these actions power is implied. (6.16.3) And again such matters in the city, either the splendour I have shown with sponsoring choruses or other things, are naturally envied by the citizens, but to foreigners this splendour also appears as a strength.

GAMES AT FUNERAL CONTESTS: 'I'M THE BEST!'

Patroclus' funeral included various contests in his honour, and the vivid description of these occupies Book 23 of the *Iliad*. Achilles announces boxing as the second contest, the prizes for which are a hard-working mule for the winner and second prize, for the loser, a two-handled cup, which must have been a trophy worth having, for when Euryalus is defeated and has to be helped home his friends return to fetch it for him. The winning blow, delivered when Euryalus lets his guard down, is clearly sharp and painful. Epeius' boast that 'I'm the best' is indicative of Greek society in which modesty was not a virtue. Homer, *Iliad*, 23.664–99:

So Achilles spoke, and at once there stood up a man brave and
    tall,
skilled in boxing, Epeius son of Panopeus,   665
and he put his hand on the hard-working mule and made a
    challenge:

'Come near whoever will carry off the two-handled cup:
I say that none other of the Achaeans defeating me in the boxing
will lead off the mule: I swear that I'm the best!
Isn't it enough that I am not up to the mark in battle?   670
Since how could it be that a man be master of all crafts?
For I'll say this, and it will come to pass:
I'll completely pulverise his flesh and smash his bones.
His relatives should stay here, huddled together
to carry him off, overpowered by my hands.'   675

So he boasted, and all of them were hushed to silence.
But god-like Euryalus alone jumped up to face him,
son of lord Mecisteus, of the line of Talaus,
who in the past went to Thebes for the funeral of Oedipus
after his downfall, and there was victorious over all the Thebans.   680
The spear-famed son of Tydeus, Diomedes, got Euryalus ready
with encouraging words, and greatly desired that he be victorious.
First of all he placed a girdle around his waist, and then
gave him leather thongs skilfully cut from a field ox.
The two girdled boxers stepped into the middle of the assembled
    crowd;   685
facing each other they put up their strong hands at the same time

and fell to, their heavy hands making contact.
A terrible grinding of teeth arose, and the sweat poured
from all over their bodies: but godly Epeius set upon Euryalus
and hit him on the jaw as he peered over his guard, and Euryalus
   did not stand   690
up much longer after that, for his glorious limbs gave way under
   him.
Just as from beneath a ripple on the sea caused by the North Wind
a fish leaps in the weeds on a sandbank, then the black wave
   conceals it,
so Euryalus struck by the blow leapt up. Then great-hearted Epeius
taking his hands stood him up. His close friends gathered around
   him   695
and they led him through the assembled crowd with his feet
   dragging,
vomiting up clots of blood, and with his head dangling to one side:
they led him, his mind wandering, and set him down among them
and they themselves went and fetched for him the two-handled cup.

THE CHARIOT RACE

The excitement of the chariot race is celebrated on numerous Athenian vases. Chariots generally had four horses and the driver had a goad or lash (see illustration 4.2). In Sophocles' *Electra*, Orestes pretends that he is dead and so an old slave describes to his sister Electra how he has been killed in a chariot race, competing at Delphi in the Pythian contests. Orestes' death may not be real, but the details here are specific and clearly some charioteers did meet their deaths in this dangerous if spectacular sport. Sophocles, *Electra*, 681–756:

Orestes came to the glorious ornament of Greece,
the contests, on account of the Delphic prizes,
and when he heard the clear voice of the man
announcing the race, which is judged first,
he entered cutting a magnificent figure admired by everyone there.   685
He made the result of the race equal with his appearance
and finished winning the all-honoured prize of victory.
So as to tell you much briefly
I don't know of the deeds and victories of any other such man.
But know this: of all the prizes in the contests which the judges
   announced,   690
of the customary races on the double track,

he carried all of them off and was called happy;
he was announced as an Argive,
by name of Orestes, son of the famous Agamemnon
who once assembled the famous army of Greece.   695
And so far, so good, but when one of the gods engages in mischief
not even a strong man is able to escape.

For on another day Orestes, when at dawn
there was a swift-footed contest of the chariot horses,
entered along with many other chariot drivers.   700
One was from Achaea, one from Sparta,
two were from Libya, masters of yoked carts,
another one, the fifth among them, possessed horses from Thessaly,
the sixth hailed from Aetolia,
with chestnut fillies, the seventh was a man from Magnesia,   705
while the eighth, from the race of Aenia, had white horses:
the ninth was from god-built Athens,
another was a Boeotian, occupying the tenth chariot.

Standing where the chosen judges   710
had designated with lots and placed their chariots,
they were off at the blast of the bronze trumpet: at this,
calling out to their horses, they shook the reins in their hands:
and the whole racecourse reverberated
with the din of rattling chariots, and the dust rose   715
in the air, all of them mixed up together.
They did not fear to use the goad, as desiring to overtake
the wheels and the violently snorting horses of the others.
For around alike their backs and wheels below
the hard foaming breathing of the horses fell upon them.

Orestes keeping near the stone marker at the end   720
every time hugged the turning post, giving rein to his right-hand
     trace horse
to shut out the pursuing chariot.
At the start all had stood up straight in their chariots:
then the hard-mouthed horses of the man of Aenia
carried him off by force on the turn   725
as they were finishing the sixth and beginning the seventh course
and smashed their foreheads against the chariot from Libya:
and then one driver in a disaster smashed
and crashed into another, and then the whole plain
of Delphi was filled with chariot wreckage.   730

Seeing this the skilful Athenian charioteer
drew his horses aside and held them back, avoiding
the heaving wave of horses thrown into disorder in the middle of the
  course.

Orestes was coming last, checking his horses
at the rear, having confidence in the outcome: 735
and when he saw that the Athenian alone remained in the race,
driving a sharp cry through the ears of his swift
horses, he pursued him, and quickly came alongside
and the two of them drove on, the head now of one, now the
  other
jutting forth from the chariots of horses.   740
And in all the other laps of the course rock-steady
the driver Orestes remained standing and the chariot upright;
then as he loosed the left-hand rein
as the horse turned he failed to notice the end of the post
and hit it: he broke the axle midway,   745
slipped over the chariot rail, and was entangled
in the reins. As he fell to the ground the horses
were scattered to the middle of the course.

And when the crowd saw him fallen from the chariot,
they broke out into lamentation for the young man,   750
that having performed such deeds such a disaster should befall,
being flung to the ground, then displaying to the heavens
his legs, until the charioteers
with difficulty stopped the course of the horses –
they released him so covered in blood that none of his friends   755
seeing him could have recognised his miserable frame.

Races on single horses were also popular. The tyrant Hieron of Syracuse
won the single horse race at Olympia in 476 BC; Pindar also composed
Olympian Victory Ode 1 for the same victory. Here, unusually, Bacchylides
praises the winning horse; the race was at dawn (note that Hieron himself
did not ride the horse). Bacchylides, *Victory Ode*, 5.37–49:

Yellow-maned Pherenicus,
horse swift as the storm,
at the broad, eddying Alpheus river of Olympia
you were seen victorious by Dawn with her golden arms   40
and also at sacred Delphi:
placing my hand upon the ground I swear

that he never yet was befouled with dust
by horses in front of him in the race
as he charged to the finishing line.   45
For obedient to his jockey
his rushes equal to the force of the North Wind,
he wins a victory that draws
new congratulations for hospitable Hieron.

THE WINNERS (AND THE LOSERS)

The following victory ode was written for an unknown Athenian who was
victorious in the foot race at the Isthmian Games, sacred to the god
Poseidon, held every two years at the Isthmus of Corinth. There is a
spectacular image of the victorious runner finishing so quickly that he
hurtles into the standing contestants (there were no seats), and the olive oil
off his back and limbs rubs onto them. Victors often had coloured ribbons
tied to their head and limbs by admirers, and could be pelted with flowers:
here the victor makes himself a crown of flowers. This runner had won races
at other games, and here at the Isthmian contests is crowned for winning
two consecutive competitions. Bacchylides, *Victory Ode*, 10.15–28:

By means of the goddess Victory once again   15
as you bound flowers into your golden hair
you brought great kudos and honour to far-spread Athens
and to your tribe there, the Oeneidae,
in the world-famous contests of Poseidon
when you revealed the swift rush of your feet to the Greeks.   20

For when at the finishing line of the race
he came to a stop, exhaling hot breath,
and in his next race wet the cloaks of the spectators with his olive
   oil
as he fell into the assembled crowd
after he had rounded the track four times,   25
the spokesman for the wise stewards of the contests
twice announced him victor
at the Isthmian Games.

This ode celebrates Automedes' victory in the pentathlon; Bacchylides
does not mention all the contests. The 'garland awarded every two years' is
the victory crown (lines 23–4), and the 'dark-leaved branch of the elder
tree' is poetic licence for 'javelin' (lines 33–4). Bacchylides, *Victory Ode*,
9.21–38:

Renowned are those mortals
who at the famous games of Nemea
crown their golden hair with the garland
awarded every two years.
Now Fortune has given victory to Automedes   25
spectacular among the pentathletes,
just as the brilliant moon
transcends the light of the stars
on the middle night of the month:
among the countless crowd of the Greeks   30
he showed his awesome body
hurling the discus shaped as a wheel,
and the dark-leaved branch
of the elder tree he sent into the high ether
from his hand, rousing the roar of the crowd,   35
and executed lightning moves in the wrestling:
with such daring prowess did he bring down
bodies of rippling muscle to the earth.

Pindar's attitude to success is made clear in this ode, composed in honour of
Alcimedon of Aegina, winner of the boys' wrestling at Olympia in 460 BC.
Pindar, *Olympian Victory Ode*, 8.1–14:

Mother of the games crowned in gold, Olympia,
Lady of truth, where mortal seers examining the burnt offerings
seek to discern the will of Zeus of the blinding lightning
and whether he has some message concerning men
who in their heart quest   5
to win great success,
and to have a break from their toils.

For the prayers of mortals are answered in return for piety.
Sanctuary of Pisa with your beautiful trees on the river Alpheus,
welcome this band of revellers and its wearing of garlands for the
    feast: 10
there is eternal glory for he whom your glorious prize follows.
Varying blessings come to different men,
and many are the paths to success
which comes from the gods.

While for the winner there was glorious fame at home, and eternal praise
in a victory ode by Pindar or Bacchylides, there was no joyous homecoming for the defeated. Aristomenes of the island of Aegina had been

victorious over four men in the wrestling in the Pythian Games at Delphi in 446 BC; Pindar praises him but also sheds light on the four unfortunate losers. Pindar, *Pythian Victory Ode*, 8.81–7:

> You fell from above
> with aggressive resolve on four bodies,
> for whom there was judged no happy return home
> as there was judged for you in the Pythian Games,
> nor returning to their mothers did sweet laughter   85
> arouse joy around them, but down the alleys they slunk,
> keeping aloof from their enemies, bitten by defeat.

THE ATHLETES THEMSELVES

Lucian here takes a comic look at Greek sports. The fictional speaker is Anacharsis, a Scythian, who finds Greek sport decidedly strange, and asks Solon what it is all about. Lucian, *Anacharsis* (or *Concerning Athletics*), 1–5:

(1) Why, Solon, are your young men doing this? Some of them are embracing each other and tripping each other up, while others are strangling and twisting one another and wallowing in the mud, rolling around like pigs. But at the start, as soon as they had stripped, for I saw it myself, they put oil on themselves and took it in turns to rub each other down quite peacefully. But after that, I don't know what got into them, as now they've put their heads down, and are shoving each other and smashing their heads together as if they were rams. Look at that! That man there picked the other one up by the legs and threw him to the ground, then fell down on him and won't let him lift his head up, forcing him down into the mud. Finally, winding his legs around the man's stomach, he's putting his forearm around his throat and is strangling the poor brute, who is slapping him on the shoulder, I suppose to call it quits, so that he won't be totally throttled. Not even for the sake of the oil do they worry about getting dirty, but in rubbing off the oil and plastering themselves with mud and a lot of sweat they make themselves ridiculous, at least to me, slipping through each other's hands like eels.

(2) Others are behaving in exactly the same manner in the open courtyard, though not in the mud. Rather, they have laid down a thick layer of sand in a pit and willingly sprinkle the dust over one another and themselves, like roosters, so that, I suppose, the sand removes the slipperiness of the oil and makes for a better grip on a dry surface.

(3) Others, standing up straight, themselves covered in dust, are attacking each other, hitting and kicking. This one wretch here at any rate seems as if he is going to vomit up his teeth, so full is his mouth of blood and sand; he's had a blow on the jaw, as you can see. But even the official here – I take his purple cloak as proof that he is one of the officials – doesn't separate them and put an end to the fight, but encourages them and praises the one who threw the punch.

(4) Elsewhere others are all being active and leaping about as if they were running, but are staying in the same spot; they leap up high and kick the air.

(5) So I'd like to know what good comes from these activities. To me at least it seems more like lunacy, and no one could easily persuade me that men who act in this way are not insane.

Wrestling was extremely popular with the spectators at festivals. The competitors were usually fairly large men, wrestling naked. A leg-trip could be used to break a neck-hold, as seen on an Athenian vase (see illustration 4.3). The career of Milon, Greece's most famous wrestler with numerous victories, spanned the period 536–512 BC. Athenaeus, *The Wise Men at Dinner*, 412e–f:

(412e) Milon of Croton, as Theodorus of Hierapolis writes in his *On Athletic Contests*, would eat twenty pounds of meat and the same amount of bread, and drink three jugs of wine. At Olympia he hoisted a four-year-old bull (412f) onto his shoulders and carried it around the stadium, after which he butchered it and ate it all himself in a single day.

Thucydides in his account of early Greece refers first to the Greeks carrying their weapons with them constantly due to the unsettled nature of the times, and then to a change in customs. Thucydides, 1.6.3–5:

(1.6.3) The Athenians were among the first to put aside their weapons, and changing to more luxurious habits to take up an easier lifestyle. Their older men of the wealthier class only not so long ago stopped wearing linen undergarments and binding their hair in a knot on their head with a golden grasshopper as a fastener, a custom that had been adopted because of their effeminacy. The same costume also prevailed for a long time among the older men of the Ionians, because of their kinship with Athens. (1.6.4) The Spartans were the first to adopt an unpretentious style of clothing such as is worn now, and the wealthy among them also took up other things to assimilate themselves with the ordinary people. (1.6.5) The Spartans were the first to compete naked, stripping in public and anointing themselves with oil for athletics. For in ancient times at the Olympic Games the athletes wore girdles around their genitals when they competed, and it isn't many years since they stopped doing so.

'I WIN'

There is less graffiti from ancient Greece than might be expected, and it falls into two main categories, amatory and athletic, and the two groups also overlap. Athletic graffiti is known from Nemea in the Peloponnese, the site of the two-yearly competitions in honour of the god Zeus, and here there is an almost perfectly preserved tunnel through which the competing athletes made their way into the stadium. Here, as they no doubt waited to be called for their events, some were bored enough to scratch graffiti into the stone walls. H.W. Pleket (ed.), *Supplementum Epigraphicum Graecum* (Amsterdam, 1992), vol. 39, no. 342:

I win!

Acrotatus [presumably written by Acrotatus].

Acrotatus is beautiful [written in a different hand by another athlete who found Acrotatus handsome].

To the one who wrote this [written by a third hand, who obviously did not share the previous graffito's opinion of Acrotatus' looks].

CELEBRATING A VICTORY

Victories in the games were honoured with wine and song, and more wine. The ancient Greeks celebrated wine in numerous poems; Pindar, *Paean*, 4.25–6 describes it as: 'Dionysus' life-giving cure for troubles.' Bacchylides, Fragment 20b, lines 6–16:

The sweet necessity of the passing cups
warms the hearts of the young men,
and expectation of love, mingling with
wine the gift of Dionysus,
sends the thoughts of men up high: 10
immediately a drinker plunders the towers of cities,
decides to be ruler over the whole human race,

his house glistens with elephant tusks and gold
and ships bearing wheat from Egypt across the dazzling sea
bring him great wealth.   15
So the drinker's heart fantasises.

The Boeotian cups mentioned in this poem would be plain with little or inartistic decoration as opposed to the beautifully decorated ones from Athens. Bacchylides, Fragment 21:

There are no carcasses of bulls here nor gold
nor carpets dyed with purple,
but present is a kindly heart
the lovely Muse of song
and sweet wine in cups from Boeotia.

Scolia were drinking songs sung by men, and many survive from Athens. Each drinker took it in turn to sing a different song. *Scolia*, 890, 900, 901, 902:

To have good health is the best for mortal man,
second is to be good-looking,
third is to have money acquired honestly,
and fourth to be young with your friends.

If only I could be turned into a beautiful ivory lyre
and handsome boys would carry me to a song and dance in honour of
   Dionysus.

If only I could be turned, without being melted, into a huge golden bowl
and a beautiful woman would carry me thinking pure thoughts.

Drink with me, be young with me, love with me, wear garlands on your
   head with me,
be possessed with me when I'm possessed, sane when I am sane.

What to serve the guests is always a problem, but with a range of delicacies to choose from, and knowing the preferences of the diners, the chef can present the perfect menu. Menander, *Trophonius*, Fragment 351:

The dinner is for entertaining a stranger.
Where is he from? For this makes a difference for the chef.
Like the little guests from the islands –

reared on fresh fishies of every kind –
they aren't in the least bit excited by dried fish
and only touch it as an afterthought
but tackle with zest the stuffing
and savoury dishes. Someone from Arcadia, on the contrary,
not living near the sea is captivated by shellfish,
while the wealthy tycoon from Ionia makes a Lydian dish
his main course, and aphrodisiac foods arousing sensual desire.

Food is needed for a feast, and couches for eating and dining on. The ancient Greeks did not sit at table and chair to eat, but reclined on couches with cushions (see illustration 4.4). They used pieces of broken pottery almost like note pads, scratching messages on them, and even shopping lists. The first graffito here is an order to arrange for some new couches for Phalanthus, who must need them for entertaining; it is scratched on a piece of a sixth-century BC vase. The second graffito is a list of ingredients, and also dishes to use, probably also for entertaining, and was scratched on a piece of a late fourth-century to early third-century BC terracotta saucer. M. Lang, *Graffiti and Dipinti. The Athenian Agora XXI* (Princeton, 1976), p. 8, B2, p. 10, B12:

Slave, bring other new couches to Phalanthus!

Kneading-dish
Long baked rolls: 20
Medium-size plates and platters: 4
Flat dishes: 5
Drinking cups: 2
Oil-jar
Half-pint jar
Bowl

DOGS AND THE HUNT

Eumaeus the swineherd does not recognise his master Odysseus, returning after twenty years, but Odysseus' dog Argus does, and then dies. Hunting was one of the pursuits of the aristocracy, and Xenophon wrote a work, *On Hunting*. However, hunting was not simply a sport, but a way of harvesting the animal resources of the land. Homer, *Odyssey*, 17.290–327:

As they were saying such things to each other,   290
a dog lying there raised its head and pricked up its ears,

Argus, belonging to patient-hearted Odysseus, which he himself once
   bred
but did not have the pleasure of before he departed for sacred Ilion.
In days gone past the young men had taken him
to the country to hunt the wild goats and deer and hares: 295
but now he lay forgotten about, his master absent,
on the high pile of dung of mules and oxen,
heaped up deep, which lay in front of the doors
until the slaves of Odysseus would take it, manuring his great
   estate:
there the dog Argus lay, quite full of dog fleas.   300
Now as he noticed Odysseus nearby,
Argus wagged his tail and dropped both his ears,
but he was not able to get any closer to his master:
then Odysseus looking away wiped off a tear,
easily escaping Eumaeus' notice, and quickly said to him: 305

'Eumaeus, it's rather strange that this dog lies here on the dung
   heap.
He has a fine frame, yet I don't know for certain
whether he also has speed to put with this appearance,
or whether he is no better than the table dogs of men
which masters pamper, to keep for show.'   310

Replying, Eumaeus the swineherd, said to him:
'Truly, this is the dog of a man who has died far away.
If he had such form and action
as when Odysseus leaving him went to Troy,
soon you'd be amazed to see his swiftness and strength.   315
For no wild beast that he came across could escape in the thick
   depths
of the wood; he also had a strong sense of smell.
But now he has come upon evil days, and his master has perished
far from the land of his fathers, and the careless women don't care
   for him.
Slaves, when their masters no longer have power over them,   320
then no longer wish to give honest service.
For loud-thundering Zeus takes away half of the virtue
of a man, once the day of slavery seizes him.'

Eumaeus went into the well-built palace when he had finished
   speaking,
and went straight to the hall to join the noble suitors.   325

But the fate of black death now immediately overtook Argus
having seen Odysseus in the twentieth year since his departure.

Here is another author on the subject of dogs. Pindar, Fragment 234:

The horse is yoked to the chariot,
the ox is to the plough, while the dolphin
darts swiftly alongside a ship,
but anyone who wants to slay a wild boar
must find a stout-hearted dog.

Dogs protected the flocks, but here a wolf makes off with a favourite
poddy. Theocritus, *Epigram*, 6:

Ah, wretched Thyrsis, what does it profit you if by mourning
you melt away your two eyes with tears?
The kid has gone, the fine poddy, departed to Hades
for with its claws a savage wolf has held her in tight embrace.
The dogs are yapping: but what's the point, since   5
nothing of bone or ashes is left now that she is gone?

Hunting was part of the overall education of the wealthy young man.
Xenophon, *On Hunting*, 1.18:

I recommend that the young not be disdainful of hunting, or of any other
teaching. For these men become proficient in war and other pursuits,
from which, as a matter of course, comes competence in reasoning,
speaking and action.

FIVE

Soldiers and Cowards

Sing, Muse, of the wrath of Achilles, son of Peleus,
which brought countless sufferings upon the Achaeans
and sent to Hades many stalwart souls
of warriors, while they themselves became prey for the dogs
and all the birds, and so the will of Zeus was fulfilled.

Homer, *Iliad*, 1.1–5.

So begins the first extant work of written Greek poetry, the climax of an
oral tradition reaching back several centuries, and arguably the greatest
work of western literature, Homer's *Iliad*. This epic was an account of the
tenth and final year of the Trojan War, the titanic struggle between the
Greeks and the city of Troy, in what is now modern Turkey. Helen had
eloped with Paris to Troy: 'Paris the wicked, Paris the dread, an evil for
Greece, that cradle of heroes' (Alcman, 77), and the Greeks fight to bring
her back to her home, and her husband, Menelaus.

For the Greeks, war was heroic, and it gave a man the opportunity of
proving his *arete*, his 'virtue' or 'excellence'. No consciences were pricked
by the thought of war, and it was in many ways an essential and
indispensable part of Greek civilisation. Homer's *Iliad* is a celebration of
the warrior ethos among the aristocrats who ruled the archaic Greek world
of the eighth century BC. In this noble epic, the mass of the combatants
fight nameless, while the great heroes of either side seek each other out for
mortal combat.

After the period of the writing of the *Iliad*, the basis of the Greek army
was the *hoplite*. This type of soldier gradually emerged after 750 BC and
remained the dominant component of Greek armies in the classical period.
A conspicuous feature was his bronze shield, the *hoplon*, from which the
soldier may have taken his name – *hoplite*. A bronze cuirass, greaves,
helmet and spear in addition to this shield were his standard equipment.
Most depictions of warriors show them without footwear, and they are to
be imagined as fighting in bare feet. The *hoplite*'s armour of bronze
protected his head, chest and calves, but the groin, neck and thighs
remained exposed. The helmet was made from a single piece of bronze, and

often had a crest to make the *hoplite* look more terrifying. The Spartan poet Tyrtaeus (Poem 10, lines 24–5) refers to a warrior 'breathing out his brave spirit in the dust, holding his bloody genitals in his own hands', and the nature of the wounds inflicted by spears and swords in the areas not protected by armour must have been horrific. A small bronze statuette of a *hoplite*, dating from about 500 BC and discovered at the sanctuary of Zeus at Dodona in northern Greece, was probably a dedication to the god by a soldier, possibly in thanks for a successful return from battle (see illustration 5.1).

As the soldier had to purchase his own armour – it was not provided by the state – *hoplites* tended to be drawn from the prosperous farming class. In addition, Greek soldiers could seek employment abroad as mercenaries, and are found serving in Egypt in the sixth century BC; and in the late fifth and fourth centuries BC the Persians employed Greek professional soldiers as being superior to their own troops. Even in the fifth century, Greek cities sometimes hired mercenaries to supplement their citizen army, but the emphasis in the classical period was on the citizen soldier. Citizens who could afford armour possessed it and marched out in defence of their city as and when required. Before joining his comrades, a soldier as he left his actual house might perform a sacrifice, and examine the entrails of the victim in the hope of finding a good omen (see illustration 5.2). Cities did not generally use slaves as soldiers, and it was only in the direst of emergencies that slaves were freed to fight in wars.

States such as Sparta had a specific training system to turn out *hoplites*, whereas the Athenians prided themselves on being good soldiers without the need to sacrifice their lifestyles. But the strength of Athens when it built up an empire in the Aegean in the fifth century BC lay in its navy, with an eventual fleet of 300 *triremes* (war ships with three banks of oars) each manned by a crew of approximately 200. The rowers were Athenians from the poorer class, the *thetes*, who could not afford bronze armour, but who could row, and were paid to do so. The involvement of the poor in the fleet, which was the basis of fifth-century BC Athenian power, strengthened democracy in Athens. The three natural harbours about 7 km from Athens were developed by the Athenians, with numerous ship sheds, and stone walls connected the harbour region to the city. The most important of these harbours, the Piraeus, became the commercial and trading hub of Athens.

A more elitist military formation was the cavalry, for those wealthier citizens who possessed land and enough money to support a horse. Particularly in northern Greece, in Thessaly, cavalry was important, as it was too in Boeotia, where the Greek mounted units served with the Persians in the invasion of Greece, 480 to 479 BC. At Athens, members of the cavalry were entitled to specific financial assistance from the state, in recognition of the importance of having cavalry, but it took third place after the navy and *hoplite* forces.

Greek warfare tended to be seasonal. For naval warfare this was particularly the case, with the sailing season from April to October; summer, with its calm seas, was the best time for sailing. Land warfare occurred in spring and summer due to the difficulties of the weather in autumn and winter; moreover, *hoplite* farmers were needed in autumn for ploughing the fields. Invaders, such as the Spartans in the Peloponnesian War, arrived in Attica just as the grain was ripening, to deny the enemy the harvest.

Warfare was important to the Greeks for a variety of reasons. Greek cities were fiercely independent, and hostilities kept encroaching neighbours at bay. Campaigning was also an important source of booty, especially human: even the enslavement of small towns was commercially profitable. It also led to political supremacy such as the leadership and influence which the Spartans exercised over their allies in the Peloponnesian League, and Athens more directly over its allies in the Delian League.

ATTITUDES TO WAR AND PEACE

In many societies the glamour of war has overshadowed the reality. Pindar in the fifth century BC was aware of this. Pindar, *Hyporchema*, 110:

> War is sweet to the inexperienced
> but at its coming anyone who is acquainted with it
> is in his heart fearful beyond measure.

The cry of battle could be personified as a deity, 'War-Cry'. Pindar, *Dithyramb*, 78:

> Listen to me, War-Cry, who introduces the spears,
> daughter of War, to whom on behalf of their city
> men offer a sacred sacrifice of death.

But Pindar was not a pacifist, and makes clear the necessity for war. Pindar, Fragment 169a, 16–17:

> It's better to die when your possessions
> are being carried off than to live as a coward.

The benefits of peace when weapons rust is conveyed in masterly fashion by the poet Bacchylides; two lines, 73–4, are missing from the original Greek text. Bacchylides, *Paean*, 4.61–72, 75–80:

Peace brings forth noble prosperity
and the flowers of honey-tongued song to mortal beings
and the burning to the gods
on embellished altars
of the thighs of oxen and fine-fleeced sheep in golden flame,   65
and turns the thoughts of young men
to the wrestling ground
and flutes and revel making.
On the handles clipped with iron to shields
reddish-brown spiders spin their webs.   70
Corrosion feasts on the point of the sharp spear
and the double-bladed sword.

The loud noise of the bronze war trumpets is silent,   75
and sleep sweet to the mind
comforting the soul at the break of day
is not plundered from men's eyelids.
The streets burgeon with the lovely feast
and the hymns sung by boys blaze forth.   80

THE BLOOD AND THE GLORY OF BATTLE

The afterlife was a shadowy and dreary place: to gain a type of immortality, warriors had to perform heroic deeds, which would be sung of by bards such as Homer and listened to by generations to come. Two heroes, Sarpedon and Glaucus, Lycians fighting for the Trojans, sum up the attitude to battle and honour. If Sarpedon and Glaucus could leave the battlefield and have immortality, they would do so, but since it is the lot of men to die, they will fight, either being killed in battle and so giving glory to someone else, or will kill, glorifying themselves. Homer, *Iliad*, 12.310–28:

'Glaucus, why is it that we two are in particular held in honour   310
with seats and feasts and full goblets
in Lycia, and everyone looks upon us as if we were gods?
And we possess a large tract of land by the banks of the Xanthus
     river,
a fine orchard and wheat-bearing fields.
And so it is necessary for us to take our place   315
among the foremost Lycians and go to meet the raging battle
so that many of the breast-plated Lycians may say:

"Truly, not inglorious are those that rule over Lycia,
our kings, consuming fat sheep
and excellent honey-sweet wine: and their strength is   320
noble, since they fight among the foremost Lycians."
O friend, if from this battle having escaped,
always we were to be immortal and deathless,
neither would I fight among the foremost
nor would I send you into battle which brings men glory: 325
but now since countless fates of death surround us
which no mortal man can flee or escape
let us go forward; we will give glory to another, or another will
    give glory to us.'

This was the quest for *arete*, excellence, so dominant here in the *Iliad*,
and which was to spur Alexander the Great on to ever greater victories
in his longing for immortal fame. The audiences of the archaic and
classical periods were educated on Homer, and the scenes in the *Iliad*
were part of the very psyche of the Greeks. The warriors in the *Iliad*
speak to each other before coming to blows, eager to prove both in
words and deeds who is the better man. So Pandarus (Aeneas is with
him) the Trojan spoke to the mighty Greek hero Diomedes. Homer,
Iliad, 5.280–93, 296:

Pandarus poised and threw his long shafted spear   280
and it struck against Diomedes' shield: the bronze point
went right through and reached the corselet.
Then at him the glorious son of Lycaon, Pandarus, shouted
    loudly:
'You are struck in the guts, and I don't think you'll
last for long, but you have given great glory to me.'   285
Then the mighty Diomedes, not at all worried, answered:
'You have missed me: but I think that
we will not stop until one of you has fallen
and with his blood satiated Ares, the warrior with the shield of
    tough bull's hide.'
So he spoke and hurled his spear: and the goddess Athena guided
    the missile
to Pandarus' nose, beside the eye, and it crashed though his white   290
    teeth,
so that the unyielding bronze cut off his tongue at its root
and the spear-point came out near the base of his chin.   293

And there Pandarus' life and his strength were undone.   296

Battle was serious and gruesome in the classical age as well. When the Thebans and the Spartans, who had earlier been allies in the Peloponnesian War (431–404 BC), fought at Coronea in 394 BC, the carnage of warfare was all too clear. Xenophon, *Life of Agesilaus*, 2.14:

> When the fighting had stopped, one could see that where they had attacked each other the earth was stained with blood. The corpses of friends and enemies lay next to each other; shields were shattered, spears were broken into pieces and daggers were unsheathed, some on the ground, others thrust into bodies, and some even still gripped in hands, ready to strike.

BRAVERY AND VALOUR

For heroic valour in the classical age and the military ethos, the Spartans surpassed all others. Sparta in two wars, one at the end of the eighth century and the other in the middle of the seventh century BC, conquered the neighbouring state of Messenia, reducing its population to the status of serfs, or in the Greek, *helots*, meaning 'those who have been seized'. This second war in which all of Messenia was conquered in a twenty-year campaign increased Sparta's territory but also imposed one major difficulty: the Spartans, not particularly numerous – probably never more than 10,000 adult males – now had to control a subject population many times their own number.

In their second war against the Messenians the Spartans had a great general, Tyrtaeus, who chose to inspire the Spartan *hoplites* with songs. Athenian boys might learn the *Iliad* off by heart, but Spartan boys were taught the martial songs of Tyrtaeus which praised fighting in war and extolled the greatness of a warrior who fell in the front line of battle. Boreas was the north wind, blowing down from Thrace (line 4); Tithonus was so handsome that the goddess Eos (Dawn) fell in love with him (line 5). Tyrtaeus, 12:

> Neither would I be mindful of nor take account of a man
> either for his excellence at running or wrestling,
> not even if he had the size and the strength of the Cyclopes,
> and in running was victorious over the Thracian Boreas,
> nor if he were more handsome in appearance than Tithonus,   5
> nor if he were richer than Midas and Cinyras,
> nor if he were more kingly than Pelops, son of Tantalus,
> and were to be more honey tongued than Adrastus,
> nor if he had a reputation for everything else except for raging battle.

For no man is good in war 10
unless he can bear seeing bloody slaughter,
and getting close can strike at the enemy.
This is excellence [*arete*], this is the greatest prize among men
and the best for a young man to gain.
This is the common good for the city and the entire people, 15
whenever a man planting his feet firmly in the front ranks steadfastly
   keeps his ground
and never gives a thought to shameful flight,
hazarding his life and valiant spirit
and standing by the man next to him speaks with encouragement.
This is the man who is good in battle. 20

With speed he repels the bristling phalanx of the enemy forces
and by his determination he checks the swell of battle.
Falling in the front line of battle he loses his dear life
and brings glory to his city and people and father,
many times through his breast and bossed shield 25
and breastplate pierced through from the front.
Young and old together lament him,
and all the city mourns with deep regret;
his tomb and children are notable among men
and his children's children and all his family after; 30
his great glory and his name will never perish,
he becomes immortal even though underground,
whoever nobly stood and fought
for country and children when raging Ares took him.

But if he escapes the fate of death that brings long woe, 35
and victorious wins the glorious boast of his spear,
all honour him, young and old alike,
and he after much contentment goes to Hades;
as he ages he has distinction among the citizens, nor does anyone
wish to harm either his reputation or his right. 40
All alike in the seats of council, both the young, his age group,
and his elders, give way to him.
Now let every man strive to reach the peak of this prowess
and in his heart let him never relax from war.

The most famous example of Spartan valour was the battle of Thermopylae in 480 BC. King Xerxes of Persia invaded Greece in 480–479 BC with a huge army and fleet, encountering his first real opposition from the Greeks at the mountain pass of Thermopylae. Before the hostilities began there, he sent a spy to find out about Greek strength. Demaratus, the son of Ariston, was an ex-Spartan king who had been living in exile at the Persian court (7.209.1). Herodotus, 7.208.1–209.4:

(7.208.1) Xerxes sent a spy on horseback to see how many Greeks there were and what they were doing. Xerxes had heard while he was still in Thessaly that a small army was collected at Thermopylae, commanded by the Spartans and their king, Leonidas, descended from the family of Heracles. (7.208.2) So the mounted spy approached the camp and surveyed it, but didn't see the whole army. For it wasn't possible to see those who were on the other side of the wall, which the Greeks had repaired and were guarding. But he observed those outside, whose arms were in front of the wall. At this time it chanced to be the Spartans stationed there. (7.208.3) Some of them were exercising naked, and the rest were grooming their hair. The spy watched this in amazement, and also learned their number. Taking precise note of all this, he rode away quietly, for no one pursued him nor paid much attention as he left. Arriving back, he reported to Xerxes about everything he had seen.

(7.209.1) Xerxes, hearing all this, couldn't comprehend the truth, that the Spartans were preparing to be destroyed and to destroy with all their might. Rather, to him what they were doing seemed ridiculous, so he sent for Demaratus, the son of Ariston, who was with the Persian army. (7.209.2) When he entered Xerxes' presence, the king questioned him about each of these things, wanting to know about what the Spartans were doing.

Demaratus replied: 'I've told you before, when we were setting out for Greece, about these men, and when you had listened you ridiculed me, even though I knew how these matters would turn out. For it is my greatest aim to speak the truth in your presence, O King. (7.209.3) So listen once again. These Spartans have come to fight with us for the pass, and they are preparing for this. For it is the custom among them to groom their hair whenever they are about to endanger their lives. (7.209.4) Understand this: if you can defeat these Spartans and the ones who have remained at home, there is no other race of men, O King, who will remain or raise a hand against you. For now you are going against the finest kingdom and city in Greece, and the best men.'

COWARDICE

But what of the Spartan coward? There was a story that the poet Archilochus from the Aegean island of Paros, who had thrown away his shield and fled before the Saians, a Thracian tribe, visited Sparta but was expelled when the

Spartans found out about his flight in battle, which for them amounted to cowardice; he described how he had thrown away his shield in one of his poems. Archilochus, 5:

One of the Saians greatly rejoices in my faultless shield
which beside a shrub against my wishes I forsook.
But I saved my own skin. Why should I care about that shield?
Away with it! I'll get another one that's no worse.

Others might dedicate a shield that had saved their life in battle. Anacreon, *Epigram*, 111d:

The shield that preserved Python in most painful battle
is hung up in the sanctuary of Athena.

In 371 BC, when the Thebans under their general Epaminondas had won an unexpected victory against Sparta at Leuctra in Boeotia, the Spartans had to confront reality, that their numbers were so small that they could not punish men whose crime was to show great fear in battle. There were so many cowards in 371 BC that the Spartans were afraid to strip them of their citizenship rights because their numbers made them a powerful group whose frustration and anger at being deprived of the status of Spartans and their rights as such might lead them to attempt a revolution. Plutarch, *Life of Agesilaus*, 30.2–4:

(30.2) Among their political woes were those Spartans who had shown fear in the battle, those who were called the 'tremblers' [cowards], and they hesitated to bring about the loss of citizenship rights for these according to the law, as the tremblers were many and powerful, fearing that they would bring about a revolution. (30.3) For not only were cowards usually barred from all offices, but also it was considered unworthy to give any woman in marriage to cowards, or take any of their women relatives in marriage. And anyone who came upon the cowards was free to strike them if he wished. (30.4) Cowards were forced to go around unwashed and with mean apparel, and they both wore a threadbare cloak patched with cloth of various colours and cut off half of their beards but allowed the other half to grow.

Theophrastus provides a light-hearted look at the coward and cowardice. A wave hitting the ship is regarded by a coward as a sign that there is someone on board who has not been initiated into the Samothracian mysteries, which promised divine assistance to those in need at sea (2). 'Go to the crows' was a proverbial expression much like our, 'Go to hell!' (5). Athenian citizens were divided into ten 'tribes', and the members of each tribe served together in war (6). Theophrastus, *Characters*, 25, *Cowardice*:

(25.1) Rest assured that cowardice would seem to be a giving way of the soul through fear. The coward is the sort of person who, (25.2) while sailing, asserts that the cliffs are pirate vessels. When a wave strikes, he asks if anyone on board is not initiated; lifting up his head he asks the ship's pilot if they are halfway there yet, and what he thinks about the appearance of the sky, and says to the man sitting next to him that he is frightened because of a dream he's had. He strips off his tunic and hands it to his slave, and begs to get put to shore.

(25.3) When the coward is serving in the army, and the infantry is going into battle, he calls everyone and tells them to stand near him and have a look around first, and says that their job is to discover which ones are the enemy. (25.4) When he hears the shouts of battle and sees men falling down, he says to those standing next to him that in his haste he has forgotten his sword, and he runs to his tent, sends out his slave, ordering him to look for the position of the enemy, hides his sword beneath the pillow, then whiles away a lot of time pretending to find it. (25.5) When from his tent he spies one of his friends being brought in wounded, he runs up to him, encouraging him to bear up, and picking him up carries him away. He takes care of him, washing him off, and sits by him to swat the flies off the wound – anything rather than fight the enemy. When the trumpeter sounds the signal for battle, he sits in his tent and curses, 'Go to the crows! He won't let a man have a minute's sleep what with his constant signalling.'

(25.6) Covered from head to toe with the blood of the other man's wound, he meets those returning from the battle and relates how, as if he'd been in danger himself, 'I have rescued one of our comrades'. Then he brings the members of his tribe inside so that they can see, and he recounts to each of them how he himself brought the man to the tent – with his own hands.

The *ephebes* at Athens were eighteen- to twenty-year-olds who underwent a period of military training. This practice began in the fourth century BC, probably in the 330s. The *ephebes* swore an oath to defend the fatherland, and not to 'bring shame upon the sacred arms'. The following oath was inscribed on stone in the late fourth century BC. M.N. Tod, *Greek Historical Inscriptions* (Oxford, 1948), vol. II, no. 204:

(1) The gods be witness. The priest of Ares and Athena the Warrior, Dion son of Dion of the *deme* Acharnae, dedicated this stone.

(5) The ancestral oath of the *ephebes*, which it is compulsory for the *ephebes* to swear: 'I will not bring shame upon the sacred arms, nor will I desert the man beside me, wherever I might be stationed. I will defend the sacred and holy, and I will not pass down a smaller fatherland, (10) but one greater and better, as much as I with all the other *ephebes* can, and I will obey those who govern sensibly, the established laws, and laws which might be sensibly established in the future. (15) If anyone undertakes to annul the laws, I with all the other *ephebes* will not yield. I will honour the sacred ancestral rites. This oath is witnessed by the gods and goddesses Aglaurus, Hestia, Enyo, Enyalius, Ares and Athena the Warrior, Zeus, Thallo, Auxo, Hegemone, Heracles, the boundary stones of the fatherland, wheat, (20) barley, vines, olive trees, figs.

Lycurgus' *Against Leocrates* was delivered in 330 BC, several years after the disastrous battle of Chaeronea in 338 BC when Philip II of Macedon defeated Athens and Thebes and destroyed Greek liberty. Leocrates, an Athenian citizen, had fled from Athens after the battle and returned in 332 BC; Lycurgus decided to prosecute him in the courts for cowardice, and Leocrates only narrowly escaped the death penalty: the vote was tied, which meant acquittal. Lycurgus, *Against Leocrates*, 1–10:

(1) Justice, Athenians, and reverence towards both you and the gods will characterise the beginning of my prosecution of Leocrates, who stands trial. I pray to Athena and the other gods and to the heroes whose statues stand in our city and the surrounding countryside. If I have justly brought this prosecution against Leocrates, and if the one I prosecute is a traitor to these, and the temples, shrines and sanctuaries and a traitor to the honours enshrined in your laws and the ceremonies of sacrifice which our ancestors have bequeathed us, (2) may these make me worthy on this day to be the prosecutor of Leocrates' wrongdoings, in the interest of the people and the city, and you, deliberating on behalf of your fathers and children and wives and ancestral land and shrines, and having in the power of your vote a traitor to all these things, be unrelenting judges, now and for the rest of time, to those breaking the laws to such an extent. But if this man here who I am bringing to this trial is not a traitor to his country, nor abandoned his city and shrines, may he be saved from danger, both by the gods and by you, the jurors.

(3) It is advantageous to the city, gentlemen of the jury, that within it there are prosecutors of those who break its laws, and in the same way I

would wish to find among the majority the same spirit of dedication to the public good. But now the contrary is the case, as he who risks danger to himself for the common good incurs hatred and is viewed, not as loving his city, but as a busy-body, which is not just or in the best interests of the city. For there are three important features that protect and preserve our democracy and the prosperity of the city. (4) The first is the system of the laws, the second the vote of the jury, and the third is the trial, handing over the crimes to the juries. The laws exist to make known what is forbidden, the prosecutor to make known those made liable to penalties under the law, and the juror to punish those these two (law and prosecutor) have brought to his attention, so neither the law nor the vote of the jurors has any power without the prosecutor to hand over to them those who have committed crimes.

(5) And I myself, Athenians, knowing that Leocrates had fled the dangers faced by his country, absconded from his fellow citizens, totally abandoned your authority, and was liable for everything written in the indictment, brought on this proceeding for impeachment, and it was not in the least through any enmity or through any love of contention that I instituted this trial. But I thought that it would be wicked to overlook his pushing his way into the market-place and sharing the public sacrifices, when he had been a disgrace to his country and all of you. (6) For the just citizen does not because of private enmities bring a public prosecution against someone who is not harming the city, but he will consider to be his personal enemies those who break the laws of the country in some way, and wrongs to the public will be for the just citizens public grounds for disagreement with wrongdoers.

(7) All public trials must be considered crucial, particularly this one in which you are now about to give your vote. For whenever you judge a case concerning an unconstitutional proposal made in the assembly, you correct this only, and your prevention of this act has an importance corresponding to the harm the proposal intends to the city. But the present case does not encompass either some small share of the city's concerns or a brief period of time, but is on behalf of the whole country and will bequeath for our descendants a decision to be remembered for all time.

(8) So terrible and of such magnitude is the crime that has been committed that it is impossible to find an indictment worthy of it, nor in the laws is there devised a fitting penalty for the crimes. For what punishment would fit a man who deserted his country, refused to defend the shrines of his forefathers, deserted the tombs of his ancestors and

betrayed the whole country into enemy hands? For the most extreme and final of punishments, death, though it is the penalty allowed by the laws, is too meagre for Leocrates' crimes. (9) The penalty for such wrongs has not been laid down, gentlemen of the jury, not because of the indifference of the legislators of the past, but because such a thing never occurred in past time, and it was not anticipated that such an event would occur in the future. So it is particularly important, men of the jury, for you to act now not only as judges but also as legislators. For where a law defines transgressions, it is easy, applying such a standard, to punish transgressors against the laws. When a number of items have not been specifically included, but are covered by a single term, and when a man has committed greater crimes than these, and is equally guilty of them all, it is crucial that your verdict be bequeathed as a precedent for your descendants.

(10) And know well, gentlemen, that not only will you punish this man by condemning him, but you will direct all the younger men to virtue. For there are two strands to the education of the young: the punishment of wrongdoers, and the reward granted to good men. With each of these things in sight, they flee from the first through fear, and are enthusiastic for the second through their desire for good opinion. So it is necessary, men of the jury, for you to be attentive to the trial and make no concern more important than justice.

WARTIME MASSACRES AND ATROCITIES

Even soldiers who fought well in battle might, of course, be captured or surrender, and the Spartan ideals about victory or death were not held by all the Greeks. It was routine for soldiers who had been captured in war to be ransomed by their relatives, and there was even a standard charge among the Greeks: two *minas*. But atrocities occurred in warfare even when there were established conventions. The first massacre of the Peloponnesian War occurred in 427 BC, when the city of Plataea, allied to Athens, was attacked. Each soldier was asked only one question, whether they had been of any assistance to Sparta: as the Plataeans had fought on the other side, they had little chance to make a positive reply. Thucydides, 3.68.1–2:

(3.68.1) The Spartans brought forward the Plataeans one at a time and asked each of them the same thing, whether they had performed any good service in the war for the Spartans and their allies. When each Plataean replied in the negative, the Spartans led them off and executed them, without any exception. (3.68.2) Not less than 200 Plataeans were massacred in this way, along with 25 Athenians who had also been besieged. The women were enslaved.

While it is clear that much of Greek warfare was of a ritualistic nature, with towns and cities sending out their armies, almost on an annual basis, to delineate the borders between two particular states, warfare could be taken seriously and might involve the sacking of cities and the inhumane treatment of civilians and belligerents alike. When one of Athens' trusted allies Mytilene, which had been treated more on an equal footing with Athens than its other allies, revolted in 427 BC, the Athenians were furious and held a debate about the prisoners from Mytilene being held at Athens. Paches was the Athenian general who was at Mytilene (3.36.3). Diodotus had argued, against Cleon, to spare Mytilene (3.49.1). Thucydides, 3.36.2–4, 3.49.1–4:

(3.36.2) The Athenians held a debate in their assembly, and being in an angry frame of mind decided to put the prisoners to death, and not only them but also all the adult males at Mytilene, and to sell the children and women into slavery. They were particularly angered that the Mytileneans had undertaken this revolt even though they were not ruled as subjects, unlike the other cities allied to Athens. . . . (3.36.3) So they sent a *trireme* to Paches to communicate their decision, ordering him to kill the Mytileneans as soon as possible.

(3.36.4) But on the following day, a change of heart and a reconsideration came over the Athenians, and they thought that the decision was cruel and severe, to destroy the whole city of Mytilene rather than just those responsible for the revolt. . . .

(3.49.1) The show of hands in the voting was almost equal for both sides, but the view of Diodotus prevailed. (3.49.2) Immediately the Athenians dispatched another *trireme* with all haste, because if the other ship arrived first, the second would find the city destroyed: and the first ship already had a head start of a day and a night. (3.49.3) The ambassadors from Mytilene provided wine and barley cakes for the ship, and promised great rewards if it overtook the first, and such was the haste of the voyage that the crew kept on rowing as they ate their barley cakes kneaded with wine and olive oil, and only slept in turns as the others rowed. (3.49.4) By chance, no adverse wind arose, and as the first ship was not sailing in haste to its unwelcome task, while the second hurried on in the manner described above, the first arrived, and Paches had just read out the Athenian decision and was about to implement it when the second ship came in and prevented the massacre. By just so much did Mytilene escape danger.

When Thracian mercenaries arrived at Athens too late to join the Athenian expedition to Sicily, they were sent back to Thrace under the command of the Athenian general Dieitrephes, and he was instructed to use them along the way to harm the enemy in whatever way he could. Accordingly he led them to Boeotia, and against the town of Mycalessus, where one of the bloodiest massacres of the war took place. Thucydides, 7.29.3–5:

(7.29.3) That night Dieitrephes escaped attention, bivouacking near the temple of the god Hermes, which was about sixteen stades from Mycalessus. At dawn Dieitrephes attacked the town, which wasn't a big one, and assaulted and captured it, as the inhabitants were not guarding it. They were not expecting that anyone would ever come up so far from the sea to attack them, and also the wall of the town was weak and in some places had collapsed, and in others was built too low. At the same time, the gates had been left open because of a lack of fear. (7.29.4) The Thracians falling upon Mycalessus plundered both the houses and temples, and slaughtered the inhabitants, sparing neither the old nor the young, but killing them all, one after the other, whoever they came across, slaying both children and women, and even the beasts of burden and whatever other living creatures they happened to see. For the Thracian race, like the most murderous of the barbarians, is particularly so when it is has nothing to fear. (7.29.5) In addition to the general confusion, which wasn't negligible, and the destruction of every sort that was occurring, the Thracians in particular attacked a boy's school, the biggest in town, into which the children had just happened to go, and butchered them all. The disaster to the whole town was in magnitude unsurpassed, falling upon it in a sudden and terrible way.

When the Syracusans defeated the great military expedition sent against them by Athens in 413 BC they were in no mood for any international niceties. The captured Athenian soldiers and their allies were put into the quarries at Syracuse, which can still be seen to the east of the ancient stone theatre. An idea can be obtained of the limited rations that the prisoners received there by noting that the Spartans besieged by the Athenians on the island of Sphacteria in 425 were allowed twice as much food by the Athenians, as well as a pint of wine, as the Athenians were given by the Syracusans. But after the Sicilian Expedition, in which Athens failed to conquer Sicily and suffered a humiliating defeat, the Syracusans were ruthless. The Athenian general, Demosthenes, had been specifically promised his freedom. Thucydides, 7.86.1–87.3:

(7.86.1) The Syracusans and their allies came together and took as many of the prisoners of war as they could and the booty, and returned to Syracuse. (7.86.2) The rest of the prisoners, that is, the Athenians and their allies, they sent down into the stone quarries, considering that this was the safest means of guarding them. But Nicias and Demosthenes they put to the sword, though the Spartan commander Gylippus objected. For Gylippus thought that it would be a stunning success if in addition to his other achievements he could take the enemy generals back to the Spartans. (7.86.3) And one, Demosthenes, was their greatest enemy, because of Sphacteria and Pylus; while the other, Nicias, was for the same reason the most friendly for he had energetically sought to have the Spartans who had been captured on the island released, persuading the Athenians to make peace. (7.86.4) For these reasons the Spartans were well disposed towards Nicias, and it was not least on account of this that Nicias himself, trusting in Gylippus, had surrendered to him. But it was said that some of the Syracusans were afraid, as they had been communicating with him (about betraying Syracuse to him), in case if he were tortured about precisely this sort of thing he might make trouble for them in their moment of success, and others, particularly the Corinthians, because since he was rich he might escape by bribery and immediately bring new troubles upon them, and so persuaded the allies to put him to death. (7.86.5) For this reason, or ones very like it, Nicias was executed, a man who of all the Greeks of my time least deserved to arrive at such a fate because his whole way of life had been governed by excellence [*arete*].

(7.87.1) At first, the Syracusans harshly treated those held in the quarries. For there were many of them in a deep and narrow place; at first the sun and the stifling heat tormented them, as there was no roof, and then the nights that followed were, by contrast, autumnal and chill, and the change in temperature brought on sickness. (7.87.2) Because of the narrow space they had to do everything in the same place, and moreover the corpses of those who had died from their wounds or the temperature variations or similar problems were heaped together, one on top of the other, so that the stench was overpowering. They were at the same time afflicted with hunger and thirst, as for eight months each man was given a half pint of water and two pints of grain a day. They were spared none of all the other sufferings that men might experience in such a place. (7.87.3) Now for some seventy days they all lived together in this way, after which all, except for the Athenians and any Sicilians or Italian Greeks that had joined in the expedition, were sold. It would be difficult to state accurately how many prisoners had been captured, nevertheless it was not fewer than 7,000.

SIEGE WARFARE

The fortifications of the small town of Mycalessus were weak, had collapsed or were not high enough, hence its destruction. Walls were the best security against invaders, forcing them to adopt more sophisticated measures to capture a town or city. Some soldiers could man the walls while others went to meet the enemy at the gates (see illustration 5.3). A major military treatise by Aeneas 'the Tactician' of the middle of the fourth century BC gives advice to the inhabitants of a city about how to deal with sieges. Among other methods, shelters and siege engines, which the enemy brought up against the walls, could be set on fire. Tow was a coarse fibre, like flax or hemp, which would burn easily (33.1). Pestles refer to the wooden tool that Hesiod instructs the reader needs to be 3 cubits long (33.2). Aeneas the Tactician, *How to Resist Besiegers*, 33.1–4:

(33.1) It is necessary to pour pitch and throw tow and sulphur over the shelters brought up by the enemy, then let down onto the shelter a burning bundle of sticks attached to a rope. Such inflammable materials as these, held out from the walls, are thrown as the siege engines are being moved up.

But this is what needs to be done to burn them up. (33.2) Prepare pieces of wood in the shape of pestles but much bigger in size, and into the end of each piece drive sharp iron spikes, smaller and larger, and around the other areas of the piece of wood, both above and below, separately fasten highly inflammable materials. The overall effect should be like the thunderbolts drawn by artists. This has to be dropped onto the siege machine as it is being brought forward, and is designed so as to fasten onto the machine, and once stuck there to keep the fire alight.

(33.3) Next, if there are any wooden towers in the city, or if the city wall is partly wooden, the parapet of these needs to be provided with covers of felt and leather so as not to be set on fire by the enemy. (33.4) If the gates are set alight, bring up wood and throwing it on make it as big a fire as possible, until you can dig a trench inside, and quickly construct a counter-defence from the materials which are available to you, and if there are none, demolish the nearest houses.

The siege of Tyre in 332 BC by Alexander the Great involved special difficulties. The island on which the city of Tyre was built was about half a mile from the shore, and the mole constructed to reach the city ended up 200 ft wide; Alexander conquered Tyre by increasing his navy to outnumber that of the Tyrians, and reducing the walls with massive siege engines. Most of the population, some 30,000, were sold into slavery. Arrian describes the construction of the mole used to reach the city walls. Arrian, *The Expedition of Alexander*, 2.18.1–19.6:

(2.18.1) It was obvious that the siege of Tyre was a massive operation. (2.18.2) For the city was an island, completely surrounded by high walls. At that time Tyre appeared to have the advantage at sea, and the Persians still ruled the seas, and the people of Tyre continued to have many ships at their disposal.

(2.18.3) Alexander's arguments prevailed, and he decided to construct a mole out from the mainland to the city. The place is a strait covered with shallow water, and near the mainland the sea was shallow and muddy, and next to the city itself where the crossing is deepest the depth is about three fathoms. But there was a large quantity of stone and wood, which they piled above the stones, and it wasn't difficult to fix stakes in the mud which itself acted to bind the stones together.

(2.18.4) The Macedonians were as enthusiastic about the operation as Alexander, who was himself present and organising each detail, and exhorted them with his words, and also encouraged with gifts those who were particularly outstanding in the quality of their work. While they were working near the mainland the construction proceeded without difficulty, where the depth was shallow and nothing impeded the work on the mole. (2.18.5) But once they got to the deeper water and simultaneously they drew near the city, they suffered badly, being shot at from the high battlements, particularly since they were properly dressed in their working clothes rather than in battle gear, and the Tyrians sailed here and there along the mole in their warships, so that since they were still masters of the sea they made it difficult in many places for the Macedonians to work on the mole. (2.18.6) The Macedonians constructed two towers at the end of the mole, which now extended far out into the sea, and put machines of war on the towers. They covered them in animal skins and hides, as a protection against incendiary projectiles fired from the city walls, and as a defence against arrows for the workers. At the same time, those Tyrians who sailed up close to harm those working on the mole could be shot at from the towers and probably easily driven off.

(2.19.1) But the Tyrians employed a counter-measure against this. They filled a horse-transport ship with branches of wood and other flammable wood, erected two masts in the bows and fenced the boat all around as high as they could, so that it could hold as much wood-chip and rubbish and as many torches as possible, and in addition stowed on it pitch, sulphur and other such things that would foment a great blaze. (2.19.2) To each of the two masts they attached a double yard-arm from which they slung in cauldrons such things as could be poured or thrown in to fuel a great blaze, and they raised the height of the bow by weighing down the aft of the ship. (2.19.3) Then they waited for a wind blowing towards the mole and having passed cables from the transport ship dragged it with warships by the stern. When they came near the mole and the towers, they set the wood alight and at the same time rowed the warships as quickly as possible, driving the ship onto the end of the mole. Those who were on the burning ship swam away without difficulty.

(2.19.4) At this point, a great flame struck the towers, and the yard-arms of the ship broke, throwing onto the blaze all the things which had been placed on them to fuel the fire. Those in the warships stayed near the mole, shooting arrows at the towers, so that it wasn't safe for anyone to approach with anything to extinguish the fire. (2.19.5) While this was going on, with the towers completely ablaze, many people came out from the city and getting into small boats which they beached here and there along the mole easily tore down the fences which had been set up for protection before it and set alight all the war machines, as many as had not already caught alight from the ship. (2.19.6) Alexander, however, ordered that the mole be made broader, commencing at the mainland, so as to have room for more towers, and that the engineers construct more war machines.

Siege warfare tended to be simplistic in classical Greece, but the Hellenistic period that followed ushered in a technological revolution in the art of siege warfare. During the siege of the island city of Rhodes in 305–304 BC Demetrius, son of Antigonus the One-Eyed, one of Alexander the Great's generals, made use of siege machinery and was given a new 'nickname', Demetrius Poliorcetes, the 'City-Besieger'. Although he failed to conquer the city, his siege weapons captured the ancient imagination. Plutarch, *Life of Demetrius*, 21.1–3:

(21.1) Demetrius went to war against the people of Rhodes . . . and he moved up against its walls the greatest of his 'city-takers'. It had a square base, each side having a length at the base of 48 cubits [72 ft], and it had a height of 66 cubits [99 ft], with the top tapering, with the upper sides narrower than at the base. (21.2) Inside it was divided into many storeys and rooms, and on the side that faced the enemy each storey was pierced with openings, and through these all sorts of missiles were thrown, for it was full of fighting men with every sort of weapon. (21.3) The 'city-taker' did not shake or tilt in its movements, but advanced straight and steady, equally balanced on its base, at the same time proceeding with a rushing noise and much impetus. At the same time it imparted to those who saw it a feeling of terror and at the same time a certain delight.

ARMOUR AND WEAPONRY

Herodotus contrasts the Persians and the Greeks, and what emerges from this is that the armour of the Greeks was a key factor in the superiority of the *hoplites* against the Persians. The differences are also made clear in a well-known Athenian vase dating to soon after the Persian War which shows a Greek *hoplite* with helmet, breastplate and shield about to deal a fatal blow to his Persian opponent, who has no armour and wears only a leather cap, as opposed to the bronze and crested helmet of the Greek. The quiver that can be seen against the Persian's left leg also points to a major difference between the two sides: the Greeks generally preferred hand-to-hand combat, using first their spears and if necessary their swords, while the Persians often used archers in the preliminary phase of the battle. The Persian archer draws a sword as a last resort in self-defence: he is clearly no match for his adversary's superior skill and armour (see illustration 5.4). At the Battle of Plataea, in 479 BC, the differences in armour and weaponry were apparent. While the Persian commander Mardonius remained alive, the Persians maintained some semblance of order. Herodotus, 9.62.2–63.2:

(9.62.2) There was a fierce drawn-out engagement, hand-to-hand, near the shrine of Demeter, at which they had come to close quarters. The barbarians would grab the Spartans' spears and break them. (9.62.3) In courage and might the Persians were not inferior to the Spartans, but they were without armour, inexperienced, and not the equal of their adversaries in skill. They darted out from their ranks, sometimes singly, or combining in groups of ten, and also in larger and smaller groups, falling upon the Spartans and being slaughtered.

(9.63.1) Where Mardonius himself was, fighting from his white horse, and surrounded by the picked best thousand of the Persians, here particularly did the Persians fall upon the enemy. And for so long as

Mardonius was alive they held their ground and defended themselves, and overcame many of the Spartans. (9.63.2) But when Mardonius died and those stationed around him who were the best of their soldiers also fell, then the rest of them fled and yielded to the Spartans. For the main cause of their destruction was that they had no armour, and they fought as light-armed foot-soldiers against *hoplites*.

Hoplites fought with their shield in their left hand and their spear in the right. This exposed the right side as the most vulnerable to a lunge from the enemy opposite. There was therefore a tendency for each man to shuffle up closer to the man on his right, whose shield, in that man's left hand, could help protect his own right, otherwise unshielded. As the right wing moved further to the right because of this, each man seeking the protection of his neighbour's shield on the right, this wing tended to overlap or envelop the enemy's left wing; this was happening on both sides of the battle. Thucydides was aware of this phenomenon, and mentions it in connection with the Battle of Mantinea in 418 BC. Thucydides, 5.71.1:

All armies are similar in this way: in coming to grips they are rather forced out onto their right wing, and each side overlaps with the right wing those opposite on the left wing, because of the fear each man has to keep his unprotected side as close as possible to the shield of the one stationed on his right, believing that the closer the shields are packed together, the more well protected they will be. And the one who is responsible for this is the first one stationed on the right wing, who is always eager to withdraw his unprotected side from the facing enemy, and the others follow him in this because of the same fear.

RANSOM FOR PRISONERS

In Homer's *Iliad*, Thersites asked if Agamemnon wants even more of the gold from the ransoms paid for Trojans captured on the battlefield (Homer, *Iliad*, 2.229–31; see p. 270). The Athenians also ransomed 700 Boeotian prisoners for 2 *minas* each at the end of the sixth century BC; 2 *minas* was 200 *drachmas*, with a *drachma* being about a day's wage. When Cleomenes, King of Sparta, attacked Argos, he tricked some of the Argives into surrendering. Herodotus, 6.79.1:

Cleomenes then acted as follows: from some deserters he learned the names of the Argives who had taken refuge in the sacred wood of the hero Argos, and sent a herald in to invite them out by name, saying that he had received their ransoms; two *minas* is the sum set by the Peloponnesians as the ransom for each prisoner. About fifty of the Argives whom Cleomenes had called forth came out one by one and were killed.

Bodies would be taken up by each side under a truce arranged for this purpose after the battle. Achilles and Hector fought to the death. That Achilles refused to accept a ransom in return for Hector's body was shocking, but much more so for the listeners was Achilles' appalling treatment of Hector's corpse. Mutilation of the war dead, while attested in other cultures, ancient and modern, was abhorrent to the Greeks. Although Homer here describes single combat between two heroes, in the classical period the *hoplite*'s use of the spear was similar, with the *hoplite* seeking to kill or wound the enemy he faced in the line of battle. Homer, *Iliad*, 22.306–54:

Hector drew a sharp sword,
which hung at his waist: massive and strong,
and gathering himself up swooped as does a high-flying eagle,
darting through the gloomy clouds to the plain below
seizing a tender lamb or a trembling hare: 310
so Hector swooped brandishing his sharp-edged sword.
Achilles rushed at him, his heart gorged with savage
anger, and in front of his chest the cunningly wrought beautiful
    shield covered him
and he nodded with the shining four-horned helmet,
and the beautiful golden plumes waved about   315
which the god Hephaestus had placed thick around the crest.
As a star goes among the stars in the night's darkness,
the star of the evening, Hesper, the fairest star set in the sky,
so the sharp point of the spear shone, which Achilles
brandished in his right hand, planning an evil fate for
    god-like Hector,   320
looking on his beautiful flesh, to see where it might best yield.
Of him all the rest of the body was sheathed in bronze armour,
beautiful, that Hector stripped when he slew the might of Patroclus,
but the flesh showed where the collar-bones support the neck from
    the shoulders,
the throat, where the destruction of life is quickest: 325
here as he rushed at him god-like Achilles drove with his spear
and the point was driven clean through the soft throat.
But the ash-spear heavy with its bronze tip did not sever the
    windpipe,

4.1. The pancration: eye-gouging and probably biting; the referee prepares to strike. Athenian vase, *c.* 480 BC. (© *British Museum*)

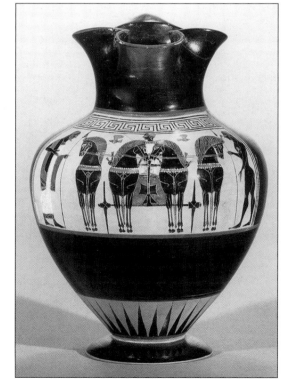

4.2. A four-horse chariot with driver. Athenian vase, *c.* 550 BC. (© *British Museum*)

4.3. Wrestlers, one
in a neck-hold.
Athenian vase,
c. 540 BC.
(*Badisches
Landesmuseum,
Karlsruhe,
Inv. 65/45*)

4.4. A symposium:
drinkers on couches
are served by
youths. Athenian
vase, *c.* 500–470 BC.
(© *British Museum*)

5.1. Greek warrior, perhaps Spartan, with a large crest on his helmet, wearing typical armour. Bronze figurine, 12.8 cm high, from the Peloponnese or north-west Greece, *c.* 510–500 BC. (*Bildarchiv Preussischer Kulturbesitz, Berlin, 2002, Johannes Laurentius*)

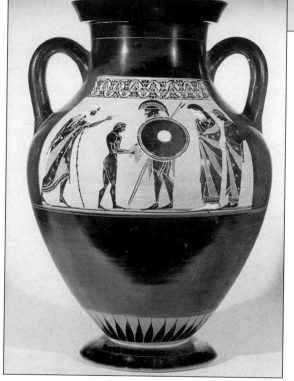

5.2. A warrior departing for battle examines the entrails of a sacrificed beast for good omens, while his wife and father look on. The boy presenting the entrails is probably a slave. Athenian vase, *c.* 530 BC. (© *British Museum*)

5.3. A city under siege; note the distraught woman in the centre of the city. From Xanthos, Asia Minor, *c.* 380 BC. (© *British Museum*)

5.4. A Greek *hoplite* stands over a Persian soldier. Athenian vase, *c.* 480–470 BC. (© *The Trustees of the National Museums of Scotland*)

5.5. Two warships, with officers of the bow. Athenian vase, *c.* 530–510 BC. (*Photo RMN, Chuzeville; Louvre, Paris*)

6.1. Achilles bandages Patroclus. Athenian vase, *c.* 510–500 BC. (*Bildarchiv Preussischer Kulturbesitz, Berlin, 2002*)

6.2. Croesus on his funeral pyre.
Athenian vase, early fifth century BC.
(*Photo RMN, Hervé Lewandowski;
Louvre, Paris*)

6.3. A seated doctor treats a
patient, who grimaces. Athenian
vase, *c.* 470 BC. (*Photo RMN,
Hervé Lewandowski; Louvre,
Paris*)

6.4. A family of worshippers approaches Asclepius (seated), behind whom stands the goddess Health. A slave girl carries on her head a large chest containing the sacrificial items and associated foodstuffs. A serpent, sacred to Asclepius, rears up under his throne. Athenian, white marble, 37 cm high, *c.* 325 BC. (*Bildarchiv Preussischer Kulturbesitz, Berlin, 2002, Jürgen Liepe*)

7.1. Stoking a furnace in a bronze foundry and assembling a bronze statue. Athenian vase, *c.* 480 BC. (*Bildarchiv Preussischer Kulturbesitz, Berlin, 2002, Ingrid Geske*)

7.2. Demosthenes; marble, 2 m high, a copy of the original by Polyeuctus of 280 BC. (*Ny Carlsberg Glyptotek, Copenhagen*)

7.3. Bust of Pericles, with his helmet, hiding his 'squill-head'. Marble, a copy of an Athenian fifth-century original. (© *British Museum*)

so that Hector could reply and exchange words with his enemy.
He fell in the dust; and god-like Achilles gloated over him: 330

'Hector, surely you said as you despoiled Patroclus
that you would be safe, and didn't think about me, far off.
You fool! Far away from him a helper much more powerful
remained behind by the hollow ships,
I who brought you to your knees. The dogs and the birds   335
will tear you to pieces, shaming you, but the Achaeans will bury
   Patroclus.'

Then Hector of the glistening helmet, spoke with his last strength:
'I beg you, by your life, your knees, and your parents,
don't let the dogs feast on me by the hollow ships of the Achaeans,
but take for yourself heaps of both bronze and gold,   340
gifts that my father and lady mother will give you,
and give my body back to my home, so that the Trojans
and their wives may give me, dead, the rites of the funeral fire.'

Then fixing him with a baneful stare swift-footed Achilles replied:
'Don't beg me, you dog, by my knees or parents.   345
Would that somehow my wrath and soul might impel me
to carve your flesh up so that I could eat it raw, for what you've
   done to me.
There isn't a man alive who could keep the dogs from your head,
not even if a ten- or twenty-fold ransom
they brought here and put in front of me, and promised more
   besides,   350
not even if Priam, son of Dardanus, offered to weigh out
your body in gold: so even your lady mother will not
arrange you on the death-bed and mourn, she who brought you
   into the world,
but the dogs and the birds will devour every scrap of you!'   354

Hector makes a last reply, predicting that Achilles himself will not escape
alive from Troy but be killed at its gates by Paris, Helen's seducer. Homer,
Iliad, 22.361–6, 395–415:

Even as Hector was speaking the last throes of death enveloped him,
and his soul soaring free of his limbs departed to the house of Hades,
lamenting its fate, leaving behind manhood and youth.
And now, even though he was dead, god-like Achilles spoke to
   him:

'Die! I'll accept my fate then, whenever Zeus 365
and the other immortal gods decide to fulfil it.'

Achilles now devised shameful treatment for god-like Hector. 395
He pierced the tendons at the back of both his feet
from heel to ankle, and threading through thongs of ox-hide
tied them to his chariot, leaving the head to dangle behind.
Then climbing into the chariot and hoisting up the glorious armour
and whipping the horses to a run, they galloped along not
　　unwillingly. 400
And the dust flew up as Hector was dragged along, his jet-black
　　flowing hair
fanning out on both sides, and all in the dust lay that head
once so handsome: but now Zeus had delivered him to his foes
to desecrate in the land of his forebears.

So all his head was covered with clouds of dust. And now his
　　mother 405
tore at her hair, and casting her shining veil far away
shrieked wildly at the sight of her child.
His beloved father groaned piteously, and around them the people
were seized with wailing and groaning throughout the city.
Most like this would it have been if all Ilion 410
was smouldering away on its heights from top to bottom.
And the people scarcely restrained the grieving old man,
Priam, hell-bent on going out through the Dardanian gates:
he entreated everyone, rolling around in the dung,
naming each man by his name. 415

THE BRAVERY OF ALEXANDER: 'A MAN IS THE MEASURE OF HIS DEEDS'

Part of India had been under Persian domination, and Alexander sought to assert his authority here, as conqueror of the Persian Empire. In 325 BC he campaigned against the Mallians, and attacked their main city. As was often the case, Alexander's progress was accompanied by wholesale slaughter and massacre. Even those who served with him considered his actions in this attack reckless. Arrian, *The Expedition of Alexander*, 6.9.1–11.2, 6.13.4–5:

(6.9.1) The next day Alexander split his army into two parts, and taking command of one part he began assaulting the wall, and gave Perdiccas command of the other half of the army. In the meantime the Indians did not receive the Macedonian attack but abandoned the walls of the city, and themselves fled as a group to the citadel. Alexander and the soldiers with him broke apart a small gate, and they entered into the city far ahead of the others. (6.9.2) But those commanded by Perdiccas fell behind, not getting over the wall easily, and most of them were not carrying ladders, as it seemed to them that the city had been captured, as they saw that the walls were deserted by the defenders. But when they saw the citadel held by the enemy and numerous fighters drawn up before it for its defence, then some began to mine under the wall, while others placed ladders against it wherever this was possible, attempting to force entry to the citadel.

(6.9.3) But Alexander, thinking that the Macedonians carrying the ladders to him were dragging their feet, seized a ladder from one of the men carrying them and put it up against the wall, tucked himself well up under his shield, and went up. Peucestas went next, bearing the sacred shield, which Alexander had taken from the temple of Athena at Troy and always kept with him, and which was borne before him in battle. After him Leonnatus the bodyguard ascended on the same ladder. Abreas, one of the soldiers of those who had been rewarded with double pay, came up by another ladder. (6.9.4) The king was now at the parapet of the wall, and leaning his shield against it shoved some of the Indians inside the wall, others he slew with his sword, stripping the wall [of defenders] in that place. But the bodyguards, becoming terrified, rushed in their zeal up the same ladders, breaking them, so that those ascending fell below, and made the ascent impossible for the rest of them.

(6.9.5) Alexander standing upon the wall was shot at all around from the adjacent towers, for none of the Indians in them were game enough to come near him, and also by those in the city, being within striking distance, for it so happened that there was earth thrown against the wall at this place. Alexander was a clear target, because of both his glittering armour and his extraordinary courage, and he realised that staying there was dangerous, but also that he couldn't achieve anything useful there. However, if he leapt down inside the wall he might by this very action strike panic into the Indians, and if not, and he had to face danger, he would perform great deeds, worth listening to by posterity, and not die ignobly. Thinking along these lines he leapt from the wall into the citadel. (6.9.6) There, with his back to the wall, he slew with his sword some of those who came within reach, including the leader of the Indians, who came at him too eagerly. Another, as he came near, he stopped by hurling a stone, and again another by the same method, but again, anyone who came close enough he killed with his sword. The barbarians no longer wanted to go near him, but standing all around him they hurled whatever projectile they happened to have or whatever came to hand.

(6.10.1) Meanwhile Peucestas and Abreas, who had both been awarded double pay, and with them Leonnatus, the only ones who chanced to climb up the wall on ladders before they broke, leapt down and themselves fought in front of the king. Abreas fell there, taking an arrow in the face. Alexander himself was struck by an arrow which went clean through his breastplate into his chest over the lung, so that according to Ptolemy's history breath and blood spurted out of the wound together.

(6.10.2) But Alexander, while his blood stayed warm, although suffering, kept at it. But he had a massive haemorrhage, which came out with his breath, in a stream, and dizziness and faintness overcame him and he fell there bending over on his shield. Peucestas stood over him where he lay, and held over him the sacred shield from Troy, and Leonnatus on the other side; they both now had missiles thrown at them. Alexander was close to collapse from the loss of blood.

(6.10.3) The Macedonian assault was now in disarray. Those who saw Alexander coming under attack on the wall and then leaping into the citadel, through zeal and fear in case their king should come to grief through hazarding danger so recklessly, smashed up the ladders and devised various other means to ascend the wall in this crisis. Some fixed pegs into the wall, made of clay, and hanging onto these clambered up the wall with difficulty, and some mounted the shoulders of others. (6.10.4) The first one to ascend threw himself over the wall into the citadel, where they saw the king lying prostrate, and they all raised a lament and the battle-cry. Already a fierce contest raged around the fallen king; now one, now another of the Macedonians raising their shield over him. While this was going on, some of them broke down the bar with which the gate of the curtain wall between the towers was made fast, and so entered in small groups. Others put their shoulders to where the gate was broken, pushed it inwards, and in this way threw open the citadel.

(6.11.1) Some now began to massacre the Indians, killing them all, and not sparing woman or child. Others carried off the king, who was in a bad way, on the shield, thinking that it was scarcely possible that he could live. Some write that it was Critodemus, a doctor from the island of Cos, by birth a member of the guild of the healing god Asclepius, who pulled the arrow out of the wound, cutting into where it had lodged. Others write that Perdiccas, the bodyguard, because there was no doctor at this critical juncture, cut into the wound with his sword and drew out the missile at the express command of Alexander. (6.11.2) The jolting as he was borne off caused a massive flow of blood, so that Alexander fainted again, and the flow of blood was checked by his fainting. Numerous other stories have been written by the historians about this disaster, and tradition has handed them down, just as the first inventors of the lies told them, and preserves them still to this day, and will never cease handing them down in succession to others, unless the account which I have written down here puts an end to them.

(6.13.4) Nearchus writes that Alexander was furious with those friends who reproached him for the danger he had faced so far out in front of the army, as this was not the role of the general, but that of the soldier. It seems to me that Alexander was indignant about what they were saying because he knew it was true, and that he had laid himself open to this charge. But on the other hand, because he was intent on battle and desirous of glory, just as others are a slave to some pleasure, he was not strong enough to resist danger. (6.13.5) Nearchus also writes that a certain old Boeotian – he doesn't mention his name – noticing that Alexander was angry at the reproaches of his friends and betrayed this in his facial expression, went up to him and said this in his Boeotian dialect: 'Alexander, a man is the measure of his deeds', and he also quoted some poetry, the overall sense of which was that, 'the man of action is bound to suffer'. By saying this he was immediately in good repute with Alexander, and from then on had his closer friendship.

In 327 BC the siege of Sogdiana (in Bactria, in central Asia Minor, between the Aral Sea and India) involved the use of 'winged soldiers' to capture an otherwise invincible rocky outcrop. Arrian, *The Expedition of Alexander*, 4.18.4–19.5:

(4.18.4) Alexander advanced to the Rock of Sogdiana at the beginning of spring, where, it was reported to him, many of the Sogdianians had fled. It was also reported that the wife and daughters of Oxyartes the Bactrian had taken refuge at the rock, Oxyartes putting them there in an impregnable place for safety when he had revolted from Alexander. Once the rock was captured Alexander thought that the Sogdianians who wanted to revolt would not have any rallying point to do so. (4.18.5) But when the Macedonians came to the rock, Alexander found that it was precipitous on all sides for attack, and the barbarians had stocked up on provisions for a lengthy siege. A great fall of snow made the ascent more difficult for the Macedonians, and also provided the barbarians with a ready source of water. But despite this, Alexander took the decision to make an assault. (4.18.6) For also an immoderate boast by the barbarians goaded Alexander on, possessed by a desire for glory. When he offered to meet them and discuss terms, to the effect that they could have safe conduct to their homes if they handed over the rock, they told him with barbaric laughter to find soldiers with wings to capture the rock for him, as no other men would be a worry to them. (4.18.7) At this, Alexander announced that the first soldier to scale the rock would be awarded a prize of twelve talents, the second, eleven, the third ten, and so on down the line, with the twelfth soldier to receive 300 Persian gold coins. The Macedonians were enthusiastic enough as it was but this announcement spurred them on even more.

(4.19.1) Those who had rock-climbing experience from previous sieges now assembled, some 300 in number, equipped with small iron pegs, which they used to make their tents secure, attached to strong linen cords to drive into the snow where it seemed frozen solid or where the bare earth was exposed through the snow. They set out at night to the part of the rock that was most precipitous and which would be the least guarded. (4.19.2) These men fixed the pegs into the earth wherever it showed, and into the snow where it was least likely to break away; they each got themselves up the rock by a different route. Of them, thirty lost their lives in the ascent, and their bodies were not recovered for burial, falling in different places in the snow. (4.19.3) The rest, ascending, reached the summit of the mountain at dawn, and waved bits of linen at the camp of the Macedonians, just as Alexander had instructed them. Alexander sent a herald and ordered him to shout at the advance guard of the barbarians not to waste any more time but to give themselves up, for he had indeed discovered winged men and the summit of the mountain was in their possession, pointing out the soldiers on the summit as he said this.

(4.19.4) Amazed at the sight of something so unexpected, and suspicious that there were more fully armed soldiers holding the summit, they surrendered themselves. In this way the sight of a few of these Macedonians struck fear into them. Many wives and children were captured, in particular, Oxyartes' wife and daughters. (4.19.5) Oxyartes had a virgin daughter ripe for marriage, called Roxane, and those serving with Alexander said that she was the most beautiful woman they had seen in Asia, second only to the wife of Darius. Alexander fell in love with her when he saw her, but although he desired her did not wish to treat her violently, although she was a captive, and thought it not beneath himself to marry her.

WAR: WOMEN'S OUTLOOK

Aristophanes' *Lysistrata* has as its plot Athenian wives forcing their husbands to make peace with the Spartans – by going on a 'sex strike'. The play was produced in 411 BC, two years after the dreadful disaster in Sicily. The main character is Lysistrata, whose name literally means, 'Disbander of armies'.

Various topical allusions in the play can be briefly explained. The Athenian men are away at war and their sexual attentions are missed (despite this the women will go ahead with their sex strike), and since the revolt of the city of Miletus in the previous year the women haven't even had the consolation of dildos, an export speciality of Miletus (lines 108–10). The tragedy about Poseidon and the tub was dealt with by Sophocles: Tyro was in love with the River Enipeus; Poseidon fell in love with Tyro, disguised himself as the river and seduced her; she abandoned the twin boys born of this union in a tub on the river, but they were rescued (line 139). When Troy was sacked, Menelaus wanted to kill his unfaithful wife Helen, but one look at her soon changed his mind (line 155). When an oath was sworn it was done over a sacrificial victim or parts of it (hence the discussion in lines 185–211). Oaths were often sworn over or by holding parts of boars, so the 'sacrificed' wine jar is referred to as a boar (line 202). Aristophanes is, of course, as in many of his plays, making a stock joke about women's propensity for drinking. Aristophanes, *Lysistrata*, 99–237:

Lysistrata: Don't you miss the fathers of your children
when they're away with the army? I know for a fact that   100
each of you has a husband who is away from home.

Calonice: Certainly my husband, poor man, has been gone five
   months,
deary, away in Thrace, guarding Eucrates.

Myrrhine: Mine's been at Pylus seven whole months.

Lampito: And mine, whenever he's released from the army,   105
strapping on his shield, he goes flying off.

Lysistrata: And there is not so much as a spark of an adulterer left.
And since the Milesians revolted against us,
I haven't even set eyes on a six-inch dildo,
which might have been a leather consolation for us.   110
Would you join with me if I hit upon a plan
to bring the war to an end?

Myrrhine: By the Two Goddesses, Demeter and Persephone, I would,
even if I had to sell this dress here, and drink up what it fetched
  on the same day.

Calonice: Count me in – I'd be prepared to cut myself   115
in two like a flatfish and hand over half.

Lampito: And I'd scale to the top of Mount Taygetus
if I could catch a glimpse of peace there.

Lysistrata: Let me speak: there's no need for secrecy about the plan.
For we, women, if we intend   120
to force our men to make peace
we must give up –

Myrrhine: What? Go on.

Lysistrata: So you'll do it?

Myrrhine: We'll do it, even if we have to die for it!

Lysistrata: Well then, we are going to have to go without . . .
  the dick.
Why are you turning away from me? Where are you going?   125
Why are you grimacing and shaking your heads?
Why are you going red in the face? Why are you crying?
Will you do it, or won't you? What are you going to do?

Myrrhine: I can't go through with it, but let the war drag on.

Calonice: By Zeus, I can't do it, but let the war drag on.   130

Lysistrata: Are you saying this, Flatfish?
Didn't you say just now that you'd cut yourself in two?

Calonice: But, but anything else that's required. And I'm prepared
to walk through fire. I'd do this, but the dick . . .
dear Lysistrata, there just isn't anything like it.   135

Lysistrata: What's your view?

Athenian wife: I'm also prepared to walk through fire.

Lysistrata: How absolutely sex mad is all our female race.
It's not for nothing that tragedies are written about us.
For we are nothing but the story about Poseidon and the tub.
But, dear Spartan, Lampito, – if even just you   140
joined me, the plan might still be saved.
Vote for my plan!

Lampito: By the Twin Gods of Sparta, Castor and Pollux,
it's difficult for women sleeping alone without a hard cock.
But all the same, we've got to do this for peace.

Lysistrata: You're the best, and the only woman out of all
this lot here.   145

Calonice: So if we did go without what you suggest –
and may it not come to this – would peace
be more likely by doing this?

Lysistrata: Without a doubt, by the Two Goddesses.
For if we sat inside with our make-up on,
and wearing our fine silk dresses   150
and with our fannies plucked in a triangle
and our husbands erect and lusting to have sex
but we didn't go near them but kept our distance,
they'd make peace quickly, I'm sure of that.

Lampito: Yes; Menelaus, when he saw a glimpse of Helen's
naked breasts   155
threw away, I understand, his sword.

Calonice: But what are *we* to do if our husbands leave *us* alone?

Lysistrata: Use a dildo.

Calonice: Substitutes are lousy!
What if they grab us, and drag us into the bedroom by force?   160

Lysistrata: Hang onto the door.

Calonice: What if they beat us up?

Lysistrata: Then you have to give in, but be nasty:
for there is no joy for them in forced sex.
Make their lives a misery in other ways: never mind, they'll
soon
be at a loss. For no husband can ever be   165
really happy if his wife is disagreeable.

Myrrhine: If you two are settled on this, then it's all right by us.

Lampito: And so we will persuade our husbands
to keep a genuine, just peace absolutely:
but how could one persuade the Athenian rabble   170
not to talk rubbish?

Lysistrata: Don't you worry yourself: we'll persuade our side.

Lampito: Not while their warships have sails
and bottomless money, by the Two Goddesses!

Lysistrata: But this has been adequately taken care of: 175
we'll seize the acropolis today.
This task has been assigned to the older women;
while we are arranging this,
they'll seize the acropolis, pretending to have gone there to make a
     sacrifice.

Lampito: Everything's under control: what you're talking about is
     great.   180

Lysistrata: Then why don't we agree to this as soon as possible,
Lampito, so that the agreement might be unbreakable?

Lampito: Disclose the oath, so we can swear it.

Lysistrata: You've spoken well. Where's the Scythian girl? What
     are you staring at?
Put the shield down, hollow side up, in front of us;   185
let someone give me the bits of the sacrificial victim.

Calonice: Lysistrata, what sort of oath will you make us swear?

Lysistrata: What sort? By slaying a sheep on a shield,
as, they say, Aeschylus once did.

Calonice: Don't, Lysistrata, swear an oath
about peace over a shield.   190

Lysistrata: So what sort of oath should it be?

Calonice: If we got hold of a white horse from somewhere
we could cut it into sacrificial pieces.

Lysistrata: Where on earth would we get a white horse from?

Calonice: So how are we going to swear the oath?

Myrrhine: By Zeus, I'll tell you, if you want to know!
We place a great black wine cup, hollow side up of course,   195
and slay a jar of wine from Thasos over it,
and we'll swear not to add any water to the cup.

Lampito: Ah, I want to praise that oath but words fail me!

Lysistrata: Someone go inside and carry out the cup and wine jar.

Calonice: Dearest women, what a huge wine jar! 200
Anyone who touches it would be instantly happy.

Lysistrata: Put this down and take hold of this boar with me.
Lady Persuasion and Friendship Cup
kindly receive this sacrifice from the women.

Calonice: Indeed the blood's got a nice colour and pours out well. 205

Lampito: And what an aromatic bouquet, by Castor!

Myrrhine: Allow me to be the first, women, to swear the oath.

Calonice: No, by Aphrodite, unless your name comes out of the
hat first.

Lysistrata: Everyone take hold of the cup, Lampito:
and one of you must say, on behalf of everyone, what I say: 210
and all of you are to swear to keep the oath.
No man, either lover or husband –

Calonice: No man, either lover or husband –

Lysistrata: will come near me with an erection. Say it!

Calonice: will come near me with an erection. Oh, 215
I'm about to faint, Lysistrata.

Lysistrata: At home I'll live my life as if a virgin –

Calonice: At home I'll live my life as if a virgin –

Lysistrata: wearing a saffron dress and all made up –

Calonice: wearing a saffron dress and all made up – 220

Lysistrata: so that my husband will be completely lustful for me.

Calonice: so that my husband will be completely lustful for me.

Lysistrata: I won't ever willingly yield to my husband.

Calonice: I won't ever willingly yield to my husband.

Lysistrata: If he should employ force to compel me, unwilling – 225

Calonice: If he should employ force to compel me, unwilling –

Lysistrata: I'll give in with bad grace and I won't snuggle up.

Calonice: I'll give in with bad grace and I won't snuggle up.

Lysistrata: I will not hold my Persian slippers up to the roof.

Calonice: I will not hold my Persian slippers up to the roof.   230

Lysistrata: I won't take up the lioness-on-a-cheese-grater position.

Calonice: I won't take up the lioness-on-a-cheese-grater position.

Lysistrata: If I stand firm and fast by this oath, may I drink from this cup here.

Calonice: If I stand firm and fast by this oath, may I drink from this cup here.

Lysistrata: But if I transgress against this oath, may the cup be filled with water.   235

Calonice: But if I transgress against this oath, may the cup be filled with water.

Lysistrata: Do we all swear these things?

All the women: By Zeus we do!

The women's plan is to deny the men sex: the women at first are horrified by Lysistrata's plan but agree. But as time wears on the women find it difficult to stick to their resolve: Aristophanes here gets comic mileage out of the male idea of the sex-crazed woman. Lysistrata comes on stage, upset at the women. The god Pan was well known for his horniness (line 721); Orsilochus is otherwise unknown, but perhaps he was a favourite with the ladies (line 725). The Third Wife uses the excuse of childbirth to attempt to leave the acropolis, as births could not take place in temples or on holy ground, such as the acropolis (lines 742–59). The helmet the Third Wife has up her dress to make her appear pregnant would have been the sacred bronze helmet of the statue of Athena on the acropolis (lines 751–2). The owl was the sacred bird of Athena, goddess of the acropolis, and the noise of owls supposedly keeps one of the women awake all night (lines 760–1). Aristophanes, *Lysistrata*, 706–80:

Leader of the Women's Chorus: Mistress of this enterprise and plan, why do you come out of the house, looking away from me so sullenly?

Lysistrata: The deeds of wretched women and the female mind make me dispirited and cause me to pace back and forth.

Leader of the Women's Chorus: What are you saying? What are you saying?   710

Lysistrata: The truth, the truth.

Leader of the Women's Chorus: What's so terrible? Tell your dear
friends.

Lysistrata: It's too shameful to talk about, but a heavy burden to
keep quiet about.

Leader of the Women's Chorus: Don't hide from me the disaster
that's befallen us.

Lysistrata: In brief: we need sex! 715

Leader of the Women's Chorus: Oh Zeus!

Lysistrata: Why cry out to Zeus? It's just the way it is.
I can't keep them separate from their husbands
any longer: they're escaping!
The first one I apprehended was near the grotto of Pan 720
burrowing out through the opening,
another, the deserter, was wriggling down a pulley,
and another one yesterday, on a sparrow,
intended to fly off down to the house
of Orsilochus but I hauled her off by the hair. 725
They're raking up every possible excuse to get home.
Here comes one of them.
You there, where are you rushing off to?

First Wife: I want to go home.
I've got some woollen garments from Miletus at home
and they're being chewed to bits by moths.

Lysistrata: Moths indeed! 730
Get back inside the acropolis.

First Wife: But by the Two Goddesses, I'll be back quickly,
all I want to do is spread them on the bed.

Lysistrata: Don't spread anything, and don't go anywhere.

First Wife: So I have to let my woollens be destroyed?

Lysistrata: If that's what's required.

Second Wife: Wretched me, wretched for my fine flax, 735
which I've left at home uncarded.

Lysistrata: Another one whose come to card
her fine flax. Go right back there.

Second Wife: But by the Goddess Phosphorus
I'll do a bit of carding and come straight back.

Lysistrata: No, no carding. Because if you were to start that,   740
another wife would want to do the same.

Third Wife: Lady Birth-Goddess, keep my baby inside
until I reach some spot not sacred to the gods.

Lysistrata: What stupid nonsense!

Third Wife: I'm giving birth right now!

Lysistrata: But yesterday you weren't even pregnant.

Third Wife: But I am today.   745
Send me home as quickly as possible,
Lysistrata, to the midwife.

Lysistrata: What story are you spinning?
What's this hard thing you have here?

Third Wife: A boy baby.

Lysistrata: By Aphrodite, it's not, but it's clear you have something,
bronze and hollow: I'll have a look.   750
Silly woman, you've got the sacred helmet
and claim you're pregnant?

Third Wife: By Zeus, I am pregnant.

Lysistrata: Why do you have this helmet then?

Third Wife: So that if the birth pains overtook me here
on the acropolis, getting into the helmet
I could give birth in it, just like the pigeons.   755

Lysistrata: What are you talking about? You're just making up
    excuses. The whole thing's obvious.
Why don't you stay here until it's time for your helmet's baptism?

Third Wife: But I can't even get to sleep on the acropolis,
since I caught sight of the serpent that guards the acropolis.

First Wife: And wretched me: I'm dying of sleeplessness, lying
    awake all night   760
with the owls always calling 'oo-hoo, oo-hoo'.

Lysistrata: Ridiculous women, enough of these tricks.
You probably do miss your husbands. But don't you realise,

they are longing for us? I know very well
that they are having troubled nights. But hang on, good wives,   765
and persevere for just a little while longer,
as there is an oracle that predicts victory for us,
if we don't quarrel among ourselves. This is the oracle here.

First Wife: Read out to us what it predicts.

Lysistrata: Silence.
But whenever the female swallows cower in one place   770
fleeing the male hoopee bird, avoiding the phallus,
there is an end of troubles, and Zeus who thunders from on high
will put what's on top underneath –

First Wife: So we'll be lying on top?

Lysistrata: – and if the swallows start arguing and flee on their
    wings
from the holy temple, then it will seem that there is   775
no bird whatsoever more lascivious.

First Wife: That oracle's clear, by Zeus.

Lysistrata: By all the gods! Now let's not give up although we're
    suffering,
but let's go back into the acropolis. For this would be a real
    disgrace,
dearest women, if we betrayed the oracle!   780

THE *HOPLITES* OF THEBES' SACRED BAND

Thebes' Sacred Band was an elite corps bound by homoerotic relationships.
It was formed in 379 BC by Gorgidas when Thebes was liberated from the
Spartans, and played a vital role in the Battle of Leuctra in 371 BC which
effectively destroyed Spartan power. The quotation of Nestor is from
Homer, *Iliad*, 2.363 (18.2). The legend of Iolaus and Heracles is interesting,
providing a mythical justification for the Sacred Band: the lovers were
imitating the ancient heroes (18.5). The Battle of Chaeronea was fought in
338 BC, with Athens, Thebes and various Greek states, against Macedon,
which won (18.7): the Sacred Band was destroyed to a man, and never
revived. The Macedonian *sarissa* was a long spear, more like a pike, about
12 cubits in length (18.7). Plutarch, *Life of Pelopidas*, 18.1–7:

(18.1) The Sacred Band, so they say, was first established by Gorgidas,
and was made up of 300 picked men, for whom the city provided
training and maintenance, and who were stationed on the Cadmeia, the

acropolis of Thebes. This is why they were also called the City Band, because in the past the correct name for 'acropolis' was 'city'. (18.2) But some say that this force comprised lovers and their beloved, and a humorous remark of Pammenes is recorded that he said Homer's Nestor was not being a tactician when he ordered the Greeks to organise their companies of soldiers by tribes and clans, 'so that clan might give support to clans, and tribe to tribes', as he ought to have stationed lover next to beloved.

(18.3) For in dire straits, tribesmen and clansmen don't have much attachment for each other, but a band which is held together by the friendship between lovers is indissoluble and cannot be broken, as the lover is ashamed before the beloved, and the beloved ashamed to be disgraced before their lover, and so they stand firm for each other in dreadful predicaments. (18.4) There is no need to be amazed by this, since men feel more shame on account of their lovers when they are absent than of others when they are present, as in the case of that man whose enemy was about to slaughter him as he lay who begged him to plunge his sword into his breast, 'So that,' he said, 'my beloved won't see my corpse with a wound in its back and be ashamed.'

(18.5) It is also said that Iolaus, beloved of Heracles, accompanied him and stood by him during his labours, and Aristotle says that even in his own day lover and beloved made vows to each other at the tomb of Iolaus. (18.6) So it is reasonable that it is called the 'Sacred' Band, just as Plato describes a lover friend as 'possessed by the god'. (18.7) It is said that the Sacred Band was undefeated until the Battle of Chaeronea. When, after that battle, Philip was viewing the corpses and stood at the place where the 300 members of the Sacred Band had fallen and were lying all entangled with each other in their armour, where they had fought against the Macedonian *sarissas*, he was amazed and learning that this was the band of the lovers and beloved, he wept and exclaimed, 'May they perish miserably, those who suspect that these men did or suffered anything shameful.'

SHIPS AND ROWERS

The Persian invasion of Greece in 480 BC went well on land at first (though there was also a naval setback at Artemision), with the Persians successfully forcing the pass at Thermopylae. But at Salamis (a small island off the coast of Athens) the combined Greek fleet, in which the Athenian ships were in the majority, inflicted a devastating loss on the Persians, thanks to the brilliant strategy of the Athenian Themistocles. Although the Persians had still to be defeated on land, which the Greeks achieved in 479 BC at Plataea in Boeotia largely due to the Spartans, Salamis was the turning point of the war, and without this victory it is doubtful that the Greeks would have won the overall campaign.

Aeschylus was an eyewitness and participant in the Battle of Salamis. His play *The Persians* was produced in 472 BC, and is the earliest account of the battle. It celebrates the Greek victory and the city of Athens, and evokes the pride of the Athenians in their victory. Salamis in a very real sense secured the history of western civilisation, preserving the west from the east at a crucial stage in the development of Athenian culture. Greek victory here was a triumph for Athenian democracy and its institutions. Athens' continued existence led to its Golden Age of literature, culture and politics, and established a legacy that still remains a priceless asset of western civilisation.

The play opens with the chorus of Persian elders describing the beginning of the battle. Aeschylus, *The Persians*, 65–80:

The royal army, annihilator of cities,	65
has made its way	
to the neighbouring land opposite,	
crossing the straits of the Hellespont	
on a bridge of boats	
bound with flaxen cords,	70
a well-bolted road-way	
as a yoke around the neck of the sea.	
The impetuous master of Asia's millions	
against the entire world	
his god-like flock does drive	75
in two parts, both on foot	
and by sea,	
trusting in his strong	
harsh commanders,	
himself the god's peer, light of a gold-begotten race.	80

The Persian Queen Atossa, disturbed by an ominous dream, asks the chorus of Persian elders about Athens. Atossa cannot understand how a city without a leader can withstand the Persians: Aeschylus' pride – and that of his audience – in the democracy is clear here. 'A treasury in the ground' refers to the silver mines near Athens, which financed Themistocles' ship-building programme of 484 BC, providing the ships that were crucial for defeating the Persians (line 238). Aeschylus, *The Persians*, 230–44:

Atossa: Friends, I would like to learn
 where is the land of Athens said to be situated?   230

Chorus of Persian Elders: Far away, in the west, where the Sun Lord
 daily wastes away.

Atossa: But why would my son desire to make prey of this city?

Chorus: For then all of Greece would become obedient to the king.

Atossa: So has their army such a mass of men?   235

Chorus: With such an army as they have, they have inflicted many blows
 on the Persians.

Atossa: What else do they have as well as the army? Do they have
 enough wealth at home?

Chorus: They have a spring of silver, a treasury in the ground.

Atossa: Is the point of the bow-stretching arrow conspicuous in their
 hands?

Chorus: Not in the least. They have spears for close fighting and carry
 shields for armour.   240

Atossa: Who is set over them as shepherd, and who is despot of their
 army?

Chorus: They are not called slaves or vassals of any man.

Atossa: How then could they stand firm in the face of an enemy army?

Chorus: Firm enough to destroy the huge and glorious force of Darius.

A messenger arrives bringing Atossa and the chorus the disastrous news of Salamis. Themistocles tricked the Persians into fighting in the narrow straits between the island of Salamis and the Athenian coast, where their numbers were a disadvantage. Aeschylus, *The Persians*, 272–9:

Messenger: The shores of Salamis and all the neighbouring coasts
are bloated with corpses destroyed by a wretched fate.

Chorus: Woe! You are saying that the sea-tossed bodies
of our loved ones, drowned,   275
are borne along lifeless
floating in their thick cloaks!

Messenger: Our bows were useless, and the whole force
is destroyed, overpowered when the ships charged each other.

The messenger recounts the fate of some leading Persians. A few lines indicate Aeschylus' powerful use of language to conjure up a scene. Aeschylus, *The Persians*, 304–5, 314–17:

> *Messenger:* Dadaces, commander of a thousand men, struck by a
>   spear
> flew with a nimble leap from his ship.
>
> Matallus of Chrysa, commander of ten-thousand foot
> and of the thirty-thousand black horse
> in death stained bloody red his thick bushy beard
> changing the colour to a deep crimson.

The messenger goes on to describe the battle. The Persian envoy's speech is, of course, written by an Athenian for an Athenian audience. There are no Persian accounts of the battle. The loop on the rowing end of the oar was put around a pin on the side of the ship to keep it in place while rowing (line 376). The 'bronze-sheathed rams' of the warships (line 415) can be seen in illustration 5.5, and often, as here, they were fashioned into animal shapes. At Marathon in 490 BC the Athenians and Plataeans had destroyed the expedition sent against them by Xerxes' father Darius (line 474). Aeschylus, *The Persians*, 337–514:

> *Messenger:* Were numbers the deciding factor, know that the
>   barbarians
> would have prevailed with their ships. For to the Greeks
> the whole number of ships was ten times thirty,
> and apart from these there was a picked force of ten ships.   340
> But Xerxes, for this I know, led a total of one-thousand ships
> and there were two-hundred and seven
> that were especially swift. That's the sum total.
> Do you think that we were outnumbered in the battle?
> But some divine power destroyed our force,   345
> weighting the scales so they were not equally matched in fortune.
> The gods preserve the city of the goddess Athena.
>
> Atossa: So is the city of Athens not yet destroyed?
>
> *Messenger:* While she has men her defence is assured.
>
> *Atossa:* Tell me of the beginning of the clash of the ships.   350
> Who commenced the battle, the Greeks
> or my son, exulting in the multitude of his ships?

Messenger: Queen, a destructive force or some evil power
appearing from somewhere or other began our total defeat.
For a Greek coming from the Athenian force   355
said to your son Xerxes that,
when the dusk of black night should fall,
the Greeks would not remain, but leaping onto the decks
of the ships would save their lives
in clandestine flight, some here others there.   360
As soon as Xerxes heard this, unaware of the treachery
of this Greek or the envy of the gods,
he pronounced this order to all the captains:
when the sun with his rays should desist from lighting up
the earth, and darkness had taken fast hold of the temple of the
   sky,   365
they were to station the ships in a compact body in three lines
and other ships in a circle around the island of Salamis
to guard the entrances and the straits where the sea surged.
If the Greeks should escape their evil fate,
finding some secret flight for their ships,   370
it was announced that each captain would lose his head.
He ordered all this from the great confidence of his heart:
for he did not understand what the gods had in mind.
Our men, not disorderly but obedient in spirit
prepared their evening meal, and each seaman   375
fastened their oars through the snuggly fitting pins.
When the light of the sun had ebbed away
and night appeared, every man who was master of an oar
and every man experienced in arms boarded ship:
the long ships encouraged each other, line by line: 380
each sailed as they had been ordered,
and all night the commanders of the ships
kept all the host of the fleet sailing to and fro.
And night was departing, and the Greek force
did not in any way attempt a secret flight.   385
When, however, day with its white horses brilliant to behold
shone over the entire land,
first from the Greeks a shout rang out
like a song of good omen, and in the same instant
the island rock opposite echoed it clearly.   390
Fear gripped all the barbarians
misled in their opinion: for not as if they were in flight
did the Greeks sing their sacred battle hymn then

but as men hastening to battle full of courage.
The trumpet blast consumed them all.   395
At once to orders with the dashing oars in unison
they struck the deep sea,
and all the ships came swiftly into view.
First the well-disciplined right wing led off in good order
and then their whole fleet sallied out against us,   400
and at the same time one heard a mighty cry in unison:

'Onward sons of Greece,
set your homeland free, liberate your children,
your wives, the temples of your fathers' gods,
the tombs of your forefathers: now we fight for everything.'   405

From us the clamour of the Persian tongue
rose up in reply, and there was no time for delay.
At once ship struck ship with bronze-sheathed ram:
a Greek vessel commenced the clash,
wrecking the entire stern of a Phoenician ship –   410
each ship was directed against another.
At first, the stream of the Persian force held its own,
but when the mass of our ships was crowded together
into the narrow strait and no assistance could be given to one
    another,
they struck their bronze-sheathed rams   415
against each other, and all their rowing gear was shattered;
the Greek ships not passing up this opportunity
formed up in a circle and struck, hulls of ships rolled over,
and one could no longer see the sea,
bloated with the wreckage of ships and the slaughter of men.   420
The shores and reefs were stocked with corpses,
and every ship began to row away in disorderly retreat
as many as belonged to the barbarian fleet.
But as if the Persians were tunny-fish or some catch of fish
the Greeks kept striking and hacking with the broken wreckage   425
of oar handles and ruined ships: groaning and screams
possessed all the open sea
until the face of murky night broke off the scene.
The plentitude of the disasters, not even if I related them
for ten days running, would I be able to tell you in their entirety.   430
For know you well, never before in history has such
a crowded multitude of men perished in the course of a single
    day.

Atossa: Alas! A mighty ocean of evils
has burst upon the Persians and the entire race of barbarians.

Messenger: Now know this well, this isn't yet half the disaster.   435
Such a misfortune of sufferings came upon them
as to outweigh these twice in the turn of the scales.

Atossa: But what fate could have befallen them still more hostile
    than this?
Speak, what is this disaster which you say
came upon the expedition, reducing them to direr straits?   440

Messenger: Those Persians who were in the prime of life,
most courageous in spirit and distinguished by high birth,
and always among those foremost in their loyalty to their king,
have died basely by a most shameful fate.

Atossa: Wretched woman that I am, friends, due to this evil calamity.   445
By meeting what doom did you say these men perished?

Messenger: There is an island, Psyttalea, in front of Salamis,
small, with poor anchorage for ships, which the dance-loving
god Pan haunts along its sea-washed shore.
There Xerxes sent these men so that when the enemy   450
had suffered shipwreck and sought the safety of the island,
they could slaughter the easily overcome host of Greeks,
and rescue their friends from the straits of the sea –
grievously misjudging the outcome. For when the god
had awarded the glory of the battle of the ships to the Greeks,   455
on that same day girding their bodies
in well-made bronze armour they leapt off their ships.
They encircled the whole island, so that our men
were clueless about where they might turn. Many times
they were struck by stones let loose from Greek hands, and arrows   460
falling on them from the string of the bow destroyed them.
Finally, the Greeks with a shout rushed them in a body
striking them, butchering the limbs of the wretched creatures,
until they had totally annihilated all their lives.
Xerxes groaned aloud beholding the depth of the disaster   465
for he had a seat with a full view of the whole force,
a high hill near the open sea.
Tearing his clothes and giving voice to a loud cry,
he gave orders at once to his foot forces,
dismissing them in a panicked rout. This disaster   470
along with the one I just now told you gives you cause to groan.

Atossa: Hateful fortune, how you have brought the plans of the
  Persians to nothing.
Bitter was the revenge my son found revealed for himself
in famous Athens, as if those of the barbarians whom
  Marathon
had previously destroyed were not enough.   475
For them my son thought to make retribution
but has drawn down such a multitude of calamities.
But tell me of the ships that escaped destruction,
where did you leave them? Do you know so as to give an accurate
  account?

Messenger: The commanders of the ships that survived   480
hurriedly in disorderly flight made sail with the wind.
The rest of the force was destroyed in the land of Boeotia,
some suffering from thirst despite being near a refreshing spring,
but others destitute, fatigued,
made their way to the land of the Phocians   485
and Doris, and the gulf of Melia, where
the Spercheus River irrigates the plain with refreshing water.
From there starving from lack of food
the plain of Achaea received us,
and the cities of Thessaly. There many died   490
from thirst and hunger, for we suffered from both of these.
Then we arrived in the land of Magnesia
and the country of Macedonia, and the ford of the Axius River,
and the reedy marsh of the Bolbe, and Mount Pangaeus
in the country of Edonia. But on that same night the god   495
awoke winter ahead of season, and froze all the stream
of sacred Strymon. Some who before this
had considered the gods of no account then prayed
with entreaties, kneeling in prostration to earth and heaven.
But when the entire army had ceased calling on the gods   500
they made their way across the frozen water.
And whoever of us started out before the rays
of the sun god were spread about found safety.
But when the radiant circle of the sun blazing with its rays
reached over the middle of the passage over the stream, melting
  the ice with its flame,
the men slipped in, one after the other. And fortunate   505
was he who quickly forfeited the breath of life.
As many of the rest who found safety and made their way

with great suffering through Thrace
escaped and reached the land of their hearths.   510
But they were few in number. So the city of the Persians
well may lament the beloved youth of the land.
This account is true. But I have left off speaking
of many of the evils that the god hurled down upon the Persians.

The Persian queen Atossa conjures up the spirit of her dead husband
Darius, father of Xerxes, after the Battle of Salamis. The Greek victory is
attributed to the *hybris* and sacrilege of the Persians punished by Zeus,
providing an important insight into the pious fears and religious mentality
of the Greeks. Darius refers to the Battle of Plataea, in the year following
Salamis, ascribing the victory to the Spartans: the Dorian spear (line 817).
Aeschylus, *The Persians*, 798–831:

Chorus of Persian elders: Won't all the army of barbarians
cross the Hellespont from Europe?

Darius: Few out of many, if – having seen events that have   800
just now happened – the oracles of the gods are believed,
for oracles are fulfilled, and not just some of them, while others
    are not.
And if this is true, he is persuaded by false hopes
in leaving behind in Greece a select force of the army.
They wait where the Asopus River with its streams waters   805
the plain, a blessed richness to the soil of Boeotia.
There it awaits for them to suffer the summit of their disasters,
payment for their *hybris* and their sacrilegious arrogance.
Arriving in Greece, they were not ashamed to carry off the images
of the gods and to burn the temples.   810
Altars were destroyed, and the statues of the gods
were wrenched right off their pedestals into utter destruction.
So having committed atrocities they will not escape a lesser
    suffering
than the ones that await them, and not yet
is the spring of their evils dry, but it still gurgles up.   815
For so great will be the clots of gore oozing
from the Dorian spear in the land of Plataea.
Heaps of corpses even to the third generation
will speak voiceless to the eyes of men that mortals
should not think presumptuously.   820
For *hybris* when it flowers forth bears fruits, a crop
of recklessness, from which is reaped a harvest of bitter tears.

Behold that such are the penalties for these things –
be mindful both of Athens and Greece,
let no one despising present fortune 825
lust after that of others, squandering great wealth.
Truly Zeus is a punisher
of arrogant thoughts, chastening with a heavy hand.

Admonish my son, who has received in these disasters a
caution
to think wisely, with well-spoken words of warning, 830
to cease offending against the gods with his arrogant impudence.

After the ghost of Darius returns to Hades, Xerxes himself appears on
stage, his robes torn in grief at the magnitude of his defeat. After the lines
given here, the chorus asks after various Persian commanders. The play
then ends in some fifty lines of weeping and mourning by Xerxes and the
Persian elders, Aeschylus stretching out Xerxes' grief to underscore the
Persian disaster, in contrast with the Greek, but especially Athenian,
triumph. Aeschylus, *The Persians*, 909–31:

Xerxes: Alas, wretched man I am, meeting
with an abominable fate that was completely unexpected. 910
How savagely has Fate fallen on the Persian race.
What might I yet suffer, wretched one?
The strength of my limbs is undone
as I look upon this chorus of ancient men.
Zeus, would that the doom of death 915
had covered me too
along with the departed men.

Chorus: Woe, king, for our mighty army
and for the great honour of the Persian name,
and for the beauty of the men 920
whom Fate has now cut off.

The land laments its native youth
slaughtered for Xerxes who gluts Hades
with Persians. For many men have gone to the house of Death,
masters at the bow, the flower of our country, 925
an entire thick multitude
of men has perished.
Alas, woe, for our trusted defence.
The country of Asia, king of the earth,

has terribly, terribly   930
been brought to its knees.

The Athenians after initial successes in Sicily had their fleet blockaded in
the great harbour of Syracuse in 413 BC. Their fleet had to break out or
face the destruction of the expedition. This is a classic description of a
naval battle. Thucydides, 7.70.3–8, 7.71.5:

(7.70.3) The sailors on both sides were very enthusiastic to sail in,
whenever this was ordered, and there was a great deal of counter-
manoeuvring by the helmsmen and rivalry among themselves. The
marines, whenever ship struck ship, took care that what was happening
on deck was not inferior to the skill shown elsewhere. Everyone, each in
his own position, was eager to appear the best. (7.70.4) Many ships
were coming into contact in a confined space, for most of these fought
in the smallest place ever, with both sides together falling little short of
200 ships, and ramming attacks were few, as there could be no backing
up or breaking the enemy's line, while collisions, as ship chanced to run
foul against ship either in flight or sailing against another ship, were
more frequent.

(7.70.5) While a ship was bearing down, the men on the decks used
great quantities of javelins, arrows and stones against it, and when the
ships met, the marines attempted to board the opposing ship, fighting
hand-to-hand. (7.70.6) It often happened that because of the narrowness
of the place a ship that had rammed another found itself being rammed,
and that two ships or sometimes even more had perforce become
entangled around one ship. The helmsmen had to organise defence
against these ships, and offence against those, and not one at a time, but
against many on all sides. The great noise arising from the clashing of
many ships simultaneously gave rise to consternation and caused the
shouted orders of the boatswains to be inaudible.

(7.70.7) For there was a great deal of calling out and shouting by the
helmsmen of both sides doing their job and arising from their zeal for
immediate victory, on the one side shouting to the Athenians they must
force their way out, and now as never before take fast hold of a safe
passage to their country, while on the other shouting to the Syracusans
and their allies that it would be glorious to stop the Athenians fleeing,
and if victorious to increase the fame of each man's country. (7.70.8)
Moreover the generals on each side, if they saw someone backing away
to the shore without being forced to do so, called upon the captains by
name and asked them, in the case of the Athenians, whether they were

retreating because they felt more at home on the most hostile shore than on the sea which they had gained possession of by great suffering, and in the case of the Syracusans if they were fleeing from the Athenians, who were clearly eager to flee in whatever way they could.

(7.71.5) The Syracusans and their allies having endured the naval battle for a long time routed the Athenians and manifestly prevailed over them, and with great shouting and cheering pursued them to the land.

Aristophanes describes the din accompanying the launching of Athens' warships, the *triremes*. Aristophanes, *Acharnians*, 544–54:

Chorus: With the launching
of three-hundred ships, the city would at once be full   545
of the uproar of soldiers, shouting around the ship commander,
the paying out of war wages, the gilding of figureheads of Pallas Athena,
noisy porticoes, the measuring out of grain,
wine skins, oarloops, bargaining over casks,
garlic, olives, nets of onions,   550
garlands for feasts, anchovies, flute-girls, black eyes,
the ship sheds with the planing of oar handles,
of ship bolts being hammered, holes hollowed out for oars,
of flutes, boatswains, whistles and pipes.

WAR MEMORIALS

It was common but not universal practice to bury the war dead on the battleground in a communal grave and pile up a huge mound of earth over them. The best example is, of course, the huge mound of earth at Marathon over the Athenian dead, but for the Athenians unlike the Spartans and some other states it was unusual to bury the war dead where they fell. The exact date of this war memorial on the island of Euboea and who it was for is unknown. The Euripus was the name of the strait of water that separated the island of Euboea from Boeotia on the mainland. Simonides, *Epigram*, 2:

In a cleft of Mount Dirphys we were vanquished
and this memorial mound has been heaped over us
near the Euripus strait at the expense of the city,
not without cause, for we forfeited lovely youth
meeting the savage cloud of battle.

An epigram to the fallen was inscribed on stone and placed on the burial mound of the Athenians at Marathon, 490 BC. Simonides, *Epigram*, 21:

> Fighting as the defenders of Greece the Athenians at Marathon
> levelled the strength of the golden-robed Persians.

Also with Marathon for its subject, this epigram epitomises Athenian fears: domination by the Persians would not have been simply a loss of political autonomy but slavery. Simonides, *Epigram*, 18:

> The sons of Athens annihilated the Persian army,
> keeping at bay grievous enslavement from their ancestral earth.

In 507 BC the Athenians defeated the Boeotians who had invaded and on the very same day then crossed from Athens over to the nearby city of Chalcis on Eretria, which had launched a synchronised attack on Athens with the Boeotians. Athens won both battles, the first victories of the democracy only recently established in 508 BC. Proud of this double success, the Athenians put the prisoners they had taken from Boeotia and Chalcis into chains. They ransomed them, and from 10 per cent of the proceeds dedicated a bronze four-horse chariot to Athena, martial and patron god of Athens. They also dedicated the iron chains as well; Herodotus 5.77 has the full story. Simonides, *Epigram*, 3:

> In iron chains the sons of Athens
> extinguished the *hybris* of the races of Boeotia and Chalcis
> taming them in the business of war;
> with a tenth of the ransom the Athenians dedicated these horses to
>   Athena.

These are the two most famous war memorial epigrams, the first applying to all the Peloponnesian Greeks who died at Thermopylae and the second to the Spartans alone. These epigrams were carved on stone slabs and placed on the earthen burial mounds of the dead. The second addresses the reader. Simonides, *Epigram*, 22, a, b:

> Once, in this place, 4,000 men
> from the Peloponnese fought 3 million men.

> Stranger, announce to the Spartans that we lie
> in this place obedient to their commands.

There was a prophecy that the Persians would not be defeated unless a Spartan king died. Leonidas willingly sacrificed his life at Thermopylae. Simonides, *Epigram*, 7:

Leonidas, King of Sparta with its wide plains,
famous are those who now concealed by the earth
died here with you, awaiting in war the prowess
of the many bows and the fleet-footed horses of the Persians.

Pericles spoke an elaborate oration over the dead, but Anacreon's four-line piece for the warrior Agathon is much more moving. Anacreon, *Epigram*, 100d:

The awesomely strong Agathon yielded his life for Abdera
and the entire city lamented at his funeral pyre,
for such a young man as this had never been slain
by blood-loving Ares in the vortex of horrible battle.

SIX

Philosophers and Doctors

That which was, always existed, and always will exist. For if it had a beginning, it is axiomatic that before it came into existence, nothing existed. Well then, if nothing existed, it's impossible that anything could come into existence out of nothing.

Melissus of Samos, Fragment 1.

Many of the first Greek philosophers came from Ionia, the west coast of what is now modern Turkey, where in the sixth century BC there was a flowering of contemplation and thought about the nature of the cosmos, the ordered universe and reality. Ionian thinkers such as Pythagoras and Xenophanes travelled to Italy and Sicily and stimulated philosophical thought there. Pythagoras himself wrote nothing, and most of the information about his philosophy comes from much later writers. All that can safely be said is that Pythagoras was greatly interested in mathematics, and (perhaps) the transmigration of the soul after death. It was only in the fifth century BC that philosophy moved on to wider concerns. Socrates, for example, started his 'career' as a natural philosopher and focused on the essence of the universe but then turned to a contemplation of wisdom and *arete* (virtue).

Herodotus would not be described as a philosopher. But in his *Histories* he shows a deep interest in moral maxims, and the rise and decline of human affairs. His portrait of Solon and Croesus is a classic example of this, as too is his account of Polycrates and his ring. As Croesus was about to be burned to death (he was saved by a miracle), he remembered what Solon had told him about the vagaries of human happiness. Similarly, poets such as Bacchylides and Pindar routinely combined praise of the subject of their victory ode with myth and moral adages. Aeschylus shows a very real awareness of what 'humanises' human beings, while Sophocles provides a more pessimistic view of his fellow mortals.

Socrates (469–399 BC) was, of course, the philosopher par excellence. His ideas are recorded by Plato and Xenophon in 'dialogues', records of conversations that Socrates had with his followers. Socrates wrote nothing himself, and so what is known about his ideas is what Plato and Xenophon chose to record. Socrates did not have the luxury of full-time speculation. He was the son of a stone sculptor and pursued the same craft. His mother was a midwife; perhaps this suggested to him the analogy that he was like a midwife, helping individuals 'give birth' to knowledge. He saw active service as a *hoplite* in the Peloponnesian War, in both 424 and 422 BC. Contemporary with him were the sophists, often itinerant, who taught a range of subjects for a fee; in the popular imagination they were associated particularly with the art of rhetoric, and making the weaker, unjust argument prevail. Socrates' main teaching method was to question, and he himself did not claim to 'know' anything. His main concern was with '*arete*' and whether it could be learned or taught.

Medicine could hardly be termed advanced in the classical Greek world. Heraclitus condemned doctors for causing as much pain as the original complaint. The Greeks of course suffered from a wide variety of ailments, and the frequency of battle led to many war wounds. A particularly fine Athenian vase shows Achilles bandaging his close friend Patroclus (see illustration 6.1). Unexpected were outbreaks of diseases such as the plague, which decimated the population of Athens in 429 BC and the following few years.

It was Hippocrates in the second half of the fifth century BC who placed medical practice on a firm basis. Numerous myths grew up around him, but there was a strong tradition that he separated philosophy and medicine, establishing the latter as an individual discipline, and evidence suggests that he considered that disease was affected by a person's way of life, and that an understanding of the whole body was necessary for any ailment affecting one part of it. Observation and diagnosis were key elements of the Hippocratic 'approach' to medicine. Hippocrates lived from about 460 to 390 BC, and he was a contemporary of Socrates. He was from the Aegean island of Cos, and like his father who trained him in medicine was an Asclepiad, a doctor whose patron was the healing god Asclepius (known in Latin as Aesculapius). There is a large body of writings attributed to Hippocrates, the so-called 'Hippocratic corpus' of sixty texts, but it is impossible that all of these writings are by him. Rather, they were probably produced by members of the school of medicine that he founded on Cos.

In the fourth century BC the professional practice of medical knowledge became more prevalent. But 'healing cults' that began to spread throughout the Greek world from 450 BC, reaching Athens in the 420s, increased in popularity. Sickness – and cure – were inexplicable to most people, and they turned to Asclepius for help. Asclepius was both the god of doctors and the god of healing by faith, and there was no competition between healing sanctuaries and medical practitioners. Asclepius had a renowned healing sanctuary at Epidaurus in southern Greece, which was famous all over the

Greek world, and pilgrims went there with a wide variety of medical complaints.

THE EARLY PHILOSOPHERS

Xenophanes of Colophon (570–480 BC) in Asia Minor left his city, probably after the Persian conquest of 545 BC, and spent sixty-seven years wandering in Sicily. He was critical of the anthropomorphic conception of the gods, and Homer and Hesiod's depiction of them as having human vices. Xenophanes, Fragments 12, 23, 27, 29:

(12) Homer and Hesiod have given voice to the greatest possible number of lawless deeds of the gods: theft, adultery and mutual deceit.

(23) One god exists, the greatest among both gods and men, not at all similar to mortals in body or thought.

(27) All things come from earth and all things return to earth at the end.

(29) As many things as come into existence and grow are earth and water.

Heraclitus of Ephesus (540–480 BC) was primarily interested in *logos*, which for him apparently meant discourse, thought and the order of the universe. He believed that everything was in a state of flux: one did not step in and out of the same river, because the water was flowing all the time. Heraclitus, Fragments 12, 27, 30, 35, 49, 49a, 89, 93, 97, 102, 135, 136:

(12) Those who step into the same rivers have different water continually flowing on them.

(27) When they are dead, things await men which are neither anticipated nor thought of.

(30) This cosmos, which is the same for all, was created neither by one of the gods nor by one of men, but it was always, and is, and will be, ever-living fire.

(35) For men who love wisdom it is necessary to enquire into very many things.

(49) One man is 10,000 to me, if he is the best.

(49a) In the same river, we both step in and step out, we are, and we are not.

(89) There is one common cosmos to those who are awake, but of those who sleep each turns to his own private cosmos.

(93) The lord Apollo whose oracle is at Delphi neither speaks plainly nor cryptically, but provides a sign.

(97) For dogs bark at those they do not know.

(102) To God everything is beautiful and good and just, but it is men who have distinguished some things as unjust, and some as just.

(135) The shortest route to fame is to become good.

(136) Souls that fall in battle are purer than those who die in sickness.

Epicharmus of Syracuse wrote between about 500 and 475 BC. He was an author of comedies, and his 'philosophy' consisted of various maxims and sayings of characters in his plays. Fragment 64 was the epigram on Epicharmus' grave. Epicharmus, Fragments 8, 48, 49, 64:

(8) The gods are winds, water, earth, sun, fire, the stars.

(48) The body is earth, but the mind is fire.

(49) Water, earth, breath and sun are the elements.

(64) I am a corpse: a corpse is excrement, and excrement is earth. If earth is a god, I am not a corpse, but a god.

Empedocles (*c.* 492–432 BC) of Acragas (modern Agrigento in Sicily) is chiefly interesting for his ideas about the reincarnation of the soul, and a cyclical history of the cosmos. Empedocles clearly enjoyed the status that his skill brought him (see 112). He was an expert in purifications, explaining why the sick flocked to him, seeking ritual prescriptions to 'purify' themselves of their diseases. Empedocles, Fragments 11, 112, 134:

(11) Idiots! For they have no long-term thoughts, since they believe that what did not exist previously comes into existence, or that something dies and is completely consumed.

(112) Friends, who live in the great town on the heights of the city, looking down on yellow Acragas, attending to good deeds, respectful harbours for strangers, inexperienced in wickedness, greetings: I go as an immortal god among you, no longer mortal, honoured by all, as is proper, crowned with ribbons and blooming garlands. When I come to them in their prosperous towns, to men and women, I am honoured, and they follow me, enquiring, in their tens of thousands, where is the path of profit, some wanting oracles, while some ask to hear some healing word for sicknesses of all sorts, long shot through with harsh pains.

(134) For he does not have the head of a man on a trunk of a body, nor do two branches shoot from his back, nor does he have feet, nor swift knees, nor any hairy genitalia, but he is Mind, sacred and beyond even a god's power to articulate, only itself, rushing throughout the entire cosmos with its swift thoughts.

TRUE HAPPINESS

Croesus thought that he was the happiest man alive, but Solon had different ideas: no one is truly happy until death, for no one ever knows what tomorrow will bring. Croesus scoffed at Solon's advice, but when he lost his empire and was facing death he remembered Solon's words. Herodotus' account is not historical as Solon and Croesus did not live at the same time. But the historical reality of the account is not what is important. Herodotus, here as elsewhere in his work (note also his account of Polycrates given below), is interested in wisdom and religious concepts: Who is happy? What is happiness? Can a man be too successful? An Athenian vase shows Croesus pouring a libation of wine to the gods on his own pyre (see illustration 6.2). Herodotus, 1.30.1–32.2, 32.4–5, 32.9, 33–34.1:

(1.30.1) Solon left Athens and visited Amasis in Egypt and Croesus at Sardis. And when he had arrived in Sardis, Croesus entertained him as a guest-friend in his palace. After this, on the third or fourth day, Croesus ordered his servants to give him a tour of the treasuries, and they pointed out to him how everything there was magnificent and rich. (1.30.2) When Solon had seen and inspected everything, Croesus at the first opportunity asked him, 'Athenian guest, many reports have come to us about you, because of your wisdom and your travels, and how in the pursuit of wisdom you have travelled and seen much of the earth. So now I am overwhelmed with curiosity to ask you if anyone, of all men you have seen, is more happy than the rest?'

(1.30.3) Croesus asked this anticipating that he was the happiest of all men. Solon did not flatter him but quite honestly replied, 'O King, an Athenian called Tellus.' (1.30.4) Croesus was flabbergasted at this statement and said in sharp retort, 'On what grounds do you judge that Tellus is the happiest?' Solon replied, 'Tellus' city was prosperous, and his children were handsome and virtuous, and he lived to see each of them have children and all of them surviving, and he had a good livelihood, as these things are reckoned among us, and ended his life in the most glorious way. (1.30.5) For in a battle at Eleusis between the Athenians and their neighbours he rushed into the fray, routed the enemy and died most bravely. The Athenians honoured him with a state funeral on the spot where he had fallen and honoured him greatly.'

(1.31.1) Now Solon aroused Croesus' interest by recounting the many ways in which Tellus was happy, so he asked whom he might have seen who was second after Tellus, thinking that at least he would surely be second. Solon answered, 'Cleobis and Biton'. (1.31.2) These men were of the race of Argives and had both sufficient means of livelihood, and they also had strength of body, as shown by the fact that both of them had carried off prizes in athletic contests, and this story also indicates this.

A festival of Hera was being celebrated by the Argives and it was really important that the mother of Cleobis and Biton be taken to the shrine in the ox-cart, but the oxen for it were in the fields and did not return in time. So these young men hindered by the lack of time harnessed themselves up to the yoke and dragged the cart, and their mother sat on the cart: they pulled it for five and forty stades, and arrived at the shrine. (1.31.3) When they had done this and were seen by all the assembled festival throng, they had an excellent conclusion to their lives: and the god showed in these men how it is better for a man to die than to live. For the Argive men crowding around congratulated the strength of the young men, and the Argive women the mother, for having such children. (1.31.4) The mother overcome with joy at the deed itself and what was said about it, standing in front of Hera's statue prayed that the goddess give her sons Cleobis and Biton, who had greatly honoured her, the greatest thing a man could have. (1.31.5) After this prayer the young men sacrificed and feasted, and went to sleep in the very same temple: but they never woke up but came to their end in this way. The Argives made statues of them because of their excellence and dedicated them at Delphi.

(1.32.1) Solon awarded the second prize for happiness to these two, and Croesus angrily replied, 'Athenian guest, is my prosperity, then, so worthless to you that you hold me as not worthy even to be compared to common men?' Solon answered, 'Croesus, I know that divinity is all-jealous and also troubles us, and you ask about mortal affairs. (1.32.2) For in the long span of our life one sees many things that one doesn't want to, and also suffers much. I define seventy years as the limit of a man's life. . . . (1.32.4) All the days of the seventy years add up to 26,250, and no single one of these days is absolutely similar to another day in what it brings. So in this way, Croesus, man is entirely subject to chance. (1.32.5) It appears to me that you are very wealthy and rule over many subjects. So on that question you ask me, I can't answer you until I hear that you have died happy. For he who has a vast fortune is not happier than one who has only enough for the day, unless good luck might wait upon him until his life draws to an end, prosperous in everything. Many men with heaps of money are unfortunate, and many with just enough are fortunate. . . . (1.32.9) We have to look at the conclusion of every matter, and how it will turn out. For there are many to whom divinity gives a taste of happiness, then overturns it utterly.'

(1.33) Solon said all this to Croesus who, however, wasn't impressed, and sent him away as someone of no consequence, thinking that Solon was stupid for disregarding present good fortune and telling him to look to the end of everything. (1.34.1) After Solon departed, a great divine nemesis overtook Croesus because, I suppose, he thought that he was the most happy of all men.

Herodotus goes on to relate the fall of Croesus' empire, including the famous enquiry to the Delphic oracle. Croesus did invade Persia, and was defeated, losing his empire. The Greeks of Asia Minor were now to swap one master, the Lydians, for another, the Persians, and so began a period of Persian–Greek interaction which only ended when Alexander the Great destroyed the Persian Empire. Croesus had tested all the oracular centres, and found Delphi and that of Amphiaraus, north of Athens, the most accurate, so he sent envoys to them with the following enquiry. Herodotus, 1.53.1–3:

(1.53.1) The Lydians who were to bring gifts to the oracles of Apollo at Delphi and of Amphiaraus were instructed by Croesus to ask the oracles whether Croesus should undertake a military expedition against Persia and if he should seek a military alliance. (1.53.2) When the Lydians came to the places Croesus had sent them to, they dedicated the gifts that they had brought, and they put their question to the oracles in these words: 'Croesus king of the Lydians and other peoples, considering that these places alone are oracles among men, has presented to you gifts worthy of your prophetic powers. Now he would like to ask you if he should lead an expedition against the Persians and if he should seek a military alliance with some other race.' (1.53.3) They put these questions, and at both of the oracles received the same answer, replying to Croesus that if he led an army against Persia he would destroy a mighty empire.

And so he did. Cyrus took Croesus' empire and founded the mighty Persian Empire, which was to so trouble the Greeks, and the conflict between them is in fact Herodotus' main theme: the struggle between the Greeks and the Persians and how the Greeks of the mainland defeated the Persians not once but twice (490, 480–479 BC). Cyrus relents of his purpose to burn Croesus alive but the pyre is too blazing to be put out; Croesus prays to Apollo, who sends a violent rain storm (on a clear day) to save him. When Croesus after his downfall sent messengers to remonstrate with Apollo about the oracle he had been given, he was told that a wise man would have asked for clarification, and also that he was being punished for the sins of one of his ancestors. The oracle's famous ambiguity was never so clear! Herodotus, 1.86.1–5:

(1.86.1) The Persians captured Sardis and Croesus was made a prisoner, having reigned for fourteen years and been besieged for fourteen days, and as prophesied he had destroyed a mighty empire – his own. The Persians captured him and led him into the presence of Cyrus. (1.86.2) Cyrus had constructed a great pyre, on which he placed Croesus, bound with shackles, as well as twice seven Lydian boys next to him: intending either to sacrifice them as a choice offering to some god of his, or wishing to fulfil a vow, or it may have been because he had learned that Croesus was god-fearing that he had set him on the pyre, wanting to know if one of the gods would rescue him from being burnt alive. (1.86.3) But at any rate, he did it. Croesus, standing on the pyre remembered, even in the midst of his misfortune, how what Solon said was divinely inspired, that no living man was happy. When he recalled this, he sighed, although until then he had been very quiet, and three times said the name 'Solon'.

(1.86.4) Cyrus heard him, and ordered his interpreters to ask Croesus who was this man he was calling on, and they came near the pyre and asked him. Croesus being asked kept silent for a while, then, as he was forced to do so, he replied: 'He is one whom I would have wished to talk to all the rulers, even if I had to pay a great deal of money.' This was a riddle to them, and again they questioned him about what he was saying. (1.86.5) They persisted and pestered him, so he said how Solon the Athenian had come to him, and seeing all his treasures had treated them with disdain, and what he said, and how everything had happened to him which that man had said, though Solon spoke rather not only to him but for all of humanity, especially those who considered themselves to be among the happy.

SOCRATES AND KNOWLEDGE: CAN VIRTUE BE TAUGHT?

Socrates is but a midwife bringing forth knowledge, like a baby, and with birth-pains. Plato, *Theaetetus*, 149b–151b:

Socrates: (149b) Consider the whole matter of midwives, and you'll have a better understanding of what I mean. For you know, I'm sure, that none of them attends a birth while she is still able to fall pregnant and have babies, but only those who are now unable to have babies are midwives.

Theaetetus: I'm well acquainted with that.

Socrates: The reason for this, they say, is the goddess Artemis, because she, a childless goddess, was allotted childbirth as her sphere of influence. For she did not ordain midwifery for barren women, (149c) because human nature is not strong enough to undertake a skill in which it is inexperienced. She gave this task to those who on account of their age did not bear children, honouring them for their similarity to herself.

Theaetetus: That's reasonable.

Socrates: So it's both likely, and necessary, that midwives rather than anyone else would know who was pregnant and who not?

Theaetetus: I'll give you that.

Socrates: (149d) And the midwives by giving drugs and incantations are able to bring on contractions and, if they choose, to make them less painful, and cause those who have difficulty in labour to give birth. They can also bring on miscarriages if they think it necessary.

Theaetetus: These things are as you say.

Socrates: So then, have you also perceived this about the midwives, that they are the cleverest matchmakers, since they are all-knowing concerning what union it is necessary to make with what man to bear the best possible children?

Theaetetus: I'm not at all acquainted with that.

Socrates: (149e) Rest assured, they think more of this ability than that of cutting the umbilical cord. Consider this. Do you think that to the same science as the care and harvesting of the crops of the earth, or to another, belongs the knowledge regarding what plants and seed should be sown in what soil?

Theaetetus: Not a different science, but the same.

Socrates: And for a woman, dear friend, do you think that there is one science of sowing, and one for gathering in the harvest?

Theaetetus: I wouldn't have thought so.

Socrates: (150a) No. But because the wrongful and unskilled bringing together of men and women is given the name of pandering, the midwives, because they are respectable women, refrain from matchmaking, afraid that they will fall under the accusation of pandering. However, for true midwives alone it is fitting and proper to be a matchmaker.

Theaetetus: That seems to be the case.

Socrates: Therefore, the work of the midwives is of such import, but their work is less important than my work. For it does not happen that women sometimes bring forth phantoms, (150b) but at other times real children, which it is not easy to differentiate between. For if it did happen, the most significant and honoured aspect of the work of the midwives would be in deciding which children were real and which phantoms. Would you agree?

Theaetetus: Indeed, I do.

Socrates: My skill of midwifery encompasses the same sorts of things as theirs, but the difference is that I act as a midwife to men not women, and I have oversight over their souls when they give birth, not bodies. But the most significant aspect of my skill is that it can make trial (150c) – in every way – of whether the mind of a young man is giving birth to a phantom, a falsehood or to fruitful and veracious offspring. For this applies to me as to the midwives: I am barren of wisdom, and many have disparaged me on this ground, that I cross-examine others, but myself give no answers to anything because I have no wisdom, and they criticise me correctly. And this is the case because the god forces me to act as a midwife, but prevents me from giving birth. So I am myself not at all a wise person.

(150d) Nor do I possess any wise invention as offspring sprung from my soul. But of those who congregate around me, at first some appear totally ignorant, yet all of them, as our association develops, at least those to whom the god permits this, improve astonishingly in both their own estimation and in that of others. It is manifest that this happens, not because they have ever yet learned anything from me, but as they themselves find within themselves many good qualities they bring these to light. However, the god and I are responsible for the midwifery. This is the proof: many who are ignorant of this and consider themselves responsible for their improvement hold me in contempt, (150e) and depart from me, either of their own initiative or convinced by others to do so, before they should have. Having left me, from that time on they have miscarried through evil acquaintance and they have reared badly and destroyed the offspring delivered by me. They have believed falsehoods and phantoms to be of more consequence than the truth, and finally it becomes obvious both to themselves and to others that they were devoid of intellect. One of these is (151a) Aristides, son of Lysimachus, and there were many others as well. Such men, when they return to me earnestly entreating me to let them associate with me again, some my inner voice (*daemon*) forbids me to associate with, but others it permits me, and these again improve. Those who associate with me suffer in this process the same as women in childbirth. They suffer the pains of childbirth and are overcome with distress, night and day, more so than the women. My skill is able to arouse this labour pang, and to still it. These men indeed experience this. (151b) When in some cases, Theaetetus, they don't seem to me to be pregnant, knowing that they don't need me, with unqualified goodwill I act as matchmaker and with the god directing me I guess quite competently with whom they can associate for their own advantage. I have directed many to Prodicus [a sophist], and many to other wise and inspired men.

Meno asks what might seem to be an easy question, 'Socrates, can you tell me whether virtue can be taught?' This leads on to a discussion about what constitutes virtue (*arete*). Meno was from Thessaly and was visiting Athens; his friend Aristippus was also from Thessaly, from the city of Larissa. Gorgias was a leading sophist, from Sicily; he visited Athens in 427 BC, and his style of oratory was very influential there (70b). Plato, *Meno*, 70a–71c, 71e–72d:

Meno: (70a) Socrates, can you tell me whether virtue can be taught? Or is it unteachable and something one must practise? Or, if neither acquired by practice or learning, whether it is naturally inherent in men? Or is it gained in some other way?

Socrates: Meno, in ancient times the Thessalians were renowned and admired among the Greeks for their horse-riding and their wealth, (70b) but now it appears to me for wisdom also, and not least of all the citizens of Larissa, where your friend Aristippus comes from. The reason for this is Gorgias, for when he went to Larissa he captivated the leading members of the Aleuadae family with a passion for wisdom, and among them your lover Aristippus, as well as other prominent Thessalians. Moreover he has given you this habit, to answer fearlessly and magnificently whatever question is put to you, as is appropriate for those who are knowledgeable, (70c) since he himself sets the precedent, offering himself to be questioned by any of the Greeks who wishes to do so, on any point, and he doesn't fail to give an answer to everyone.

But here in Athens, dear Meno, the opposite state of affairs applies. (71a) A drought, as it were, of wisdom has occurred, and it appears as if wisdom has departed from our country and gone to yours. If at any rate you wanted to put that question to someone here in Athens, he would definitely laugh and reply, 'Stranger, you must consider me to be particularly blessed, to know whether virtue can be taught or in what way it arises. I myself am so lacking in knowledge as to whether or not virtue can be taught, that I do not happen to at all know what this thing itself, virtue, actually is.'

(71b) And I myself, Meno, am in the same quandary, sharing the poverty of my fellow citizens about this matter. I reproach myself that I am totally without comprehension of what virtue is. And if I don't know what something is, how can I know what sort of thing it is? Or does it seem possible to you that someone who has absolutely no idea of who Meno is, can know whether he is good-looking or wealthy or well born, or is the opposite of these? Do you think that this is possible?

Meno: Not I, at any rate. But is it true Socrates that you don't even know what virtue is, (71c) and that we are to take home this report about you?

Socrates: Not only that, friend, but also that in my opinion I never yet met anyone who did know.

Meno: (71e) But it is not difficult to define virtue, Socrates. First, if you wish to define the virtue of a man, it's easy: the virtue of a man lies in managing the affairs of the city competently, and doing so for the benefit of his friends and to the detriment of his enemies, and being cautious not to suffer any wrongs himself. Or if you wish, the virtue of a woman is easily described: it is necessary for her to manage the household capably, looking after the property inside the house, and being subject to her husband. A child has another virtue, one for the female and one for the male, and there is another for the elderly man, and one, if you will, for the free, and one for slaves. (72a) There are a great many other types of virtue as well, so that one cannot be in any sort of perplexity to say what virtue is. For according to each action and age, with regard to every deed, there is a virtue for each of us. And the same would hold true, I suppose, for vice.

Socrates: I appear to be extremely fortunate, Meno: in seeking one virtue I have uncovered a swarm of virtues in your care. Yet, Meno, to pursue this analogy of the swarm, (72b) if I should ask you about the nature of the bee, and what exactly it is, and you replied that there were many different kinds of bees, what would you say to me if I were to ask you, 'Do you say it is in being bees that there are many and various kinds of bees, different from each other, or is the difference of some other kind, such as either in beauty or size or some other characteristic?' Tell me, what would you reply to such a question?

Meno: This: that they do not differ, as bees, from one to another.

Socrates: (72c) So if I then said, 'Well then, this is just what I want you to tell me, Meno: in what don't they differ but are all the same? What would you say this is?' You would have something to say about this, wouldn't you?

Meno: I would.

Socrates: And so too about the virtues. Even if they are many and varied, yet in some way they all have the same characteristic by reason of which they are virtues, and one which it would be a good idea to keep an eye on by someone answering the question about what virtue really is. (72d) Do you understand what I am saying?

Meno: I think I understand, but I don't yet have the grasp of the question that I would like to have.

After a long discussion, it is agreed that virtue is not learned; Meno is no longer confident about defining virtue. Plato, *Meno*, 99e, 100b:

Socrates: (99e) Now if in our discussion everything we have enquired into and said is correct, then virtue would neither be innate nor learned, but is granted by divine grace, without understanding, in those who receive it. . . . (100b) But we won't know this for sure until, before asking in what way man acquires virtue, we attempt to find out what virtue is, in and by itself. Now it's time for me to go. . . .

SOCRATES PARODIED

In Aristophanes' *Clouds* (produced in 423 BC, and subsequently revised), Socrates and the new learning of the second half of the fifth century BC are satirised. There were sophists who taught how to make the 'weaker' argument the 'stronger'. The whole of the *Clouds* is a brilliant parody of the 'new learning' (ironically, Socrates was not a sophist), as well as making fun of the natural philosophers who speculated on the nature of the cosmos (one of whom was Thales, line 180). Socrates refers to the *Clouds* in his own defence speech, and his execution in 399 BC on a charge of corrupting Athens' youth shows that while Aristophanes is simply making fun of Socrates and the other new thinkers, traditionalists were concerned about the new ideas and the way they challenged traditional notions, especially concerning religion.

Strepsiades' son will not enter Socrates' school to learn so his father does so, to find out how to get out of paying his debts. (Socrates in fact did not have an academy or school.) Strepsiades has been up all night worried by his debts, and now must wake his son and reveal his plan to send him to Socrates' school to learn how to make the unjust argument win. There is a play here on the word 'compass', which was colloquial language of the street for a homosexual: Socrates 'picked up a compass', stole his cloak and sold it to provide dinner for the students (line 179). Strepsiades refers to the crushing of the revolt of the island of Euboea in 446 BC (line 213). Aristophanes, *Clouds*, 75–216:

Strepsiades: So, now I've been thinking all night 75
and I've found one road out, a marvellously divine road,
and if I can persuade this boy here, I'll be saved.
But first, I need to wake him up.
Now what would be the nicest way to rouse him? How?
Pheidippides, dear little Pheidippidy. 80

Pheidippides: What is it, Dad?

Strepsiades: Kiss me. Give me your right hand.

Pheidippides: There. What is it?

Strepsiades: Tell me, you do love me?

Pheidippides: Yes, by this statue of Poseidon here, god of horses.

Strepsiades: Don't give me any of that god of horses stuff!
For this god is the reason for all my problems. 85
But if you love me from the bottom of your heart,
son, obey me.

Pheidippides: What should I obey you about?

Strepsiades: Change your way of life as quickly as possible,
and go and learn what I advise you to.

Pheidippides: Tell me, what are you ordering me to do?

Strepsiades: Will you obey?

Pheidippides: I'll obey, by Dionysus. 90

Strepsiades: Now, look over there.
Do you see that little door and that little house?

Pheidippides: I see. So what exactly is it, Dad?

Strepsiades: It is a Think-tank for clever minds.
Men live in there who argue that the sky 95
is an oven, and this oven surrounds us,
and we are the coals for the oven.
These men teach you, if you give them money,
how to win an argument, whether your case is just or unjust.

Pheidippides: Who are these men?

Strepsiades: I don't know the precise term. 100
Meditative thinkers; fine, good men.

Pheidippides: Uggh! A good-for-nothing lot, I know that much.
You're talking about charlatans, pale-faced, barefoot,
like that evil-genius Socrates and his friend Chaerephon.

Strepsiades: Hey, steady on, be quiet. Don't talk like a child.   105
But if you care about your father having something to eat,
become one of these men, and give up the horses.

Pheidippides: No, by Dionysus, not even if you were to
    give me
the pheasants which Leogoras breeds.

Strepsiades: Come on, I'm entreating you,   110
dearest of all men to me, go and learn!

Pheidippides: And what will I learn for you?

Strepsiades: It's said that they have both arguments in there,
the Better, whatever it is, and the Worse.
One of these arguments, the Worse,
it's said, can argue and win an unjust case.   115
So if you would learn this unjust argument for me,
then any of the debts I've got because of you
I wouldn't have to pay back, not a penny of them to anyone.

Pheidippides: I won't obey you. For I couldn't stand the other horse
    riders
seeing my suntan all faded away.   120

Strepsiades: Then, by Demeter, you won't eat any of my food,
not you, nor your chariot horse nor your pedigree!
I'll throw you out of the house and you can go to hell!

Pheidippides: But my Uncle Megacles won't let me be horseless.
I'm going inside, and I don't give a damn about you!   125

Strepsiades: But I'm not going to take this fall lying down,
but with a prayer to the gods, going to the Think-tank,
I'll get an education myself.
But how am I, an old man, forgetful and stupid,
to learn the finer points of complex arguments?   130
But I've got to go. Why do I keep loitering about,
why don't I knock on the door? Boy, little boy!

Student: Go to hell! Who's knocking on the door?

Strepsiades: Strepsiades, son of Pheidon, from the *deme*
    Cicynna.

Student: A moron, by Zeus, who in such a way   135
and without any consideration kicked the door so hard
he caused a newly discovered thought to miscarry.

Strepsiades: Forgive me, for I live a long way out in the country.
But do tell me about the thing that's miscarried.

Student: It's not permitted to tell anyone but the students.   140

Strepsiades: Then tell me, you've nothing to worry about:
for I've come here as a student of the Think-tank.

Student: I'll tell you, but you have to consider these things sacred
    mysteries.
Just now Socrates asked Chaerephon
how many of its own feet a flea could jump,   145
because one, biting Chaerephon's eyebrow,
then jumped onto Socrates' head.

Strepsiades: How did he measure this?

Student: Extremely cleverly.
He melted wax, then taking the flea
he dipped both of its feet in the wax,   150
and when the wax cooled, the flea had Persian slippers around it.
He took these off the flea and measured the distance.

Strepsiades: Zeus the King, what a subtle mind!

Student: What would you say if you heard of another idea of
    Socrates?

Strepsiades: What idea? I beg you, tell me.   155

Student: Chaerephon asked him
what opinion he had about whether gnats
sing through the mouth or through their bum.

Strepsiades: What did Socrates have to say about the gnat?

Student: He replied that the gut of the gnat   160
is narrow, and that the air goes through this narrow place
with violent force straight to the rump:
then the anus, attached to this narrow tube,
makes a noise because of the force of the wind.

Strepsiades: So the anus of gnats is a trumpet.   165
Thrice-blessed man, for such gut examination!

He'd easily avoid conviction in a lawsuit
when he has such information about the gnat's guts.

Student: Earlier on he had a great idea snatched away – by a lizard.

Strepsiades: In what way? Tell me.   170

Student: He was doing some investigation into the paths
and orbits of the moon, and when he was gaping upwards
a lizard on the roof crapped on him in the dark.

Strepsiades: That makes me laugh, a lizard crapping on Socrates.

Student: And last night there wasn't any dinner for us.   175

Strepsiades: My, my. So how did he manage to get you something to eat?

Student: Over the table he sprinkled a thin layer of ash,
as if he was going to draw a geometrical problem on it,
then he bent a spit, then picked up a 'compass' from the wrestling school
    and stole his cloak.

Strepsiades: Then why do we marvel at the great philosopher Thales? 180
Quickly, open up, open up the Think-tank
and show this Socrates to me,
for I must learn. Open up the door!
[Seeing the students.] By Heracles, what country do these creatures come from?

Student: Why are you amazed? What do they seem to look like
    to you?   185

Strepsiades: Like the Spartans from Pylus who are in prison.
But those there, why are they looking into the ground?

Student: They are seeking what's under the earth.

Strepsiades: Ah, they're hunting for truffles.
But don't worry about that any longer
because I know where there are large delicious ones.   190
And what are these ones doing, all bent over like that?

Student: They are groping about in the darkness of hell.

Strepsiades: Then why are their backsides looking up into the sky?

Student: The backside is learning astronomy of its own accord.
But inside, students, don't let Socrates find you outside.   195

Strepsiades: Not yet, not yet. But let them stay, so that
I can share a little problem of my own with them.

Student: But it is not allowed that they should spend
much time outside in the open air.

Strepsiades: By the gods, what are these things here? Tell me.   200

Student: This one here is for astronomy.

Strepsiades: And this one here?

Student: Geometry.

Strepsiades: What's that good for?

Student: To measure out land.

Strepsiades: Do you mean land for colonists?

Student: No, for land generally.

Strepsiades: What you're saying is so clever! It has universal applicability
and usefulness.   205

Student: Here is a map of the entire world for you. Do you see it? Here's
Athens.

Strepsiades: What are you talking about? I don't believe you,
because I can't see the jurors sitting on their benches.

Student: This really is Attica.

Strepsiades: Then where are the men of Cicynna, my fellow villagers? 210

Student: They're in that part. And Euboea, as you can see,
is stretched out here over a long distance.

Strepsiades: I know. For we and Pericles stretched it out.
But where is Sparta?

Student: Where? Here.

Strepsiades: How near us! Change your minds about this,   215
and move it much further away from us!

SOCRATES ON TRIAL

Socrates was put on trial in 399 BC and put to death (by drinking hemlock).
He notes at his trial that he was seventy and had never been involved in a
lawsuit before. His defence as reported in Plato's *Apology* is important for
revealing his approach to his teaching: he always represented himself as
only being wise in realising how ignorant he was. Aristophanes' *Clouds* is
referred to in (19c). Plato, *Apology*, 19a–20c:

(19a) Let us resume from the beginning, with the nature of the accusation that has caused my unpopularity, (19b) which Meletus relied on when he brought this lawsuit against me. Well, then, what did the critics, those who caused my unpopularity, say to bring it about? So I am compelled to read out the affidavit as if they were plaintiffs: 'Socrates is a wrongdoer and a busy-body, examining what is under the earth and in the heavens, and makes the weaker argument prevail, and teaches others these very things.' (19c) It's something of that sort. You yourselves saw these things in the comedy by Aristophanes, where a Socrates goes swinging about, saying that he was walking on air, and blabbering a lot of nonsense, about which I know nothing, neither much nor little. And I say this, not to cast aspersions on such knowledge, in case someone is wise about such things (may I never be accused by Meletus of such a thing), but because, men of Athens, I have no interest in such matters. (19d) And I present the majority of you as witnesses to what I have said, and I call upon you both to inform and speak to each other, as many of you who have ever heard me in conversation, and there are many such among you who have. Tell each other if any of you ever heard me talking – at length or briefly – about such things. And you'll realise from this that all the other things that people say about me are the same.

For none of these things are true; and if you have heard from someone that I undertake to educate people and do so for money, (19e) that also isn't true. It strikes me as wonderful if someone is able to teach people, as do Gorgias of Leontini and Prodicus of Ceos and Hippias of Elis. For each of these is able to go into any city and persuade the young men, who are able to associate with whomever of their own citizens they please, at no cost, (20a) to desert their friends, associate with these men and to pay money to be their pupils and be thankful for the privilege. And I've heard there's another wise man, from Paros, here in town. For I chanced to meet Callias, the son of Hipponicus, a man who has spent more money on sophists than everybody else put together, so I asked him (for he has two sons), 'Callias,' I said, 'if your sons had been colts or calves, we would find and hire a trainer for them, (20b) who would make them fine and good in the qualities appropriate for them, and he would be either a horse-trainer or a farmer. Now since your sons are human whom do you have in mind to engage as their supervisor? Who is experienced in the qualities of the man and citizen? For I suppose that you have considered this, given that you have two sons. Is there someone like this, or not?'

'Certainly,' he said. 'Who is he, where does he come from, and how much does he charge?' I asked. 'Evenus from Paros,' he replied, 'and he charges five *minas*, Socrates.' And I said Evanus was blessed, (20c) if he really possessed this skill and taught for such a reasonable sum. I myself, if I understood such things, would pride myself on this and put my nose in the air, but, men of Athens, I don't understand them.'

THE NATURE OF MAN

There were various myths of Prometheus, a titan (giant) who disagreed with Zeus' plans to annihilate humanity and to replace it with a superior race. Prometheus, pitying humanity, gave it various gifts. Zeus, angered, punished him by having him bound to a rock (hence the title of Aeschylus' play). Arts, crafts, civilisation and urbanisation distinguish humanity from the beasts. Aeschylus, *Prometheus Bound*, 447–69, 476–83:

Prometheus: At first mortals saw but lacked discernment,
they heard but did not distinguish sounds, but all the length
of their days resembling the shapes in dreams
they confused everything randomly. They knew not brick-built   450
houses facing the sun, nor any woodwork:
they dwelt like little ants underground
in the nooks of caves not lit by sunlight.
They had no secure means of knowing the precise beginning of winter
nor of flowering spring nor of summer bowed down with fruits,   455
but lacking in knowledge they carried out all their enterprises,
until I taught them the risings and the settings
of the stars – a complex art.
Moreover numbers, the principal of sciences,
I invented for them, and the combinations of letters   460
providing a means for remembering everything, and the mother of
   the Muses' art.
I first harnessed under a yoke the wild beasts,
enslaving them to both the collar of the yoke and the saddle
so that they might relieve men of the heaviest burdens,
and I harnessed horses to the chariot and made them   465
obedient to the rein, an adornment of luxury and wealth.
It was no one but me that discovered
the sail-winged ocean-wandering wagons of the sailor.
Wretched as I am it was me who revealed such inventions for
   mortals.   469

Hear the rest and you'll be even more amazed   476
at the sorts of skills and crafts that I devised.
The most important one is that if someone fell sick

there was no cure, no special diet,
no ointment, no tonics. But for want of drugs				480
they wasted away until I showed them
how to blend soothing remedies,
with which they now ward off all sicknesses.

There follows a section in which Prometheus describes how he gave mortals
the art of prophecy, and then he sums up his gifts. Aeschylus, *Prometheus
Bound*, 505–6:

Learn the sum of everything in a brief sentence:				505
all the skills man has came from Prometheus.

The ancient Greeks were conscious of the uniqueness of the human
being. Sophocles, *Antigone*, 332–71:

There is much that is awesome
but nothing more so than man,
who traverses over the grey sea
blown by the winter wind,						335
cleaving through
the surging waves which engulf him;
and the first of the gods, untiring
Mother Earth, man wears away,
his ploughs furrowing year after year,				340
with his breed of horses ripping up the soil.

He ensnares the witless race
of birds, the tribes
of the wild creatures he captures
and the marine life of the ocean					345
in the woven meshes of the net:
man the thinker, cogitating;
he masters with his devices
the wild beast
that haunts the mountains, binding				350
the shaggy-maned horse and the untiring bull
of the mountains
around the back of the neck
with a yoke.

Speech and thought swift as the wind he has learned			355
and the temperament that allows cities

to be ruled by law, and how to avoid
being unsheltered in the inhospitable hills
and the watery shafts of storms:
truly a genius. He equips himself   360
to meet all future outcomes. Hades alone
proves the inescapable,
but he has procured cures
from impossible sicknesses.

Skilful beyond expectation   365
are the devices of his art –
sometimes to evil, sometimes to good
he proceeds. If he observes the laws of the earth
and the justice the gods have sworn to impose
he is honoured in his city. But without a city   370
is he whom wickedness attends because of his audacity.

Pindar praises the powers of the intellect. Pindar, *Nemean Victory Ode,*
1.25–8:

Different men have different skills: it's vital to make your way
    along straight paths, striving with the gifts you've been given.   25
Strength gets results through action,
and the intellect through cogitations
for those attended by the innate ability to foresee into the future.

Sophocles posited a very pessimistic view not just of old age but of life in
general in a play about the end of Oedipus, probably the most wretched of
creatures in Greek mythology, exposed as a baby on a hillside, murdering
his father, sleeping unknown with his mother and having children by her
and ending his life as a fugitive after he has blinded himself. Here the
chorus of old Athenian men sings. Sophocles, *Oedipus at Colonus,*
1211–38:

That man who yearns
to live for a longer time
dissatisfied with his moderate portion
harbours – it's plain to me –
a delusion. For the long   1215
days ordain many things
closer to grief
and one cannot see where any pleasure lies

for someone who falls into a longer
than necessary length of life. The deliverer who visits all and
   sundry,   1220
the doom of Hades, shows up
with no strumming of the lyre, no singing
and dancing, no wedding hymns – and death comes as the end.
Not to be born wins out over everything by any reckoning.
But once one has seen the light of day   1225
the next best thing is to return
as quickly as possible
to where one came from.
While youth which bears
empty-headed thoughtlessness is present,   1230
what greatly grievous calamity
is far distant? What trouble
isn't there? Murders, factions,
strife, battles,
and envy. Despised old age falls to one's lot   1235
last of all, powerless, unsociable,
friendless, where evil of evils
live all together with us.

Sophocles, *Tyro*, 664:

Old age and the wasting effects of time teaches everything.

Bacchylides, Fragment 25:

But Divinity has given to only a handful of mortals
that all their days they act to advantage
and arrive at old age with temples grey
without having met with anguish.

'TRY NOT TO BE WORRIED' AND OTHER PRACTICAL ADVICE

Bacchylides provides advice found in many cultures: worry can't change
anything. But, as Pindar notes below, action can. Bacchylides,
Processionals, Fragments 11–12:

One road sign, one road to happiness for mortals:
if one is able to spend life with an unbroken heart;
the person whose mind is preoccupied

with a thousand worries
through night and day   5
his heart ever wounded
for the sake of the future
has fruitless grief.

Pindar's maxim on the need to attempt in order to gain could perhaps be translated as: 'You've got to be in it to win it.' Pindar, *Isthmian Victory Ode*, 4.30:

For those who don't try to do anything, there is the obscurity of silence.

Next to nothing survives of the work of the women poets Corinna, Praxilla and Telesilla, though Sappho is better represented. Praxilla here provides advice on choosing the company one keeps. Praxilla, 749:

Stay away from base men, knowing that the base have little goodwill.

One of Pindar's best-known maxims concerns accepting our humanity and doing what we can with the means put at our disposal. Pindar, *Pythian Victory Ode*, 3.61–2:

Do not, my beloved soul, aim for the life of the immortal gods
but use to the full the gifts within your power.

Pindar, *Isthmian Victory Ode*, 8.15a:

A man needs to keep his hope high.

Pindar advised not to share one's troubles, but to show only the prosperous side of one's affairs. Pindar, *Hymn*, 42:

Do not reveal to strangers the labour with which
we are burdened. This at least I will advise you:
it's important to display our share
of the beautiful and delightful before all the people,
but if any god-sent insufferable calamity
chances upon men, it is best to conceal this in the dark.

Sophocles, *The Mysians*, 410:

No one is free of trouble, but whoever has the fewest is the most blessed.

Sophocles, Fragment 948:
  For hope is the nurturer of most mortals.

Bacchylides, Fragment 24:

  Mortals do not have free choice
  either of wealth or inexorable Ares
  or all-consuming civil disorder,
  but Destiny giver of all blessings throws a cloud
  now over this land, now over another.

LIFE'S KNOTTY PROBLEMS

Whoever undid the Gordian knot would rule Asia, so went the prophecy. The Gordian knot attached a wagon to a wooden yoke and stood in the city of Gordium, in Phrygia in Asia Minor, modern Turkey. Alexander in 333 BC couldn't see how to undo the knot, and was afraid that if he failed to do so there would be political repercussions, as it would mean that he was not to be the ruler of Asia. As with many of life's taxing problems, the solution was to take a broad perspective and tackle the issue from a new angle. Arrian, *The Expedition of Alexander*, 2.3.6–8:

  (2.3.6) There was a legend that whoever untied the knot of the wagon's yoke would rule Asia. (2.3.7) The knot was made from cornel tree bark and neither the end nor the beginning of the rope was visible. Alexander was perplexed as to how he could loosen the knot, but he didn't want to leave it knotted, in case this caused a disturbance among the people. Some say that he struck it with his sword and cut the knot, and that he said he had undone it. The historian Aristobulus writes that he drew out the pole peg, which was the bolt going right through the pole, holding the knot together, and so took the yoke from the pole. (2.3.8) At any rate I am unable to state certainly the method which he actually used to undo the knot. But he and those with him left the wagon as if the prophecy about the loosing of the knot had come to pass. During that night, there was thunder and lightning, a further confirmation from heaven, and on the next day Alexander sacrificed to whichever gods had shown him these signs and the means to untie the knot.

HIPPOCRATES, FATHER OF MEDICINE, AND HIS OATH

Prior to and even after Hippocrates, Greek doctors did not always enjoy a good reputation, as Heraclitus, writing in about 500 BC at Ephesus, makes clear. A vase that shows a doctor treating a man's arm has the patient 'backing-off' and grimacing (see illustration 6.3). Heraclitus, Fragment 58:

> Doctors cutting, burning, grossly tormenting the sick in every way demand payment from the ill, though they do not deserve it as they cause the same pains as the illness.

In the *Regimen in Health*, one of the medical writings attributed to Hippocrates, a surprisingly modern 'holistic' approach to life is evident. Hippocrates(?), *Regimen in Health*, 1.2–3:

> (1.2) It is necessary to make the regimen suit age, season, habit, environment and physique, to counteract the prevailing heat or cold. For in this way the best health will be enjoyed. (1.3) It is necessary to walk quickly in winter, and slowly in summer, unless walking in the burning heat. Overweight people need to walk faster, and thin people in a rather relaxed way.

Plato also records the Hippocratic notion that the nature of the whole body needs to be understood for one part of that body also to be understood. Plato, *Phaedrus*, 270c:

> *Socrates:* Now do you think that one can gain any useful knowledge of the nature of the soul unless you know something about the nature of the man as a whole?
>
> *Phaedrus:* If Hippocrates the Asclepiad can be believed, it is not possible to understand the nature of the body with any other method.
>
> *Socrates:* He speaks correctly, my friend.

It is not clear that this is the actual oath which Hippocrates had his students swear when he accepted them into his school (for a fee), but the 'Hippocratic Oath' surely reflects his concerns as a medical practitioner. Several areas are covered which are still relevant for the practice of medicine, and the oath provides against the sexual exploitation of patients and deals with professional as opposed to irresponsible care of patients.

> I swear by Apollo the doctor and Asclepius and Health and Panacea and all the gods and goddesses, making them my witnesses, that I will abide by this oath and this covenant as far as it is within my ability and judgement: to consider the one who taught me this skill as equal to my

parents, to hold my life in common with his, when he is in need of money to share mine with him, to hold his sons to be the same as brothers, and to teach them this skill, if they desire to learn it, without fee or covenant, and to provide precepts, lectures and all other forms of learning to my own sons and those of my teacher and to indentured students who have sworn the doctor's oath, but to no one else.

I will employ treatments to assist the sick according to my ability and judgement, but will abstain from injury and wrongdoing. Nor will I give a deadly drug to anyone who requests it, nor will I suggest such a course of action. Similarly, I will not give a woman a pessary for an abortion. But I will keep both pure and holy both my life and my skill. I will not use the knife on anyone, not even those suffering from the stone, but will leave this to men skilled in this art.

Into whatever houses I go, I will enter to assist the sick, abstain from all intentional wrongdoing and harm, and of all other things especially from sexual abuse of the bodies of women and men, both free and slave.

Whatever I might see or hear in the course of my treating the sick, and even apart from this, in my dealings with men, I will keep silent about, considering such matters to be sacred secrets.

So if I abide by this oath, and not break it, may I gain a reputation for my way of life and skill among all men for all time. But if I transgress and perjure myself, may the opposite happen.

THE GREAT PLAGUE AT ATHENS

The great plague at Athens, which raged for several years from 429 BC, was made worse by the fact that the Athenians had crowded into the city as the Spartans were ravaging the countryside at the beginning of the campaign season (war between Athens and Sparta had broken out in 431 BC). People were even living in temples due to lack of space. Pericles himself died of the plague in 429 BC. The 'Great Plague' at Athens has fascinated medical writers and doctors ever since, with controversy about exactly what it was continuing to this day. Thucydides, 2.49.1–8, 51.4–6, 52.2–53.4:

(2.49.1) This year, as all agreed, was particularly disease-free as far as other illnesses were concerned. If people did suffer from other diseases, all finished with this one. (2.49.2) Others from no obvious cause, but suddenly while they were enjoying good health were seized with an acute head fever, and redness and inflammation of the eyes, and internally both the throat and the tongue immediately became bloody and their breath unnatural and foul. (2.49.3) Then sneezing and hoarseness arose after these symptoms, and not much later the disease descended to the chest, with violent coughing. And when it reached the stomach, it upset it and vomiting of every kind of bile named by doctors ensued, (2.49.4) and this was accompanied by acute pain, and in the majority of cases an ineffectual retching occurred which produced violent spasms, which stopped soon after for some, but continued long after for others. (2.49.5) The body's exterior was not very warm to the touch, nor pale, but reddish, livid and had broken out into small blisters and sores. But internally the body burned so fiercely that the sufferers could not bear to wear even the lightest coverings and linens, and wanted nothing other than to go naked, and desired most of all to throw themselves into cold water, and many of those who were not cared for threw themselves into cisterns, tormented by an unquenchable thirst. But it made no difference whether they drank a lot or a little.

(2.49.6) They suffered from restlessness and sleeplessness throughout the duration of the sickness. The body, while the sickness was raging, was not wasted away, but contrary to what would be expected resisted its ravages, so that most died on the seventh or ninth day from when the internal inflammation began, while they still had some strength. If they survived that, the disease progressed down into the bowels where severe ulceration occurred and at the same time completely watery diarrhoea assailed them: most people perished from weakness in this second stage. (2.49.7) The sickness went through the whole body, starting at the head where it was first established, and if one survived its most serious attacks it spread to his extremities and at the least left its mark there. (2.49.8) For it attacked the genitals, fingers and toes, and many people survived but lost these, and some lost the sight of their eyes. Some, as soon as they recovered, suffered complete memory loss, and did not remember who they were or their relatives.

(2.51.4) They caught the disease by nursing each other, and died like sheep. This caused the greatest mortality rate. (2.51.5) For if they were afraid, and didn't want to visit each other, they died deserted, and many houses were emptied of the living because there was no one to care for them. When they did visit, they died, and especially those who had a claim to virtue. For they did not spare themselves in visiting their friends and made it a point of honour to do so, when in the end the relatives of the dying were overwhelmed by the enormity of the disaster and grew weary of making lamentations. (2.51.6) Nevertheless, it was more often those who recovered from the disease who pitied the dying and the sick, because they themselves knew what it was like and were feeling confident, for the disease did not attack a person a second time, at least not fatally.

(2.52.2) The corpses of the dying lay on top of each other and half-dead people staggered in the streets, and near all the springs, in their desire for water. (2.52.3) The temples, in which people were living, were full of the corpses of those who had died in them, and men because of the enormity of the plague and not knowing what would become of them gave little thought alike to the sacred and everyday. (2.52.4) All the customs which they had previously used for funerals were thrown into disarray, and they buried the dead as each one could. Many, because in their families there had already been numerous deaths, lacked the requisite materials for burial, and resorted to shameful practices, and anticipating those who had actually raised a pyre they threw their own corpse on and lit it, while others would throw their corpse on top of an already burning pyre and go away.

(2.53.1) In other ways too the plague first caused a greater lawlessness in the city. For what men had previously concealed – that they were not simply living their lives for pleasure – everyone dared to show, with fewer misgivings. They saw the sudden changes of fortune both for the prosperous who suddenly died and of those who previously had nothing, but who immediately acquired the property of others. (2.53.2) So they decided to pursue pleasures that were quick and gave satisfaction, considering their bodies and wealth alike as ephemeral. (2.53.3) And no one was enthusiastic about taking additional trouble for what was thought right, considering that it was doubtful that he would achieve it before he died. Whatever was instantly gratifying or in anyway conducive to that was accepted as honourable and useful. (2.53.4) Fear of the gods or the law of men restrained no one, judging that the pious and those who were not pious were all seen to be perishing alike. No one expected that they would live long enough to pay the penalty for misdemeanours, and they considered that the penalty that had already been decreed against them, and was hanging over their heads, was far greater, and before it fell it seemed reasonable to derive some enjoyment from their life.

MIRACLE CURES

Those who could not afford doctors or whom medicine had failed could spend the night at one of the shrines of the healing god Asclepius, hoping that the god would appear to them in a vision and place his healing hands on them while they slept. Numerous small marble reliefs from Athens survive showing families coming to worship the god Asclepius (see illustration 6.4); at Athens he had a shrine just beneath the acropolis and one at the Piraeus. At Epidaurus in the Peloponnese, the cures that the god 'performed' were recorded. While some of the cures described at Epidaurus are far-fetched, some of them are credible enough to indicate that a form of faith healing operated at this shrine. One of the reasons that the priests at the shrine set up the inscriptions was not only to advertise the power of the god but also to encourage all who were sick, no matter how hopeless their case. M. Fraenkel (ed.), *Inscriptiones Graecae*, vol. IV.1, 2nd edn (Berlin, 1902), nos 121–2, cures 3, 5, 6, 7, 16, 39:

(Cure 3) A man whose fingers of his hand, except for one, were without strength came here to the god as a suppliant. Looking at the tablets in the shrine, he did not believe the cures, and he mocked the inscriptions. But while sleeping he had a vision. It seemed to him that while playing at dice near the temple and when he was about to throw them the god appeared and leapt on his hand, stretching out his fingers. When the god stepped out of the way, he seemed to bend his hand, and his fingers stretched out one by one. And when they had all straightened, the god asked him if he still disbelieved the inscriptions on the tablets in the temple, and the man said that he did not. 'Well, then, since you didn't believe them before, though they were not incredible, from now on,' the god said, 'your name will be "Unbeliever".' When day came, he went out healthy.

(Cure 5) A mute boy. He came to the shrine on account of his muteness. When he had carried out the preliminary sacrifices and completed the customary rites, then a temple servant who looked after the fire for the god, looking at the boy's father, ordered that he undertake to make the thanksgiving offering for the cure, within the year, if he received what he came for. The mute boy suddenly said, 'I promise to do this.' His father, astounded at this, asked him to say it again, and the boy said it again, and after this he became well.

(Cure 6) Pandarus from Thessaly had scars on his forehead. As he slept, he had a vision. It seemed to him that the god bound a bandage of cloth around the scars and ordered him, when he left the sleeping shrine, to remove the bandage and dedicate it in the temple. When day came he woke up and removed the bandage, he saw his forehead clear of the scars, and he dedicated the bandage, which now had the scars which had been on his forehead, in the temple.

(Cure 7) Echedorus received the scars of Pandarus in addition to the ones he himself already had. He had been given money by Pandarus as an offering to the god at Epidaurus in his name, but Echedorus didn't dedicate the money. While he slept he had a vision. It seemed to him that the god stood beside him and asked him if he had the money from Pandarus to give as an offering to Athena in the temple. But Echedorus replied that he had received nothing from Pandarus, but that if the god would make him well, he would dedicate a painted image to him. After this the god fastened the bandage of Pandarus around Echedorus' scars and ordered him, when he had left the sleeping shrine, to take off the cloth and to wash his forehead at the spring and to examine himself in the water. When day came, going out of the sleeping shrine he removed the cloth, on which the scars were no longer to be seen. Looking into the water he saw his own forehead – with not only his own scars but having received those of Pandarus as well.

(Cure 16) Nicanor, a lame man. While he was sitting awake, a boy seized his crutch, and ran off. But Nicanor stood up, pursued him, and so became well.

(Cure 39) Agameda, of Ceos. She slept in the sanctuary for the sake of children, and saw a vision: it seemed to her that in her sleep a snake lay on her stomach. And from this five children were born to her.

SEVEN

Citizens and Officials

Man is a political creature.
Aristotle, *Politics*, 1253a2–3.

A ristotle is often quoted as having written, 'man is a political creature' (or animal). But the Greek itself is a little more subtle and meaningful than that. What he actually writes is that 'man by nature is a creature of the *polis*', the *polis* being the city, or more correctly, the 'city-state'. Our word politics, and its various derivatives, comes from this word *polis*, the city. But a Greek city was more (but not in size) than a modern city is. It was, ideally, self-sufficient, or having enough resources of its own to import what it could not produce itself. It was politically independent as well, having its own calendar, armed forces, customs, rites and in many cases its own currency. But it was much more. It was the basic political unit of ancient Greece, composed of various households. Humans, as the Greeks saw it, banded together into villages which turned into cities because of the need to cooperate in the provision of services that each person required.

But how was the city to be governed? From the eighth to the fourth centuries BC a wide variety of political systems were in operation throughout the Greek world. In the archaic world of Homer of the eighth century BC, many cities were governed by aristocracies, and the ordinary man did not criticise his political leaders, or if he did so, ended up with a drubbing, as in the case of Thersites in the *Iliad* (see below). But in this period there did exist the political assembly, the body of adult male citizens, and although in the archaic period it seems to have largely been a 'sounding board', testing the level of support for military campaigns or called by the aristocrats to inform the citizens of a decision, this assembly had the potential to develop into a democratic body, and it did just this at Athens (in 508 BC).

Forms of monarchy, aristocracy, oligarchy ('the rule of the few') and democracy were found throughout the Greek world (and all four of these words are Greek words). Sparta had two kings (a unique feature), an aristocratic council of elders and an assembly which could vote on issues brought before it but could not put forward proposals. Athenian democracy is the best known of the political systems in ancient Greece, with its powerful assembly of male citizens which made nearly all decisions, and its system of juries which often decided important constitutional matters. What has to be emphasised is that these political structures relied on speeches rather than writing or other means of communication familiar to the modern world. To persuade, one had to speak. In the assembly and jury courts, the ability to speak was vital. Demosthenes the great Athenian orator of the second half of the fourth century BC relied on his rhetorical abilities as well as his arguments to persuade his fellow citizens in the assembly and jury courts.

'Men are the city, and not walls and ships without men', the general Nicias tells the Athenians and their allies in Sicily in 413 BC (Thucydides, 7.77.7). The backbone of the *polis*, the city, was the citizen, who was prepared to fight and die for the city, and who had political power in it. But who was to be a citizen and have a say in the running of the state? For the Athenians after the democratic revolution of 508 BC a citizen was any free Athenian, and they all had the same political and legal privileges – in fact the citizens became more and more equal over time. Of course, the voting citizenry excluded their wives, and foreigners and slaves had no political rights. So the majority of the actual population living in a city such as Athens never attended the assembly, acted as a juror or held political office. But it was a democracy to the Athenians because all male Athenians were classed as citizens and ran the state, rather than just a minority of Athenians forming an aristocracy or oligarchy and denying full political rights to the other Athenians.

For Aristotle, the citizen body could not in fact include many of those who were citizens at Athens. For him the citizen had to have leisure time to devote to the art of government. Those who worked for a living, the so-called *banausic* class, could not be expected to have the time to commit themselves seriously to the art of government. Work, for Aristotle, should be carried out by slaves or hired labourers, enabling the citizen to have the time to participate in the running of the state. But the Athenian democracy, many of whose citizens were craftsmen or farmers, nevertheless operated successfully for over 200 years. Payment for political office and service on the juries, and in the fourth century BC payment for attending the assembly, enabled the poor to participate in the political life of the city. As Pericles noted, 'no one because of poverty is prevented, by the obscurity of his rank, from offering the city some good benefit' (Thucydides, 2.37.1).

The state was the citizen. And the citizen owed something to the state. President J.F. Kennedy's famous remark, 'Ask not what your country can do for you, ask what you can do for your country', is a comment that Pericles would have understood – and approved of (see illustration 7.3). Towering over democratic politics but not above being fined for it or being unpopular, in his Funeral Oration for the war dead in 431 BC he defined the privileges of Athenian citizenship, but also its obligations: those who had nothing to contribute to the city had no business being in the city.

'HOW EVER DID YOU LEARN TO SPEAK SO WELL?'

In Aristophanes' *Women in Assembly* (produced in 392 BC) the women of Athens plan to disguise themselves as their husbands, take over Athens and govern it more wisely than the citizen men. Here one of the women, Praxagora, rehearses a speech she will make in the assembly, disguised as a man, to put the motion that women as the more prudent sex, conservative and doing what's tried and proven, rather than pursuing new ways of doing things, should run the state instead of the men, whose policies are always changing. Aristophanes uses the speech to make various scurrilous remarks about women to raise a laugh with his audience. Aristophanes, *Women in Assembly*, 214–44:

Praxagora: That women are superior in their ways to we men
I will demonstrate. First, they dye their wools in hot water, all of
   them,   215
in the timeless fashion, and you won't see them
ever changing. And the city of Athens,
wouldn't it have been saved, if it had stuck to what had been tried
   and proven,
instead of meddling with some other new fangled way of doing
   things?
They do their cooking sitting down, as they have always done,   220
they carry their loads on their heads, as they have always done,
they celebrate the Thesmophoria festival, as they have always
   done,
they cook their cakes, as they have always done,
they annoy their husbands, as they have always done,
they have their lovers hidden at home, as they have always done,   225
they buy themselves delicacies, as they have always done,
they love undiluted wine, as they have always done,
they like sex on the side, as they have always done.
So, gentlemen, let's give them the running of the city,
and don't talk endlessly about it, nor enquire into   230
what they intend to do, but let's allow them
to govern in a straightforward way; let's consider this thing only:
that as mothers, firstly they will

be eager to protect the soldiers; then, as to rations,
who would supply a soldier better than the one who bore him?   235
For a woman is more resourceful when it comes to providing for
  needs,
and when they're governing they won't ever be cheated,
for they themselves know how to cheat.
I'll allow myself just these few points. If you'll be convinced by me,
you'll spend the rest of your lives happy men.   240

First woman: Well spoken, sweetest Praxagora, and right on the
  mark.
How ever did you learn to speak so well?

Praxagora: In the flight back to Athens at the end of the
  Peloponnesian War, we lived near the assembly place,
and overhearing the speeches I learned from the orators.

The ability to speak well was crucial in a society that was largely illiterate. The main method of persuasion was the spoken word. In Athens, and other democratic cities of Greece, the main political decisions were made in the assembly. Laws that were passed here could be indicted as unconstitutional and the issue decided by a court, and so the courts too could become political battlegrounds. In both places one had to be able to speak. It is a trite criticism to say that the assembly and courts were swayed by clever speakers, as there were plenty of these on both sides of politics. Demosthenes' difficulties in establishing himself as a speaker are instructive for the importance of the spoken word in a democracy (see illustration 7.2). Plutarch, *Life of Demosthenes*, 6.3–4, 7.6, 11.1:

(6.3) When Demosthenes first addressed the people in the assembly, he was interrupted by heckling and ridiculed because of his inexperience. His speech seemed confusing with its long sentences, and contorted with its over-harsh and excessive arguments. (6.4) He had also, so it seems, a weak voice and indistinct speech and a shortness of breath which broke up the sense of what he was saying by cleaving his sentences apart.

(7.6) He built himself an underground study, which has been preserved down to our own time, and each and every day he would go down into it to practise his delivery and to exercise his voice. He would often remain there for two or three months at a time, shaving one side of his face so that it was not possible to go outside, even if he wished to, because of embarrassment.

(11.1) The weakness and lisping of his voice he corrected and cured by putting pebbles in his mouth while reciting his speeches, and he exercised his voice by running and going up steep hills while speaking, and by declaiming certain words or lines without drawing breath. He had a large mirror in his house, and standing in front of this he would practise his exercises.

JURORS AND JURIES

The juries were an essential part of the Athenian political system. There were 6,000 jurors chosen each year, appointed by lot to serve on particular cases. The number of jurors was large by modern standards: the least important case called for 201 and important public cases required 501 jurors. Jurors were paid three *obols* a day, half a day's wage, and service was attractive to the poor and men past their prime. Aristophanes' *Wasps* is a parody of the entire jury system, satirising the jurors as vicious old men out to convict: 'wasps', with a sting in their tale. Xanthias and Sosias are the two slaves of Hater-of-Cleon, the son of Lover-of-Cleon; the father is addicted to jury service, and the son wants to cure him of this habit. The jurors voted by using pebbles, placing them either in the urn for acquittal or conviction. If the defendant was found guilty, the defendant and the prosecutor each proposed a penalty, which the jurors then voted on, using a wax-covered tablet. A short line meant a vote for the defendant's proposed (lighter) penalty, but a long line for the harsher prosecution's penalty: Lover-of-Cleon always votes for the harsher penalty, drawing such long lines in the wax that his finger-nails are full of it (lines 107–8). Despite the satire on the courts here, the system worked very well and few complaints are heard. Cleon was a democratic politician active in the 420s, hated and parodied by Aristophanes in other plays as well. Aristophanes, *Wasps*, 54, 64–167:

> *Xanthias:* Come on, and let me tell the audience the storyline.   54
>
> *Xanthias:* Ours is a little tale which has an opinion –
> it's not more clever than you yourselves   65
> and it's more sophisticated than vulgar comedy.
> That's our master sleeping up there,
> the big man on the roof.
> He's stationed us two to guard his father,
> who's shut up inside, so that he won't escape outside.   70
> His father is sick with an unusual malady
> which no one will be able to recognise or guess
> unless we tell you. Well then, have a guess.
> Amynias there, son of Propanes, says he loves to throw dice.

Sosias: But his guess is worthless, by Zeus: 75
he's judging by the symptoms of his own addiction!

Xanthias: He's wrong, but the name of the malady does begin with
'loves to'.
Now Sosias here is telling Dercylus
that he loves to drink.

Sosias: No way, as that sickness only affects honest men. 80

Xanthias: Nicostratus of the *deme* Scambonidae says
that he loves to sacrifice, or loves to entertain strangers.

Sosias: By the dog, Nicostratus, not someone who loves
entertaining strangers, he's not Philoxenus the faggot.

Xanthias: You're talking nothing but rubbish. You'll never
guess it. 85
If you want to know what it is, shut up now.
I will tell you what sickness the master has.
He loves jury service more than anyone else does.
He loves to judge lawsuits, and groans
if he can't get a seat on the front bench. 90
During the night he doesn't get a wink of sleep, not a scrap,
and if he closes his eyes for even an instant, nevertheless
his mind flutters all night around the water-clock there used to
time the speeches.
He's so used to holding the voting pebble that he wakes up
with three of his fingers squeezed together, 95
like someone making an offering of incense at the new moon.
And, by Zeus, if he sees some graffito
written on a door, that, 'Demus, son of Pyrilampes, is beautiful',
he goes over and writes next to it, 'Beautiful is the verdict box'.
And the rooster that crowed late in the evening, 100
so that he rose late, he said had been bribed
by the officials being examined for maladministration.
Immediately after supper he yells out for his sandals,
and then going to the courts he sleeps before them in the dawn
hanging onto the door post like a leech. 105

Out of sheer perversity he scratches a long line for
punishment
for all the defendants, and he comes home with wax
plastered under his nails like a honeybee or a bumblebee.
Terrified that he might run out of voting pebbles

to cast his vote with he has a whole beach of them in the house.   110
That's how jury mad he is: and the more you reason with him
the more lawsuits he judges. So we've shut him up behind bars
and we're guarding him to make sure he doesn't escape.
For his son has taken his father's illness very badly.
First he tried to persuade him with honeyed words   115
not to put on his worn-out cloak
and go outside, but he couldn't make him see reason.
Then the son tried water purifications and exorcisms: but they were a
    failure.
Then he initiated him into an ecstatic cult, but the old man
burst into the New Court with his ritual drum and all, and started
    judging cases.   120
When these rituals were of no avail,
his son sailed over to Aegina, and having seized his father made him lie
    down
in the healing shrine of the god Asclepius:
but when it was still dusk he was at the gates of the law courts.
After that we didn't let him out anymore.   125
But he kept getting out through the gutters
and the pipes. We stuffed up every hole with rags
and blocked them up.
But he hammered pegs into the wall of the house
and then he leapt forth just as if he was a crow.   130
We spread nets out over the whole courtyard
and we stand guard in a circle.
The old man's name is Lover-of-Cleon,
and, by Zeus, his son's name is Hater-of-Cleon;
this son has some high and mighty habits.   135

Hater-of-Cleon: Xanthias and Sosias, are you asleep?

Xanthias: Oh dear!

Sosias: What is it?

Xanthias: Hater-of-Cleon is up.

Hater-of-Cleon: Why don't one or the other of you run around here
    quickly?
My father's got into the kitchen,
slinking and scurrying around like a mouse. But watch   140
the drain hole so that he doesn't get out.
And you, keep your weight against the door.

Xanthias: As you say, master.

Hater-of-Cleon: By the Lord Poseidon, why is the chimney making
  that noise?
You there, who are you?

Lover-of-Cleon: I am the smoke coming out.

Hater-of-Cleon: Smoke? From what kind of wood?

Lover-of-Cleon: Informing wood.   145

Hater-of-Cleon: By Zeus, that's the most pungent smoke.
But you'll no longer waft about. Where's the cover for the
  chimney?
Back in there! There, I'll put this log on top as well.
There now, look for some other scheme.   150
I'm more wretched than any other man is,
now I'll be called the 'son of Smokey'.

Lover-of-Cleon: Slave!

Xanthias: Now he's pushing on the door.

Hater-of-Cleon: Push against it, strong and good. I'm coming
  over.
And watch the bolt and bar,
and careful that he doesn't gobble up the bolt pin!   155

Lover-of-Cleon: What are you doing? Why won't you let me out,
  you vile scum,
so that I can serve on a jury? Do you want people to get off
  scot-free?

Xanthias: Wouldn't you be able to bear that?

Lover-of-Cleon: I once consulted the god Apollo at Delphi and he
  prophesied
that if I once acquitted someone, then I'd wither away!   160

Xanthias: Apollo, keep harm away from us, that's a prophecy
  and a half.

Lover-of-Cleon: Come on, let me out, I beg you, or I'll burst!

Xanthias: By Poseidon, Lover-of-Cleon, never!

Lover-of-Cleon: Then I'll gnaw through this net with my teeth.

Xanthias: But you don't have any teeth!

Lover-of-Cleon: What a wretched situation.   165
How can I kill you? How? Give me a sword,
quickly, or a wooden voting tablet to record my penalty on.

THE DUTIES OF THE CITIZEN AND PRAISE FOR ATHENS

Pericles was chosen to speak the eulogy over those who had fallen in the first year of the war with the Spartans, 431 BC. Traditionally such a eulogy praised the dead and their deeds in battle, but Pericles chose to laud Athens and its way of life, emphasising that Athens was a city worth dying for. He also reminds the citizens of their obligations to the city. When Pericles says 'We who are alive now and are in the established part of life', he means those in their 'middle years', between the ages of forty to sixty years (2.36.3). Thucydides was almost certainly present at this speech. Thucydides, 2.34.1–8, 36.1–40.2, 41.1, 41.4–5, 42.2–43.6, 45.2–46.2:

(2.34.1) In the same winter, the Athenians according to their ancestral custom conducted a public funeral, in the following way, for those who had been first to die in the war. (2.34.2) The bones of the fallen are laid out two days before the funeral in a tent which is put up, and each man brings to his kin whatever he wishes. (2.34.3) When the funeral procession takes place, coffins of cypress are carried on wagons, one for each tribe: in each coffin are the bones of the tribe of which each soldier was a member. One empty bier is carried, laid out for the missing, who could not be found to take away. (2.34.4) Anyone who wishes can attend the funeral, both citizens and foreigners, and women who are related to the dead are present to mourn at the funeral. (2.34.5) In this way they are buried in the public tomb, which is in the most beautiful suburb of the city, and those who die in war are always buried in it, except for those who died at Marathon. The virtue of those was judged to be exceptional and a tomb was erected for them on the spot.

(2.34.6) When they have been covered over with earth, a man chosen by the city for his intelligence and with a pre-eminent reputation delivers fitting words of praise over them, and after this the people depart. (2.34.7) That is how they bury them, and they employed this custom during the course of the war whenever the occasion arose. (2.34.8) Pericles, son of Xanthippus, was chosen to deliver the eulogy over these first casualties of the war. And when the time came to do so, he came forward from the grave onto a high platform which had been built so that he might be heard by as many of the crowd as possible. This was his speech . . .

(2.36.1) First, I will commence with our ancestors. It is fitting on such an occasion as this one that honour be paid to their memory. For the same race of men has always lived in this land through the generations and they have bequeathed it as a free land through their valour until our present age. (2.36.2) They are worthy of praise, and our own fathers are even more so. For they added to the inheritance that they had received, taking possession of the empire that we have, and left it not without toil to us who are alive today. (2.36.3) We who are alive now and are in the established part of life have increased the size of most parts of the empire, and in all respects have provided the city with resources sufficient for both war and peace. (2.36.4) The deeds in war by which our empire was won, whether by ourselves or by our fathers enthusiastically repulsing the onslaught of war from barbarians or Greeks, I don't wish to dwell on at length to those who know about them, so I will not deal with this. What I will deal with first are the practices which have led us to these things, and the form of government and the outlook from which arose our greatness; then I will go on to praise the dead, as I consider that in the present situation it is not unfitting to speak of these things, and that the whole crowd assembled here, both citizens and foreigners, will hear it to advantage.

(2.37.1) We have a constitution that does not emulate our neighbour's laws; we ourselves provide a model for them, rather than being imitators of others. The name of our government, because it is not the few but the many who manage its affairs, is democracy. In accordance with the laws, all share equality in private disputes, and as to reputation it is not belonging to a certain class that counts but rather personal merit, as each man is distinguished in some way. And no one because of poverty is prevented, by the obscurity of his rank, from offering the city some good benefit.

(2.37.2) We act with tolerance in our public life, and also with freedom of suspicion of each other's practices in our daily lives, for we are not angry with our neighbour if he acts to suit his own pleasure, nor do we put on expressions of distaste which while harmless are hurtful. We conduct our private affairs without giving offence, and in public affairs it is fear especially that restrains us from lawlessness; we are obedient to the officials who are in office as well as to the laws, and especially to those laws established for the assistance of the wronged and the unwritten laws which bring a recognised disgrace on those that break them.

(2.38.1) Moreover, we have organised the greatest number of relaxations from work for our spirit, having games and sacrifices throughout the year, and our private dwellings are tastefully prepared, so that daily delights drive away sorrows. (2.38.2) Because of the great size of the city everything is imported from all over the world, and it is our luck to enjoy as a matter of course the advantages of the fruits of all other men just as much as those grown at home.

(2.39.1) We differ from our opponents in our training for war in the following ways. We keep our city open to everyone and do not sometimes have expulsions of foreigners to prevent anyone learning or watching anything, when seeing something which, were it not hidden, might benefit an enemy, trusting not so much in preparations and deceits as in our innate quest for action. In education, our enemies the Spartans start exercising immediately from youth in pursuit of manliness through harsh training, but we with our unrestricted lifestyle are none the less ready to face equivalent dangers. (2.39.2) Here is proof. When the Spartans invade our land, they do so not by themselves but with all their allies, but when we attack our neighbours, fighting in foreign territory, we usually conquer without difficulty men who are protecting their homes. (2.39.3) No enemy has yet met with the full force of our power because of our simultaneous maintenance of our navy and the dispatch of many of our men on land. And if they come against a portion of our forces and overwhelm some of us, they boast that they have conquered all of us, and if they are defeated that they were overcome by all our forces. (2.39.4) And yet if by living a relaxed life rather than by painful training, and not from rules but rather than from our way of life we face danger courageously, the result is that we don't suffer in advance for the sake of future pains and when we come to the test we prove ourselves no less daring than those who are always labouring. The city in this respect is worthy to be admired, as in other respects as well.

(2.40.1) We are lovers of beauty, yet without extravagance, and of wisdom without effeminacy. We use wealth for action rather than as an opportunity for boasting, and to be poor is not something shameful to admit, but rather it is disgraceful not to take measures to avoid it. (2.40.2) The same people take an interest in both their private concerns and those of the state, and in others who are busy about their work there is no lack of knowledge of political affairs. We alone consider that someone who takes no interest in the political affairs of the state is not minding his own business but rather is useless. We judge and consider political matters correctly ourselves, and we do not consider words as an impediment to action, but rather that debate is an essential instruction before taking action.

(2.41.1) Summing up, I assert that our city as a whole is a teacher to Greece . . .

(2.41.4) We provide many proofs of our power and it does not lack witnesses, and we will be held in awe both by men today and those yet to come. We do not need a Homer to sing our praise, or anyone whose poetry delights for the time being but whose version of the facts truth will frustrate. But we have coerced every land and sea to give access to our daring, and everywhere we have established eternal memorials of our vengeance and successes. (2.41.5) Such is the city for which these men fought and died considering it their duty not to allow it to be taken from them, and it is right that every man who remains behind should want to labour for her . . .

(2.42.2) When I have sung the praises of the city, it is the virtues of these men and men like them that have adorned it, and it couldn't be the case for many Greeks that what was said about them matched up with reality. It seems clear to me that the death of these men now confirms their courage, whether this was the first indication of this or its final testimony. (2.42.3) For even for those who were worse in other respects, it is only just to give priority to the courage shown on behalf of their country in war. For they have obliterated the badness of their lives with good, and the harm of their private lives is obliterated by the assistance they rendered in common.

(2.42.4) None of these men acted in a cowardly way, preferring the enjoyment of his wealth, or if he was poor in the hope that if he escaped poverty he might become wealthy, by putting off the terrible day. They accepted that the punishment of our enemies was more desirable than these things, and at the same time considering this to be the finest of dangers, they were willing – with this danger as the price – to relinquish wealth, committing themselves to hope for the obscure prospect of success, but in the action that was before their very eyes they decided to trust in themselves. In the struggle itself, they considered it better to defend themselves and suffer than to yield and save themselves. They fled only from the word disgrace, they remained and put their body to the task, and in the briefest of moments ordained by fate, at the acme of glory, not of fear, they departed.

(2.43.1) And so these men acted in a manner befitting our city, but as for those who remain behind you must, though you pray for a safer result, make up your mind to be not less courageous against the enemy. But do not consider the advantages on the basis of one speaker's words alone, who could present to you at some length the benefits of warding off the enemy, as you know these already. Rather, in your actions every day rest your gaze upon the power of the city, and become its lovers, and whenever it seems great to you, reflect in your heart that audacious men who realised what had to be done and who acted with a sense of honour acquired these things. And whenever they failed in anything attempted, they decided that the city should not be deprived of their courage, but gave the city this, their finest offering.

(2.43.2) For they gave their bodies to the common good, and won an imperishable fame and the most distinguished of tombs, not the one in which they lie buried, but rather the one in which their glory remains forever, whenever an occasion occurs for speech and action. (2.43.3) For the entire earth is the tomb of famous men, and it is not the inscription on their gravestone alone in their native land that commemorates them, but also in foreign lands an unwritten memorial of reputation, rather than a physical one, dwells in every breast.

(2.43.4) So now emulate these men, judging that happiness is freedom, and freedom is courage, and don't be anxious about the dangers of war. (2.43.5) For it is not those who are unsuccessful, for whom there is no hope of anything good, who are more justified in being unsparing with their lives, but for those who risk an about face in their fortune if they go on living, and those who in particular risk the greatest disaster if they fail. (2.43.6) For to a courageous man disgrace accompanied by cowardice is more bitter than a death he hardly notices attended at the same time by strength and hope for his country.

(2.45.2) If it is necessary for me to mention the virtue of women, referring to those of you who will now be widows, I will say it all in a brief piece of advice: great is your reputation if you are not worse than the nature you have been given, and great is her reputation of whom there is the least talk among men concerning either her virtue or faults.

(2.46.1) In my speech I have said, in accordance with custom, such words as were appropriate. Those being buried have already been honoured by the act of burial, and the city will raise their children at public expense until they are eighteen years old, bestowing a valuable crown on the fallen and their survivors in conflicts such as these. For those who establish the greatest prizes for excellence have the best men as citizens. (2.46.2) Now having mourned, each for his own dead as is proper, depart.

Hyperides in his eulogy for the fallen in the Lamian War, which concluded in 322 BC with the defeat of Athens by the Macedonians, opens with praise of the city. Hyperides, 6 (*Funeral Oration*), 4–5:

(6.4) Concerning this city, there is not sufficient time at hand to speak in detail of all the benefits that she has conferred on Greece in the past, nor is the occasion suited to a lengthy speech, nor is it easy for one man to go through and call to your mind such great achievements. But I will not hesitate to speak briefly about Athens. (6.5) For as the sun travels the entire world and distinguishes the seasons, as is fitting, and establishes everything for the best, taking care of wise and prudent men, with regard to their birth and sustenance, and the crops and all the other necessities of life, so our city always carries out the punishment of the wicked, comes to the assistance of the just, and impartiality instead of injustice she distributes to all, and at her own individual risk and expense she provides a common security for the Greeks.

THE STATE VERSUS THE INDIVIDUAL

Creon has decreed that no one is to bury Polynices who has attacked his own city, Thebes, and been killed on the battlefield. His body is to be left for the birds and dogs to feast on. His brother Eteocles, who has died in defence of Thebes, is given due burial. But Creon's decree forbidding Polynices' burial is against natural, divine law, a law so eternal that no one knows where it came from (line 457), while Creon's is a mere mortal creation. Antigone's struggle (she is Polynices' sister) is that of the individual motivated by natural justice against the ruthlessness of the state, or indeed any institution, that seeks to secure its own interests against its own citizens and what is right and just. Antigone stands for all those who have been tortured, maimed and killed in human history for what is right, and for their own principles and beliefs. She goes to her death, but argues that she prefers this to being a complacent bystander. In a world of globalisation and terrorism, she is still a reminder to western civilisation, as she has been for centuries, that some values are eternal and worth suffering for, and in the extreme case, dying for. Sophocles, *Antigone*, 446–70:

Creon [to Antigone]: Tell me, not with some long tale but quickly,
were you aware that it had been proclaimed that this act was forbidden?

Antigone: I knew. How could I not know? It was public knowledge.

Creon: And yet you had the audacity to transgress these laws?

Antigone: In my view, it was not Zeus who proclaimed these laws,   450
nor was it Justice who lives with the gods of the underworld,
that legislated these laws among men,
nor do I think that your decrees since they are invented
by a mortal were strong enough to be able to overturn

the unwritten and indestructible laws of the gods.   455
For these divine laws live not just for now or yesterday
but for eternity, and no one knows where they came from.
I don't intend to disobey divine law and pay the penalty
before the gods for fear of any man's judgement.
I knew that I would die, why not?   460
Death would eventually come to me, even if you had made no such
    proclamation.
If I am to die before my time, I consider that a gain.
For anyone who lives in the middle of many sorrows
such as I do, how can dying not come as a gain?
So for me at least meeting this doom   465
is not distressful. Yet if I had stood by
and let the son of my mother go unburied,
that would have desolated me. But this way
brings no pain. If what I do seems foolish to you,
then this is like the reproach of folly from a fool.   470

Sophocles' democratic tendencies are evident in this extract and highlight the communal nature of the city. Sophocles, *Antigone*, 734–7:

Creon: Is the city to tell me what commands I ought to give?

Haemon: Do you realise that you have just spoken like a very young
    man?   735

Creon: Should I rule this land for someone else's benefit, or for my own?

Haemon: A city for one man is no city at all.

Pericles in his Funeral Oration extolled the grandness of Athens and its benefits. In Plato's *Crito*, Socrates' friends urge him, sentenced to death, to flee from Athens. But Socrates argues against this, as to do so would not be to observe the laws of the city. Socrates argues his position with Crito, and personifies the laws of the state as 'the laws', who argue their point of view. The opening question of the laws here is rather long. A defendant, if found guilty, proposed his own punishment, as did the prosecution, and then the jury voted for which to accept (52c). Plato, *Crito*, 51a–52d:

Socrates: (51a) If the laws say, 'Is your wisdom of such a kind that it has escaped your notice that your country is more precious and to be (51b) more reverenced and is holier and held in greater honour among the gods and those men of good sense than your mother and father and all your other ancestors, and that you ought to be more reverent and compliant and abject when your country is angry than when your father is, and must either persuade it otherwise or else do whatever it commands, and to suffer whatever it commands you to suffer, silently, and if it orders you to be flogged or put in chains, and if it marches you out to war to be maimed or slain, you must do these things, and that this is quite just, and not give up or retire from or desert your position, but in war, in the law courts, (51c) and everywhere you ought to do whatever the city and your country commands, or persuade it as to what really is just, but that it is impious to use violence against your mother and father, and much more impious when used against one's country?' How will we respond to this, Crito? Are the laws speaking the truth, or not?

Crito: It seems that they are.

Socrates: Perhaps the laws would say, 'Therefore consider, Socrates, that if we speak truthfully, what you are undertaking to do to us now is not just. For we brought you into being, raised you, educated you and gave as much of a share of all the good things of life as we could to you and to all the other citizens. (51d) Nevertheless, we publicly proclaim, by having given the chance to any of the Athenians who wants, that when he comes of age and observes the administration of the city and us, the laws, and is not pleased with us, that he may leave, taking his possessions with him, going wherever he likes. And none of we laws impedes or forbids anyone of you who desires to go to a colony of Athens, if we laws and the city don't please him, or from going wherever he likes and living as a foreigner, taking his possessions with him.

(51e) But whoever of you stays in the city, observing how we administer justice and how we manage the city's other affairs, we maintain that person to have entered into an agreement with us to do whatever we might command, and we say that the person who doesn't obey is wrong on three counts: firstly, because he refuses to obey us, the ones who are his parents, secondly, because he refuses to obey us, the ones who raised him, and thirdly, because having agreed to obey us he neither obeys, nor convinces us that we are doing wrong, (52a) and although we put forward proposals and don't brutally order him to do what we command, but we permit him two choices, either to obey us or to persuade us otherwise, he does neither of these.

'We the laws say, Socrates, that you will be open to these charges, if you do what you plan to, and you will not be less guilty than other Athenians, but more so.' If then I were to say, 'Why would that be so?', perhaps they might justifiably attack me, saying that I in particular of the Athenians had reached this agreement with them. For they would say,

(52b) 'Socrates, we have tangible proof that we laws and the city satisfied you, for you would not have stayed in the city, at home, more than all the other Athenians, if you hadn't been more satisfied with it than they. You never left the city as part of a festival delegation, or went anywhere except when you were serving in the army, and you never unlike all other people made any other journey, and you had no desire to know another city or laws, but we laws and the city were satisfactory to you. So specifically did you choose us (52c) that you agreed to be a citizen under our jurisdiction, and in addition to all of this you begot children in this very city, showing that it pleased you. And then, at your trial itself you could have suggested exile as your punishment if you wished, and what you are now attempting to do against the city's wishes, you could have done with its blessing. But at your trial you put on a display to the effect that you weren't unwilling to die if that was necessary, and your preference – you said so – was death rather than exile. And now neither are you ashamed by those words nor do you give any heed to us laws, but are trying to destroy us, (52d) and you are doing something worthy of the basest slave, attempting to run away in defiance of contractual arrangements and agreements, in which you agreed to live as a citizen. So first answer this very question for us: do we speak the truth, or not, when we allege that you agreed, in deed and not just in word, to live as a citizen under the jurisdiction of us laws?' What will we say to that, Crito, other than that we did agree to do so?

Crito: We are forced to agree, Socrates.

ARISTOTLE ON THE CITY AND CITIZENSHIP

The size of the city-state (*polis*) was important for its proper functioning. A city had ideally to be large enough to be self-sufficient in the necessities of life. But if a city became too large, the citizens would not know each other, so that deciding legal cases and appointing officials according to merit would suffer as a result. Outsiders would find it easy to infiltrate this rather anonymous citizen body. A city such as Athens was too large by Aristotle's criteria. Moreover, a modern western city would not have been recognised as a city by Aristotle: it would be a tribe (an *ethnos*, an ethnic grouping) and no longer a city. Aristotle, *Politics*, 1326a40–1326b11, 1326b14–1326b24:

(1326a40–1326b2) A boat that is the size of the span of an outstretched hand will not be a boat at all, nor one that is two stades in length, and there will be a certain size when on account of its smallness or largeness it will not be seaworthy.

(1326b2–1326b7) It is the same with the city-state when because of not having enough inhabitants it is not self-sufficient, for a city-state is self-sufficient. The city-state with too many people is necessarily self-sufficient, but as a tribe of people, rather than as a city, because it is not easy for a constitution to thrive in such a city. For who will be the military commander of such an excessive number of people, and who will be their town-crier except a person with an exceptionally powerful voice?

(1326b7–1326b11) So when the population first reaches the least size to be self-sufficient in all the good things of life, it becomes an early state, in the manner of a political association. It is possible to go on further, and exceeding this in size it will become a larger city-state, but this process of growth cannot, as I have said, go on indefinitely.

(1326b14–1326b24) For the judging of legal cases and for the allocation of political positions on the basis of merit it is vital for the citizens to know each other and what kind of people they are, and so, where this isn't the case, as a matter of course the allocation of political positions and the judging of legal cases suffers. For it is not just to be casual in both these areas, which obviously does happen when the population is too great. It is also easy for foreigners and aliens who are residing in the country to gain citizenship: for it is not difficult to escape detection on account of the size of the population. So clearly this is the best limit of the city-state: having the greatest population for self-sufficiency in the requirements of life, and easily taken in at a glance.

Citizenship was not defined by simply living in a place. *Metics* were the foreigners and offspring of foreigners living and resident in a city, and even third-generation descendants of foreigners at Athens were denied access to citizenship. Aristotle, *Politics*, 1275a1–1275a33, 1275b17–1275b21:

(1275a1–1275a22) It is necessary to ask whom we are to call a citizen and who is a citizen. There is much disagreement about defining a citizen, for not everyone reaches the same conclusion about what a citizen is. For someone who is a citizen in a democracy is often not a citizen in an oligarchy. . . . Someone is not necessarily a citizen of where he lives, for *metics* and slaves have a place of domicile, and a citizen is not defined as someone having access to the privileges of the law so that they can prosecute and be prosecuted, for this is also provided for those covered by mutual treaties between states. *Metics* in many places do not have a full share in these matters, but must choose a citizen patron, and so in this way they have a common share, however incomplete, in these matters. Also boys who are not yet old enough to be enrolled as citizens, and old men who have given up active political duty, must be said to be somehow citizens, but not unreservedly but with the qualification 'not yet of age' and 'past the age' or some such term – for it doesn't make any difference, what I'm arguing is clear enough. What we are looking for is the citizen, plain and simple, without having any deficiency that must be qualified. Such problems must also be gone through and settled concerning disenfranchised and exiled citizens.

(1275a22–1275a33) Simply put, what distinguishes the citizen from any others is in their share of making judicial decisions and holding political office. Some offices are differentiated by their length of tenure, and some absolutely cannot be held by the same person twice, or only after a length of time has elapsed. Some, such as being a juror or member of the assembly, don't have such limits. It might perhaps be said that jurors and members of the assembly are not officials, and that participation in these is not holding office. But it would be ridiculous to argue that the most powerful are bereft of rule. But it doesn't make any difference for this is just quibbling over definitions, for there is no common name that ought to be used for both service in the juries and assembly: for the purposes of definition, I suggest it be 'unlimited office'. So we define citizens as sharing in this.

(1275b17–1275b21) So who is a citizen is clear from these deliberations. For whomever there is a share in office, deliberative and judicial, we say he is a citizen of this city-state, and we say plainly that a city is the number of such citizens as to be self-sufficient in the necessities of life.

The Greek word *banausoi* (the singular is *banausos*) is often translated as mechanics, but this translation does not adequately convey the full meaning of *banausoi*. It covers all those who are engaged in working with their hands. There was prejudice among the elite against this class: how could *banausoi* really participate in the affairs of the state when they were too busy to cultivate virtue (largely consisting of the ability to spend time holding political office) and the art of politics? Aristotle would exclude *banausoi* from citizenship entirely, but at Athens and other cities, they were a key element in the citizen body. The prejudices of the elite against those who actually have to work for a living (!) are clear in this passage. In the fourth century BC the Athenians allowed all citizens to hold political office and paid them to do so, as well as paying for those serving on the council, attending the assembly and being members of a jury. This equates with the practice of modern liberal western democracies. Aristotle, *Politics*, 1277b33–1278a2, 1278a6–1278a13, 1278a17–1278a26:

(1277b33–1278a2) There still remains something of a problem about the citizen. For is a citizen really one who is able to share in the holding of political office, or are the *banausoi* to be included as citizens? So if the *banausoi* are included in the citizen body although they do not participate in the holding of political office, then since the *banausos* is a citizen it is not possible for every citizen to have the virtue of holding political office. But if he is not to be a citizen, in which category must he be placed? For he is neither a *metic* nor a foreigner. But we will not say that this argument is a paradox. For slaves do not belong to any of the mentioned categories, nor do the freedmen.

(1278a6–1278a13) In ancient times in some places the *banausoi* were slaves or foreigners, and therefore many of them are still so. But the best city will not make the *banausos* a citizen. But even if the *banausos* is to be a citizen, then what we have argued is the virtue of the citizen cannot in fact be said of every citizen, nor applied to everyone who is free, but only to those of the citizens who are relieved of the compulsion of work. Some of this necessary work is performed for the individual by slaves, and some by the *banausoi* and hired labourers who serve the public.

(1278a17–1278a26) In one constitution it is necessary for the *banausos* or a hired labourer to be a citizen. But in another it is impossible, such as in a constitution known as aristocratic, and in any in which honours are awarded on the basis of virtue and merit. For it is impossible, living the life of a *banausos* or a hired labourer, to devote onself to the requirements of virtue. In oligarchies a hired labourer would not be admitted as a citizen because of the high property qualification required of those sharing in the political offices, but a *banausos* might be admitted: for many of the craftsmen become wealthy. However, in Thebes there was a law that not until ten years had passed since giving up one's trade could one share in political office.

Xenophon puts similar sentiments into Socrates' mouth. For some *banausoi* who spent the day by the fire, see illustration 7.1. Xenophon, *Oeconomicus*, 4.2–3:

(4.2) *Banausic* skills, as they are termed, are spoken against and are also, rightly so, held in particular contempt in our cities. For they totally wreck the bodies both of the workers and foremen, compelled as they are to sit and stay inside, and in some instances to pass the day by the fire. The weakening of the body causes a marked deterioration of the mind. (4.3) The *banausic* skills, as they are termed, provide no leisure time for attending to one's friends or the city. So these *banausoi* are considered to treat their friends badly and to be feeble defenders of the fatherland. In some cities, in fact, particularly in those considered to be warlike, it is prohibited for any of the citizens to work at *banausic* occupations.

DEMOCRACY, OLIGARCHY OR MONARCHY? THAT IS THE QUESTION

Herodotus admits that some Greeks do not believe that the following conversation took place. Clearly it is an invention of his own, and the Persian setting is an exotic touch: he uses the devices of the speeches to present ideas about types of government in the Greek world, democracy, oligarchy and monarchy, political systems that could be found in various Greek cities and states when he was writing. The ideas presented here almost certainly reflect political discussions carried on among the Greeks, and found fuller expression later in Plato's writings and in Aristotle's *Politics*. Those who had rebelled against the Persian Magus, who was ruling the empire, gathered for a discussion about how now best to govern; the historical setting is just before 521 BC, when one of the rebels, Darius, became king. Herodotus, 3.80.1–82.4:

(3.80.1) The rebels against the Magus began to discuss the entire state of affairs and words were spoken that are incredible to some of the Greeks, but these were indeed said. (3.80.2) Otanes urged that affairs of state be placed in the hands of the Persians as a whole, arguing as follows: 'I am of the opinion that no longer should one of us become sole ruler (monarch). This would be neither enjoyable nor good. For you have seen the *hybris* of Cambyses and to what lengths it went, and you have had your share of the *hybris* of the Magus. (3.80.3) How can monarchy be a well-adjusted thing when the ruler, not being held accountable, is able to do whatever he wants? For the best of all men alive, raised to such a position, would be stirred to thoughts which he would otherwise never have contemplated. For the good things that are present breed *hybris* in him, and from the beginning jealousy is innate in mankind.

(3.80.4) 'Possessed of these two flaws – *hybris* and jealousy – he commits all wickedness: for he commits many outrages, some because he is satiated with *hybris*, and others through envy. And yet a tyrant ought to be without jealousy, for indeed he has all good things. But he treats his fellow citizens in exactly the opposite way: he is jealous that the best of them are in good health and alive, and rejoices in the worst of the citizens, and no one is readier to give an ear to slanders. (3.80.5) Of all men, he is the most incongruous: court him in moderation, and he is annoyed that he is not sufficiently honoured, and if you honour him sufficiently, he is annoyed that you are a flatterer. But I have saved the worst to last: he disturbs ancestral laws, rapes wives and has people put to death without a trial. (3.80.6) But if the people rule, first, it has the most excellent name of all, equality before the law, second, it carries out none of the things that a monarch does. The magistrates are chosen by lot, a magistracy is held liable to audit, and all deliberations are carried out in the common assembly. So I state my opinion, that we abolish monarchy and increase the power of the multitude: for everything is in the hands of the majority.'

(3.81.1) This was the opinion put forward by Otanes. Megabyxus recommended a change to oligarchy, arguing along these lines: 'I agree with what Otanes said about putting an end to tyranny, but when he advises that the majority hold power, his opinion deviates from the best one. For nothing is more stupid or more violent than the useless mass of the people.

(3.81.2) 'And further, to escape the *hybris* of a tyrant and to fall into the *hybris* of the undisciplined people is in no way bearable. For whatever the tyrant does, he does so knowingly, but the people do not have even that comprehension. For how could someone do so, who has never been taught or seen anything right personally, but rushes madly into politics without thought, like a flooded river. (3.81.3) Those who wish to harm the Persians, let them be ruled by the people, but let us choose a group out of the best men, and delegate power to them. For we ourselves will be in that group, as it is reasonable that the best men will arrive at the best decisions.' Megabyxus put forward this opinion. Darius declared the third opinion, saying:

(3.82.1) 'It seems to me that Megabyxus speaks correctly about the people, but what he says about oligarchy isn't correct. There are three possibilities lying before us, the rule of the people, oligarchy and monarchy, each of them meant to be in its own way the best, but I say that monarchy is preferable by far. (3.82.2) Nothing would appear to be better than the one best man: and his judgement will match his character, he will govern the people without fault, and best keep silent about plans made against enemies. (3.82.3) In an oligarchy with many men striving in the public sphere for distinction [*arete*], strong personal enmities arise. For each one himself wishes to be the top dog and for his counsels to prevail, and they come to great enmities among themselves, and factionalism is the outcome, and from factionalism comes bloodshed. And from this bloodshed comes monarchy, and in this very way it is shown by how much monarchy is the best. (3.82.4) Then again, the rule of the people is unable to prevent the occurrence of bad government. Well then, with evils prevalent, common enmities do not arise among the bad men, but strong friendships: for the wicked men put their heads together to harm the state. This reaches a certain point, then someone stands up as champion of the people to put a stop to democracy. And for this he is idolised by the people, and so with the people worshipping him he is made monarch, so in this way Otanes' case also clearly shows that monarchy is the best.'

'THE RULE OF MANY IS NOT A GOOD THING'

The world of Homer was aristocratic, and certainly not democratic. The nobles of the Phaeacians could summon the king to assembly. Even Agamemnon must take his place in assembly among the Greeks and be argued against and listen to the advice offered (though he can choose to dismiss it if he wishes, with disastrous results for the Greek expedition at Troy when he does ignore it). Achilles can withdraw his services from Agamemnon if he wants to, and does so. The political situation seems to be that of a feudal monarchy, with the various leaders only as complaisant as they wish to be. The ordinary men, the fighting ranks, the 'people' as they are called, attend the assembly, but as followers, to obey what is decided by their leaders. The incident concerning Thersites below makes this clear. But nevertheless, it was from the assembly that the Greek democracies were eventually to spring, and their presence here in the world of Homer of the eighth century BC is crucial for our understanding of Greek politics of the classical period. Thersites the common soldier would have had more say in the assembly of classical Athens. As the passage opens, the Greek soldiers have been running away from an assembly to their ships in order to sail home, but Odysseus brings them back. Homer, *Iliad*, 2.198–270:

But when he saw a person of the common folk and found him shouting
   out
Odysseus hit him with his sceptre, and threatened him so:
'Soldier, sit still and listen to what others have to say,   200
those who are better men than you, you shirker in battle and
   weakling,
not reckoned as anything in either war or council.
Surely not all the Achaeans can be kings here.
The rule of many is not a good thing: let there be one ruler,
one king, to whom Zeus, the son of crooked-counselling Cronus,
   gives   205

both the sceptre and power of judgement, so that he can deliberate
  on behalf of his people.'
Giving out orders in this way he organised the army: and the
  soldiers again rushed back
to the assembly from the ships and from the huts
with a tumult, as when a wave of the loud-roaring sea
churns on the long beach, and the open ocean thunders.   210

Now the rest had sat down, and were staying in their places:
but still Thersites alone, of immeasurable speech, ranted on,
who knew many words in his head, but inappropriate and
  numerous,
thoughtlessly, without decency, railing against kings
with whatever he thought would make the Argives laugh.   215
He was the ugliest man to come beneath the walls of Ilion,
he went bandy-legged, and lame in one foot; his rounded
  shoulders
curved over his chest, and above them
his head was pointed, and only thin hair sprouted on it.

He was particularly hated by Achilles, and also by Odysseus: 220
for these two he constantly abused: but now against god-like
  Agamemnon
he uttered sharp reproachful cries. The Achaeans were really
angry against him and were indignant in their spirit.
Now he, shouting loudly, abused Agamemnon in a speech:

'Son of Atreus, are you really complaining again? What don't you
  have?   225
Your huts are stacked high with bronze, and there are plenty
of choice women in them too, which the Achaeans
give to you first whenever we sack a city.
Or do you desire even more gold, that one of the
horse-taming Trojans will bring out of Ilion as a ransom,   230
for a son which I or some other Achaean has bound and led off,
or is it a young woman, so that you can lie with her making love,
whom you'll keep away from others, for yourself? It isn't right
that you, a leader, bring the sons of the Achaeans into misery.
Ah, soft friends, base reproaches, women of Achaea, no longer
  Achaean men,   235
let's go home with our ships, and let us leave this fellow
by himself here in Troy, to wallow in his loot, so that he might
  realise

whether we have come to his aid, or not.
Now also Achilles, a man far better than he,
he's dishonoured, for he has taken away his prize, and robs him
    of it. 240
But rather, there is no wrath in the heart of Achilles: he lets go
    of it,
for otherwise, son of Atreus, now for the last time would you
    behave outrageously.'

In this way Thersites taunted Agamemnon, the shepherd of the people,
but god-like Odysseus swiftly came to Agamemnon's side,
and scowling from underneath his brows berated Thersites with
    harsh words: 245

'Thersites of ill-considered words, although you are a clear speaker,
stop, and don't desire to strive alone against kings.
For I say that there is no other creature lower than you
of those that came with the sons of Atreus under the walls of Ilion.
So don't lift up your voice to harangue kings, 250
throwing reproaches in their teeth, on the lookout for the chance to
    return home.
We don't yet clearly know how these things will turn out,
whether the homecoming of the sons of the Achaeans will be good
    or bad.
But now you in this way throw abuse at Atreus' son Agamemnon,
the shepherd of the people, because the warriors of the Greeks 255
give him much, but whom you address with taunts.
But to you I'll speak out, and it will come to pass:
if ever I come across you behaving stupidly, even as you are now,
no longer afterwards may the head of Odysseus be on his shoulders,
and no longer may I be called the father of Telemachus, 260
if I don't take your own clothes and strip you
of both cloak and tunic, which hide your nakedness,
and as to yourself send you weeping to the swift ships,
beaten from the assembly place with shameful blows.'

Odysseus said this, and with his sceptre beat both his back and
    shoulders: 265
and Thersites doubled over, and let fall a heavy tear:
a bloody swollen bruise raised itself proud on his back
beneath the sceptre of gold. He sat down, terrified,
full of pain; looking around helplessly he wiped away the tear.
But the Achaeans although sick at heart laughed happily at him. 270

Theophrastus provides another comic sketch, this time of the oligarch, who quotes Homer, *Iliad*, 2.204 that 'one ruler is best' (2), spoken by Odysseus in the passage above. Theophrastus, *Characters*, 26, *Oligarchy*:

(26.1) Oligarchy would appear to be the lust for office which strives for power and gain, and the oligarchic man is the sort, (26.2) who when the people in assembly are debating which men to appoint as assistants to the chief magistracy to organise the procession for a religious delegation, coming forward to the speaker's platform states bluntly that they need to have autocratic powers, and if other speakers propose ten assistants, he declares, 'One man is enough, but he must be a *man*.' And of the works of Homer he can recite by heart this line alone, 'The rule of many is not a good thing: let there be one ruler', and he is not versed in any of the rest.

(26.3) Without a doubt he's the sort who employs these sorts of arguments, that, 'It's vital for us to get together and talk these things over, and to get away from the crowd and the market-place, and to stop being abused or honoured as we are now when competing for the public offices', and, 'It has to be either them or us when it comes to running the city.'

(26.4) He goes out at noon with his cloak thrown over his shoulder, his hair cut moderately, nails meticulously groomed, and he struts around delivering the following lines as if he was performing in a tragic play: (26.5) 'It's impossible to live in the city because of informers', and, 'It's monstrous what we suffer in the jury courts at the hands of the bribed!', and, 'I can't understand what those who go into politics really want', and that, 'The common people are ungrateful: they are always taking their lead from whoever has something on offer or to give away.' He remarks how embarrassed he is in the political assembly whenever some weedy, unwashed citizen comes and sits next to him.

(26.6) He says, 'When will we be spared financial ruin from paying for public events and maintaining warships?', and, 'How hateful is the breed of demagogues!' He complains that it was Theseus who first set the city on the road to ruin, for he joined twelve towns into one city, and abolished the monarchy. But he was hoisted on his own petard, since he was the first one they killed. He says other things of the same colour to both foreigners and citizens who share his outlook and these political notions.

In Athens a 'right-wing ideologue' known to historians as *The Old Oligarch* wrote a pamphlet about Athens which was falsely attributed to

Xenophon under the title *Constitution of the Athenians*. Even this 'old oligarch' has to admit that the poor are the basis of power in Athens. *The Old Oligarch*, 1.2:

> It is only just that the poor and the people as a whole in Athens have more than the aristocrats and the wealthy because it is the people who row the ships and confer power on the city – the ship pilots, the boatswains and the ship's officers and the officers in charge of the ship's bow and the ship carpenters. These are the ones who confer power on the city, far more than the *hoplites*, the well born and the good men.

LIVING IN 'SACRED ATHENS'

Pindar describes Athens as a crowded ('much-trodden') city, and refers to it as 'sacred Athens'; the city's 'navel' where incense was burnt at the Altar of the Twelve Gods in the *agora*. The *agora* was much more than its literal translation 'market-place' might imply: it was the hub of the city where citizens would meet to chat and shop, and where they exchanged news and views before attending meetings of the political assembly. Pindar, Fragment 75, *Dithyramb*, 4.1–5:

> Come to the dance, gods of Mount Olympus,
> and send over it glorious grace,
> coming as you are to the much-trodden
> incense-burning navel of the city of sacred Athens
> and to the famous *agora* with its finely carved buildings.   5

Wealthier Greeks, such as Odysseus, took baths in their private homes, but most Greeks did not have this luxury. *The Old Oligarch* complains how the people of Athens provide facilities for themselves out of the taxes from the wealthy. They even build baths: for the oligarch, if there are to be the great unwashed in Athens, he'd prefer them to stay that way rather than get clean at the expense of the rich! *The Old Oligarch*, 2.9–10:

> (2.9) The Athenian people know that it isn't possible for every poor man to make sacrifices, to hold magnificent feasts and build shrines and to manage a beautiful and large city, and yet it has discovered a way of offering sacrifices, building shrines and sanctuaries, and holding feasts. The city sacrifices many victims at public expense: and it is the people who hold magnificent feasts and share among themselves the sacrifices. (2.10) Some wealthy people have gymnasiums, baths and dressing rooms in their private homes, but the people themselves have built for their own

use many wrestling schools, dressing rooms and baths. The mob has more benefit from these than the wealthy few.

KEEPING THE CITY CLEAN AND TIDY

Plato in the *Laws* sets out a series of laws and regulations for the ideal state. Everything comes under scrutiny, from the child in the womb to the question of walls for the ideal city-state. The dialogue of the *Laws* is between an Athenian 'stranger' and Megillus of Sparta and Clinias of Crete. In this section the Athenian does the talking but refers to Megillus and Spartan practices: Sparta did not have walls in the classical period. Many states had the laws and officials concerning buildings which Plato refers to. Plato, *Laws*, 778c–779d:

Athenian: (778c) The temples have to be constructed all around the market-place and on high ground around the perimeter of the whole city, for the sake of security and sanitation. Next to the temples will be the houses of the magistrates and the law courts, in which, because these are most holy places, (778d) partly because they deal with matters of piety, and partly because the temples of the gods are at hand, judgement will be given and sentences received. And among these buildings will be the courts in which cases about murders and such crimes as deserve the death penalty may fittingly be held.

Concerning walls, Megillus, I concur with the Spartan view of letting the walls lie asleep in the earth, and not waking them up, for the following reasons. The poet has a fine saying, which is often quoted, that walls should be of bronze and iron, rather than of earth. (778e) Our plan would justly deserve great derision, if every year we sent young men into the countryside, some to dig, some to construct trenches, and others to build structures to keep out the enemy, to prevent them crossing into the borders of the country, and then we were to build walls around the city! Firstly, a wall is in no way advantageous for the health of a city, and usually makes for a habit of softness of soul in the inhabitants, by inviting them to take refuge within the wall instead of repelling the enemy and (779a) instead of keeping watch continuously, day and night, and in this way gain security; fenced in with walls and gates they think they have means of safety and they go to sleep, as if they were born not to toil, not knowing that leisure is really the product of toil. I think, in fact, that from slothfulness are born again the toils caused by shameful laziness.

But if men really must have a wall, (779b) the building of private residences must from the beginning be arranged so that the whole city forms a wall, all of the houses being well constructed, regularly built and similar, facing the road, having the form of a single house, not unpleasant to look at, and for ease of defence and security it would be totally and completely superior. To ensure that the original buildings would be preserved would properly be a task for the occupants, (779c) but also the city wardens should supervise this and with fines compel those who are negligent, and supervise the cleanliness of everything in the city, and ensure that no private individual encroaches onto any property belonging to the city with either buildings or by digging. The city wardens must also oversee that the rainwater drains away properly, and over all such matters either inside or outside the city they are to manage as is appropriate. (779d) The law-givers are to see to all such matters and any others that the law neglects through an inability to do so, promulgating additional laws as necessary. Since these buildings, and those of the market-place and gymnasium, and all the schools have been constructed, and await their occupants, and the theatre its audience, let us move on to the next item of legislation.

The stone slab on which the following law was carved was discovered in 1984 during a rescue underwater archaeological dig on the island of Thasos before the harbour was deepened. The law dates to about 470–460 BC. Water had damaged the stone but careful study of this one-metre-high block has revealed a law dealing with the maintenance and cleanliness of streets. The decree is important as it is one of the first pieces of evidence showing concern for 'city hygiene' in ancient Greece. Householders were to keep the outside of their houses fronting onto the road tidy, and in addition the officials known as *epistatai*, which can be translated as 'supervisors', will also clean the road once a month. It is interesting that no one is liable to pay a fine if his offence is not written down: there is protection against corruption on the part of officials. The fines are expressed in Thasos' currency: the *hekte* and *hemiekton* were worth 1/12 and 1/24 of a *stater* respectively. A *stater* was 200 *drachmas* (the equivalent of 200 days' wages for an unskilled labourer). The fines are therefore quite steep: one offence brings a fine of 100 *drachmas* for Apollo and 100 for the city, another for a *stater*, one for a *hekte* and another fine is for one *hemiekton*. That magistrates could keep half of an exacted fine was a common practice and has numerous parallels; this procedure was meant as an inducement for them to carry out their duties, though abuses might well have occurred. Women are presumably not to look from the windows when processions for Heracles are taking place along the road; his shrine is mentioned in the inscription, and several cults of Heracles that prohibited the presence of women are known. The inscription does not state why the road is to be kept clean, but the mention of shrines hints at primarily maintaining it so for processions. A few words have been added in brackets to complete the sense of the text, and there are a few damaged gaps in the inscription, indicated here by ellipses. H.W. Pleket (ed.), *Supplementum Epigraphicum Graecum* (Amsterdam, 1995), vol. 42, no. 785:

From the road of the bank . . . of the shrine of Heracles; from the road of the shrine of the Graces, in this road no one is to make a threshold [for his house] nor draw water from the . . . nor to dig a well . . . nor place . . . nor make . . . Whoever does anything against what is written down here will owe 100 *drachmas* to Apollo and 100 *drachmas* to the city. The magistrates who are in office when the offence occurs are to exact the fine. If they don't, they will owe the amount themselves, but double, to the god Apollo and to the city. And if the penalty of the wrongdoer is not recorded, he doesn't have to pay it. . . .

Each householder is to keep the road in front of his property clean. If no one is living in the house, the owner is responsible for this, and in addition the supervisors themselves will clean the road each month. And if something falls [into the street], they will take action.

The supervisors will keep this road clean from the shrine of Heracles to the seashore. When the magistrates request an individual to take away the household rubbish and what is on the road, let him do so. Whoever does not do what is written down here is to owe a *hekte* per day to the city. The supervisors are to exact the fine and keep half of it themselves. No one is to go up onto the roofs of the publicly owned houses along this road in order to get a better view, and no woman is to look from the windows. Whoever does these things will make the occupier of the building owe one *stater* to the city for each offence. The supervisors are to exact the fine and keep half of it themselves.

From a projecting balcony he is not to make a water gutter onto this road. If anyone does this he will owe a *hemiekton* per day, half of this is to go to the city, and half to the supervisors, who are to exact it.

From the shrine of the Graces up to the buildings where the money exchange and the symposium are, and along the road to the town hall, into this area no one is to throw or put excrement. Whoever does any of these things will owe a *hemiekton* to the city for as many times as he does so. The supervisors are to exact the fine and keep half of it, and if they don't, they are to owe double to Artemis Hecate.

TEACHING THE ART OF GOVERNMENT

When the political assembly of male citizens at Athens wanted professional advice on a building project they sent for an expert: a builder. If someone who didn't know anything about building attempted to give guidance on this, he would be howled down or dragged away. But when it came to government itself, the Athenians gave everyone an equal opportunity to speak. So the Athenians obviously believed that the art of government could not be taught. What then of those who claimed that it could be? Plato, *Protagoras*, 317e–319d:

(317e) When we had all sat down, Protagoras said, 'Now you can speak, Socrates, since these gentlemen are here, about what you mentioned to me a little while ago on behalf of the young man.'

And I said, (318a) 'I'll begin in the same way as I did a moment ago, Protagoras, concerning why I have come. For Hippocrates is feeling enthusiastic about becoming one of your pupils. So he says he would be pleased to learn, if he joined you, what results he could expect. Such is the sum of our enquiry.'

Protagoras seized the point and replied, 'Young man, you'll gain this, if you join me as a pupil, that on the day you join me, you'll go home as a better person, and on the next day the very same. And every day after that you will keep on improving more and more.'

(318b) And I said when I heard this, 'What you've just said doesn't surprise me, Protagoras, but is to be expected, since even you, although you are advanced in years and therefore wise, if someone were to teach you what you didn't happen to be familiar with, you would be better for it. But let me put it like this, if Hippocrates quite immediately redirected his enthusiasm, and became desirous of the company of that young man who has just now arrived in the city, Zeuxippus of Heraclea, and should go to him, just as he has now come to you, (318c) and heard the very same things as from you, that on each day he spent with him he would be a better person and improve, and if he then asked him a question, "At what will I be better, as you say, and in what will I progress?", Zeuxippus would say to him, "At painting". And if he joined Orthagoras the Theban, and heard the very same thing as from you, and then asked at what he would become better, going to him every day, he would reply, "In playing the flute". (318d) So you, Protagoras, must also tell this young man, and me putting this question on his behalf, if Hippocrates joined Protagoras as a pupil, in what would he, on the very day he joined you and on each subsequent day, go away improved and in what sphere would he advance?'

Protagoras, when he heard me put this question replied, 'You frame your questions nicely, Socrates, and I enjoy replying to those with sensible questions. For Hippocrates if he comes to me will not suffer as those who join one of the sophists. For on the whole they maltreat the young: (318e) for the young men, who have fled from the arts, the sophists lead back again unwillingly, throwing them into the arts, teaching them mathematics, astronomy, music,' – at which he glanced at Hippias – 'but if he comes to me, he won't learn anything except what he has come for. My teaching concerns both good judgement about his personal affairs so that he might best manage his own household, and also about the affairs of the city, (319a) how he might most powerfully act and speak in matters concerning the city.'

'Am I following your arguments?' I asked. 'For you appear to me to be speaking of the art of politics and to be pledging to make men good citizens.'

'This is the very profession that I profess,' he said.

'This is a fine accomplishment you have mastered,' I said, 'if you have mastered it. For you won't hear anything from me except what I think. For I didn't think this could be taught, Protagoras, (319b) but when you say so I can't disbelieve it. How I came to consider that this could not be taught or imparted by men to men, is incumbent upon me to explain. I consider, as do the rest of the Greeks, that the Athenians are wise. For I see that whenever we are gathered together in the political assembly, when it is necessary for the city to deal with some building matter, we send for builders to give advice about the construction project, and when we deliberate about ship-building, we send for the shipwrights, and this is the case for everything (319c) that the assembly thinks is teachable and learnable.

'But if anyone else tries to give advice to them, whom the assembly doesn't consider to be an expert, even if he is very handsome or wealthy or well born, they don't put up with it, but they ridicule him and shout at him, until he either gives up his attempt to speak, is drowned out, or the public slave-archers drag him off, or the presiding officials order his expulsion. This is the way they act in matters that they consider require skill, but when they are deliberating on some matter concerning the administration of the city, (319d) the man who gets up to advise them concerning this is just as likely to be a builder, or just as likely to be a blacksmith, shoemaker, merchant, ship-owner, or wealthy, poor, aristocratic, or low born. And no one would, as in the former cases, when someone attempts to give advice, rebuke him on the grounds that he has nowhere learned anything, nor that he didn't have a teacher. For it is obvious that they don't consider this to be something that can be taught.'

The Authors Themselves

Hesiod instructed us in the working of the land,
the seasons of the crops, and ploughing. And the divine Homer
how did he achieve honour and fame if not by teaching useful things:
tactics, valour and the arming of men?

Aristophanes, Frogs, 1033–6.

A ristophanes in the fifth century BC indicates the importance of Hesiod and Homer for the Greeks, and earlier in the same century Herodotus had pointed out the significance of these two writers for Greek beliefs about the gods (see Homer below). For the Greeks, Homer and Hesiod were teachers, in addition to being authors of literature. The Greeks themselves did not produce their literature for our edification (of course), but wrote to instruct and entertain their listeners and readers, and their work reveals their priorities and what they regarded as of consequence.

This volume is a collection of some of the writings of the Greeks, including Homer and Hesiod, but other authors as well. In addition to the surviving literature of the ancient Greeks (and much has been lost), what is known about Greek history and society can be supplemented by archaeology and the physical remains of buildings such as houses and temples. Athenian vases, which were often decorated with mythological and everyday scenes, are a crucial addition to the written record. The Greeks also recorded material on stone, or scratched on broken pieces of pottery, and in this way laws, decrees, funerary inscriptions and graffiti all survive.

As this volume has largely been about the culture rather than the politics of the Greeks, many questions of historical bias in the works of Greek authors have been avoided. For example, Herodotus and Thucydides each have biases for and against certain individuals: no historical document can be taken completely at face value. The historical writings of the Greeks, while important and revealing of the Greek mentalité, must share the stage with the non-historical writings. For, in a very real sense, it is the plays and poetry that reveal as much about the Greeks' past as the works of political history.

In reading a passage from an ancient Greek writer there are often points of difficulty which even people who have studied these writings for years cannot explain. Despite this, asking a few simple questions can reveal a great deal about a particular extract. Who wrote the text from which the passage comes, and when? What does the quotation tell the reader about a certain topic or topics? What points in the extract are specially interesting? What questions does it leave unanswered about a particular topic? Is there any bias (cultural, historical or otherwise) in the passage? What is the author's aim in presenting his or her narrative? What specific audience (if any) is it directed towards?

Any culture is exposed through its writings. The ancient Greeks reveal themselves to us in their written words, and these words are evidence, material with which to reconstruct (however flawed) some sort of overall picture about ancient Greek society and the Greeks themselves. A short cut in this process is to pick up a standard textbook on Greek history. There is nothing wrong in this itself, and often such an account is invaluable and necessary. But how much more interesting it is to read about the Greeks 'in their own words' than some dry, dusty collection of facts. And at any rate, any textbook on Greek history is only as good as the way in which a modern author handles the ancient Greek authors. How could the excitement of Aeschylus' dramatic account of the defeat of the Persians at Salamis and their flight back home in his play *The Persians* ever be equalled by any modern historian?

THE ANCIENT AUTHORS

Achilles Tatius, writing in about the middle of the second century AD, was a novelist from Alexandria, author of *Leucippe and Clitophon*, a love story involving numerous adventures: elopement, shipwreck, pirates, faked deaths, separation and the like. The couple's love survives it all.

Aeneas the Tactician, or Aeneas Tacticus (fourth century BC), was the first author of a manual of military practices. His *How to Resist Besiegers* is an invaluable guide to martial practices of the time. Other military manuals in Greek also survive, but are later, from the first century BC to the third century AD. One of the longest of these is Polyaenus' *Stratagems of War*, written in the second century AD. Polyaenus' work consists of summaries of the ruses and stratagems used by dozens of military commanders, both Greek and Roman, as well as fifty-eight sections on how to conduct warfare. There was even material on psychological warfare, such as 'Terrifying the enemy', and 'Causing a lack of sleep for the enemy'.

Aeschines (397–322 BC) the Athenian orator was the main political opponent of Demosthenes' policy of an aggressive approach to the growing power of Macedon under Philip II. Demosthenes eventually gained the upper hand in this political contest in 330 BC. The contest was fought in the courts (in addition to the assembly). In 346 BC Aeschines prosecuted Timarchus (with the speech *Against Timarchus*) because Demosthenes and Timarchus commenced proceedings to prosecute him. Aeschines frustrated this prosecution by successfully bringing a court case against Timarchus on a charge of male prostitution. The speech is a central source for Athenian social history and attitudes towards sexuality.

Aeschylus (525?–456 BC) wrote several tragic plays, the best known of which are *The Persians* and the trilogy *Oresteia* (*Agamemnon*, *Women Bearing Libations* and *Eumenides*). *Prometheus Bound* may not be by him. He fought at Marathon and Salamis, and *The Persians* produced in 472 BC is clearly partly an eyewitness account. Herodotus drew heavily on it for his own description of the Battle of Salamis. Aeschylus' plays centre on events, such as the Persian defeat in *The Persians*, or Agamemnon's murder in *Agamemnon*, rather than on character (unlike Euripides). But *The Persians* is unusual in that it details historical events, whereas most tragedies dealt with mythological traditions.

Alcman was a poet writing at Sparta in the mid-seventh century BC; his work survives mainly in fragments, in particular two songs written for young (virgin) women to sing.

Anacreon (575–490 BC) was born on the island of Teos. He spent time in Abdera (Thrace), and then at the court of Polycrates of Samos, and after Polycrates' death, Hipparchus who ruled Athens as tyrant with his brother Hippias brought him to Athens. This patronage was crucial for his career. He wrote heterosexual and homosexual love poetry, and of the joys of wine. Some of his work was abusive.

Antiphon (480–411 BC) was an Athenian orator, and the first to have his speeches preserved.

Archilochus (seventh century BC) was born on the island of Paros, in the Aegean; much of his poetry is invective in nature.

Aristophanes (460 to 450–386 BC) was clearly the best of all the Athenian (and Greek) comic poets. He was the master of Old Comedy, the style of comedy of the fifth century BC. He was above all a satirist and a creator of fantastic worlds. The *Clouds* (produced in 423 BC) satirises Socrates and the new teaching of the sophists, and that of the philosophers who speculated on the nature of the universe and the gods; the *Wasps* (422 BC) satirised Athens' jury system; and his *Women at the Festival of the Thesmophoria* (411 BC) lampooned Euripides. He had imaginative plots: the *Lysistrata* (411 BC) brings peace with Sparta via a women's sex strike, and in the *Women in Assembly* (392 BC) women disguised as men pass a decree that Athens will be ruled by women from now on. In the *Acharnians* (425 BC) an Athenian citizen, tired of the Peloponnesian War, makes a private peace treaty with the Spartans. His other surviving plays are as equally fascinating. Jokes about sex, wine, slaves, women, homosexuals and Athenian politicians abound in his work.

Aristotle (384–322 BC) was born in northern Greece, but spent many years at Athens. Aristotle and his pupils were responsible for writing individual works on the constitutions of about 150 cities, and one of these was Athens. But he is better known as a philosopher and student of Plato. His *Politics* is a crucial work for information on Greek political institutions. He also wrote extensively on flora, fauna and the environment. Some works are falsely attributed to him, including the *Oeconomicus*, and it is debatable whether the *Constitution of the Athenians*, preserved on a papyrus discovered in 1890, is by him. He spent some time in Macedon as Alexander the Great's tutor.

Arrian (AD 86–160), born in Bithynia, consciously emulated Herodotus, Thucydides and Xenophon in his account of the exploits of Alexander the Great; his account of Alexander was entitled *Anabasis* ('Expedition' or 'Expedition Inland') after Xenophon's *Anabasis*. The *Expedition of Alexander* ('Anabasis') deals with events from Alexander's succession to his death. Arrian drew on numerous sources written by those who had served with Alexander, but preferred those favourable to Alexander. His account is lively and fascinating; while he attempts to 'set the record straight' on some points, he is not always historically accurate.

Athenaeus wrote the *Deipnosophistae* (*The Wise Men at Dinner*), in the third century AD. He was from Naucratis, an old Greek colony in Egypt, which Herodotus provides detail about. Over dinner (lasting several days) the diners discuss a wide variety of topics, and in doing so often quote works of literature that are now lost. His work is therefore a 'mine' of extraordinary value.

Bacchylides (529–450 BC), of the Aegean island of Ceos and nephew of Simonides (see below), wrote poems (victory odes) in honour of those who won contests at the Greek festivals, as well as hymns.

Callimachus of Cyrene (the Greek colony in Libya) wrote in the third century BC. Among other works, his *Hymns* were not actually written for performance (unlike the Homeric Hymns they emulate to an extent).

Demosthenes (384–322 BC) was a prominent Athenian opponent of Philip II and Macedonian expansion; his chief political rival was Aeschines (see above); he committed suicide in 322 BC rather than fall into Macedonian hands and be executed. After initial difficulties in establishing a career as a speaker in the assembly, he became the foremost of Athenian orators. His political speeches are crucial for an understanding of fourth century BC history, but he also wrote many speeches for clients in civil cases; many others are attributed to him but are probably not his work (such as the *Against Neaera*). These speeches in civil cases provide a wealth of information about Athenian social life.

Empedocles see p. 219.

Epicharmus see p. 219.

Epicrates (about the middle of the fourth century BC), of Ambracia in western Greece, wrote comic plays. His work survives only in fragments.

Euripides (480s–406 BC), the Athenian tragedian, has been frequently labelled a misogynist, but a close reading of his plays indicates that he was empathetic and sympathetic toward women. The many jokes in Aristophanes about Euripides' negative portrayal of women (see especially Aristophanes' *Women at the Festival of the Thesmophoria*) in fact reflect Euripides' strong interest in the situations in which women because of their gender and sexuality are placed or find themselves (see especially his *Medea* and *Alcestis*). Women as victims and avengers fascinated him. After his death, his plays were preferred to those of the other two great Athenian tragedians, Aeschylus and Sophocles.

Heraclitus p. 218.

Herodotus (*c.* 480–420 BC), born at Halicarnassus in Asia Minor, wrote a history of the Persian invasions of Greece (490 BC, 480–479 BC) and dealt with how the Greeks and Persians came into conflict, leading him to discuss sixth-century BC Greek history. As there were no written records for the sixth century BC he had to rely on oral traditions, with all its hazards. But his main narrative deals with the Persian Wars, and he relied on eyewitness accounts for many of the details he includes. He is sometimes referred to as the 'Father of History' as his is the first lengthy historical work. Yet he was not averse to recording various improbable stories, for which he has earned the title 'Father of Lies'. But he himself points to his method, and leaves the readers to decide for themselves: 'I am under an obligation to say what I have been told, but I am not obliged to believe everything, and this statement is applicable to my entire work' (7.153.2). His account is trustworthy, and he is of crucial importance for early Greek history to 479 BC. He makes clear why he wrote his account: 'Herodotus of Halicarnassus gives here his investigations [*historia*], so that the achievements of men may not be forgotten over time' ('Preface' to his work). It is often said that there is a strong religious element in his work, and the gods are often present in the narrative, but he is also very much interested in the vagaries of human existence, as seen in his stories about Solon and Croesus, and Amasis and Polycrates: 'The prosperity of men does not remain long in the one place' (1.5.4).

Hesiod (*c.* 700 BC), from Boeotia, wrote after Homer, and these two are often considered to be the major two early Greek writers. He wrote two main works: *Works and Days* and the *Theogony*. The *Works and Days* provides advice of a practical sort about farming, especially ploughing and harvesting, as well as sailing and maritime trading. The *Theogony* is concerned with the genealogy of the gods. In addition to the quotation from Aristophanes' *Frogs*, 1033–6, at the beginning of this chapter, the comment attributed to Cleomenes (King of Sparta, 520–490 BC) is instructive. Plutarch, *Sayings of the Spartans* (*Moralia*, 223a): 'Cleomenes son of Anaxandridas said that Homer was the poet of the Spartans, and Hesiod of the *helots*; for the first had given instructions as to how to fight, and the second as to how to farm.'

Hippocrates see p. 217.

Homer is the greatest poet of western literature and author of two epics, the *Iliad* and the *Odyssey*, arguably the greatest written masterpieces of European civilisation. (Some scholars claim, however, that the *Odyssey* is the work of a different author.) The *Iliad* concerns the tenth year of the siege of Troy by the Greeks (and ends before the actual sack of the city), while the *Odyssey* deals with Odysseus' ten years of adventure in reaching home against the odds and the implacable wrath of the god Poseidon. The *Iliad* probably dates from about 750 BC, and the *Odyssey* from about 725 BC. They reflect an aristocratic world, though ostensibly the setting is the siege of Troy in the Mycenaean age of kings such as Agamemnon and Menelaus. It is the Greek world of the emergent *polis*, of burgeoning trade and the embryonic political assembly.

Homer provides brilliant insights into humanity, writing imaginatively and with beautiful, powerful language. For the Greeks he was the greatest writer, and schoolboys were set the task of learning the two epics by heart. Within the plots of the two poems he provides information about farming, trading, social values and religious beliefs. His value for the nature of Greek warfare is difficult to assess (note the presence of war chariots on the battlefield of the *Iliad*, while the Greeks of the archaic and classical period did not use these in battles). Herodotus gave Homer and Hesiod the credit for organising the Greeks' religious beliefs (Herodotus, 2.53.2): 'Hesiod and Homer were the poets who composed the genealogies of the gods, and gave the gods their titles and their spheres of influence, relating their skills, and described their forms.'

Homeric Hymns. These were clearly not written by Homer, but composed in the same metre. They were written for performance, probably in the sixth century BC.

Hyperides (389–322 BC) was a powerful Athenian orator, and champion of Greek freedom against the Macedonians, who executed him in 322 BC. The ancients themselves considered his oratory second only to Demosthenes.

Isocrates (436–338 BC) wrote rather than delivered his speeches. An Athenian, he was particularly concerned with panhellenism, the unity of the Greeks, and advocated solidarity against Persia.

Lucian (born *c.* AD 120) was a prolific writer of satirical works. These included the *Anacharsis*, which parodied Greek athletic practice but is an invaluable source on this topic. His *True Story*, about an adventure to the moon and the underworld, inspired Swift.

Lycurgus (*c.* 390–326 BC) was the main Athenian politician from 338 to 326 BC, dominating the administration of finances; he aimed to revitalise Athens. His sole surviving speech (though there are extant quotations from his other speeches) is the *Against Leocrates*, delivered in 330 BC.

Lysias (459–*c.* 380 BC) was a foreigner (*metic*) living in Athens; his father had moved there from Syracuse. He composed speeches for others to deliver in court, and these reveal numerous details about Athenian life. His strength was in writing speeches to suit his client's character. His greatest speech is his *On the Murder of Eratosthenes*, written for one Euphiletus who had killed Eratosthenes for committing adultery with his wife.

Lysippus was an Athenian comic poet of the Old Comedy period, with an attested victory in 409 BC. Only a few fragments of his work remain, of which his description of Athens (see p. 6) is justly famous.

Melissus of Samos as admiral in 441 BC defeated the Athenians. He was also a philosopher and argued against the notion of change in the cosmos.

Menander (?344–292 BC) of Athens was the most important comic poet of New Comedy, the style of comedy from 325–250 BC. His work, unlike the Old Comedy of Aristophanes with its many political overtones, is very 'domestic' in nature, dealing with private problems. Most of his hundred plays were lost in late antiquity but papyrus finds from Egypt have rescued substantial parts of some of these.

The Old Oligarch is the modern name given to the author of a brief pamphlet entitled *The Constitution of the Athenians*, probably written in the 420s BC and falsely attributed to Xenophon (probably to increase its circulation). Hostile to democracy, the work provides many details of its workings, and the relationship between the democracy and the role of the poor as rowers in the navy. It contains useful information about Athenian society.

Pausanias (writing in about the middle of the second century AD) was from Asia Minor and composed a geographical description of mainland Greece. It is an invaluable and reliable source of information on religious architecture, cults, geography, customs and even history. He toured Greece personally to write his work.

Pindar (*c.* 520–446 BC) was from Boeotia in central Greece. He is best known for his victory odes (*epinicia*), poems written in praise of the victors in the athletic events at the Olympic, Pythian, Nemean and Isthmian festivals, all of which attracted competitors from all over the Greek world. These odes were performed either at the games themselves or later when the victor returned home. They often have a mythological section (usually about the mythical heroes of the victor's home city) and generally include moral maxims. In addition he wrote hymns, paeans (songs in honour of the gods, especially but not exclusively Apollo) and songs to be performed by maidens, as well as *encomia* (eulogies, singular *encomion*) and *threnoi* (dirges, singular *threnos*).

Plato (429–347 BC) was an Athenian and Socrates' main pupil, as well as a prolific writer. He was particularly affected by Socrates' execution in 399 BC, and the various dialogues he wrote could be interpreted as an attempt to present the 'real' Socrates who did not deserve death. The works of Plato's early career deal with Socrates' philosophy, but clearly later works, such as the famous *Republic* and *Laws*, although including Socrates, seem to reflect Plato's own philosophy. These works are written as dialogues, in which Socrates questions and has discussions with his listeners. The *Republic* concerns the definition of justice and dates to the middle period of Plato's writings. The *Laws*, dealing with the establishment of the ideal state, belongs to the later period, and it provides a wealth of detail on Greek social organisation. The *Apology*, a presentation of Socrates' defence in court in 399 BC on the charges of corrupting the minds of the young and introducing and worshipping deities of his own creation, is perhaps the most accessible of the works and the most informative about Socrates.

Plutarch (*c.* AD 50 to after AD 120) lived in Boeotia and wrote pairs of biographies (the *Lives*) about famous individuals, one Greek and one Roman, who had similar careers (Alexander and Caesar is one such pair; Demosthenes and Cicero is another). He was an armchair historian drawing on existing written sources and sometimes he cites or quotes these. His biographies are not strict histories, and he was less interested in historical accuracy than in making a moral point on the basis of an individual's life. But he is nevertheless invaluable as a historical source. He wrote numerous other works which are collected under the title *Moralia*.

Praxilla of Sicyon wrote in about the middle of the fifth century BC. Little survives of her work.

Sappho was born on the Aegean island of Lesbos some time after 650 BC. In antiquity she was known as the tenth Muse, in addition to the nine divine ones. Despite this, relatively little of her work survives: only one complete poem (see pp. 95–6) and some fragments. Most of her poems were of a homoerotic nature, of the love between women or girls. She had a circle of girl and women friends which changed as the girls married. But hymns and wedding songs also formed part of her repertoire.

Simonides was born in about 556 BC and was said to have lived till he was ninety. He came from the Aegean island of Ceos, like his nephew Bacchylides. He wrote several epigrams, especially for those who fought in the Persian Wars. Many epigrams were attributed to him in antiquity but appear not to have actually been composed by him. He wrote historical elegies on the battles of Artemesium and Plataea, newly discovered on papyrus in 1992 and historically invaluable.

Solon was *archon* (chief official) in Athens in 594 BC. Prior to that year he had written several poems criticising the state of affairs there, in which the rich were oppressing the poor, and after 594 BC wrote other poems justifying his actions. His work contains many moral maxims.

Sophocles (*c.* 495–406 BC) wrote tragedies over a long career at Athens. His most famous work is the *Antigone*, followed in importance by *Oedipus the King*. He had a sense of the theatrical, such as in the *Electra* when the disguised Orestes, who is pretending to have been killed in a chariot race at Delphi (see pp. 153–5), brings in his own cremated ashes in an urn and hands them to his sister who mourns him.

Theocritus was an early third-century BC poet from Syracuse, who composed at Alexandria in the 270s BC. His main works are the *Idylls*, of which the second is a mime: the love-sick Simaetha carries out a magic ritual (see pp. 36–9); this is said to find echoes in Eliot's *The Waste Land*.

Theognis of Megara was active in about 550–540 BC, and writes at a time of political upheaval of which he does not approve and from which he suffered dispossession and exile. He writes of numerous themes, including life, friendship and drinking.

Theophrastus (372–288 BC) of Lesbos succeeded Aristotle in the school of philosophy he had established at Athens. He wrote extensively on botany, philosophy and cosmology. His best-known work is the *Characters*, a humorous collection of thirty character sketches pointing out the defects of various personality types, such as those suffering from superstition or cowardice.

Thucydides (*c.* 450–390 BC) of Athens wrote a history of the Peloponnesian War (431–404 BC) but did not complete it, with his narrative breaking off in 411 BC. In the introduction to his work, he sketched an outline of the early history of Greece, and an important digression on the approximately fifty years between the end of the Persian Wars in 479 to 431 BC, but with next to nothing on the Persian Wars themselves, and so acknowledging the masterpiece of Herodotus' treatment of this period. He was conservative in his politics, admiring Pericles but inaccurately considering that Pericles enjoyed one-man rule over Athens. His history is a political and military one, though there is information on religious topics. He wrote so that his history would last forever, and was not designed to please an immediate audience. His work contains several speeches, which he either heard himself or that were reported to him: 'Concerning the speeches in this account, either those made on the eve of the war or while it was going on, it was difficult for me to recall precisely what was spoken when I heard them myself, and also for those who related them to me from elsewhere' (Thucydides, 1.22.1). He admits that in the speeches he supplies words that he believed would have suited the occasion of the speech.

So while he reports (at length) Pericles' Funeral Oration, these were not Pericles' exact words, but what Thucydides remembered Pericles to have said: the essential themes and outline of the speech would have been as recorded, but many of the actual words will be Thucydides' rather than Pericles'. He was exiled from Athens in 424 BC for failing to arrive at Amphipolis in northern Greece in time to prevent its surrender to the Spartan general Brasidas. His historical account is indisputably weaker after this date due to his absence from Athens, although it is frequently said that his exile would have enabled him to access a greater variety of sources than might otherwise have been the case. His work remains as the best account of a period of hostilities ever written, and as a model for historical enquiry.

Tyrtaeus (a Spartan general in the mid-seventh century BC) wrote poetry to encourage the Spartans in their second war against the Messenians. The poems were learned by Spartan youths to inculcate Spartan military ideals, and it is possible that his poetry was sung on the battlefield before fighting began.

Xenophanes see p. 218.

Xenophon (*c.* 430–360 BC), an Athenian writer who in his *Hellenica* picked up from Thucydides' history (which breaks off, incomplete, in 411 BC), and continued Greek history to 362 BC. He also wrote social and philosophic texts, and was interested in Sparta, about which he also wrote. The *Anabasis* is an account of the return to Greece after the Battle of Cunaxa (near Babylon) in 401 BC of the 10,000 Greek mercenaries employed by Cyrus in his rebellion. Other works, especially the *Oeconomicus*, are important for political and social history, with material on 'wife-training' and the treatment of slaves. He was an admirer of Sparta but was aware of its faults.

Glossary

Achaeans	Homer uses this word for the Greeks.
aegis	A large circular object with snake heads around the perimeter; it had protective powers, and was associated with Zeus and Athena. Athena used it to terrify the suitors when Odysseus was fighting them (Homer, *Odyssey*, 22.297).
archaic	The period from the eighth century BC (when writing was rediscovered and the so-called previous Dark Age period concluded) to 479 BC (the Greek defeat of the Persians).
arete	Virtue or excellence, whether in war, athletics or government.
Argives	Men of Argos, in the Peloponnese, ruled by Agamemnon from the city of Mycenae in Homer's *Iliad*.
Attica	The land of the Athenians around the city of Athens, some 2,400 sq km.
chorus	A group of singers in a play (a tragedy or a comedy).
classical	The period from 479 BC to 336 BC. It was followed by the Hellenistic period (336 BC, the accession of Alexander the Great to the throne of Macedon, to 31 BC, Octavian's defeat of Mark Antony and Cleopatra).
Danaans	Homer uses this word of the Greek forces at Troy.
deme	Attica was divided into 140 political units (*demes*), the villages and towns, and the suburbs of Athens itself.
dithyramb	A choral song, in honour of the god Dionysus. Simonides, Bacchylides and Pindar were the main writers of dithyrambs.
Dorians	The Greeks mainly of southern Greece, the Peloponnese.
drachma	A *drachma* was a day's wage for an unskilled worker.
elegy	A song of mourning or lament.
encomion	A poem of praise, usually for a victor, sung at a revel (comas) or banquet.
fragment	Many of the writings from ancient Greece do not survive in their entirety. Sometimes only quotations from these works made by later authors survive. Other parts of works have been discovered on papyrus from Egypt, especially of Menander.
Hades	The underworld.
hecatomb	Technically an offering of a hundred oxen to the gods, but also used generically of any animal sacrifice, regardless of number.
helots	People, especially the Messenians, enserfed by the Spartans.
Hermes	The Greek messenger god, also patron of thieves, and guide of the souls of the dead to Hades.
hoplite	Infantry soldier armed with shield (*hoplon*), spear, helmet, greaves and breastplate; the backbone of the classical Greek army.

hyporchema	A song with dancing.
Ilion	Troy (Ilium).
Ionians	The Greeks of Athens, the Aegean islands and of many of the cities of the Asia Minor coast.
mina	A hundred *drachmas*.
Olympus	A mountain in Thessaly, nearly 3,000 m high, home of the main gods and throne of Zeus.
Peloponnese	Southern Greece, separated from the rest of Greece by the Isthmus of Corinth.
phalanx	The tight formation of Greek *hoplites*, usually eight ranks deep.
Phoebus	Cult epithet (title) of Apollo, meaning 'bright' or 'pure'.
Piraeus	The main harbour of Athens, some 7 km from the acropolis and the heart of the city.
polis	A Greek city, or more precisely city-state, the word is also used for an urban centre which we would describe as a town; plural: *poleis*.
Smintheus	Cult epithet (title) of Apollo, from Sminthys, a town near Troy.
'sons of Atreus'	Agamemnon and Menelaus.
sophist	A teacher of wisdom (*sophia*).
stade	A measure of distance, about 200 m.
stater	200 *drachmas*; 2 *minas*.
talent	An abstract unit of currency (like 'a million dollars'); sixty *minas*.
Thracians	Barbarians from Thrace, north of Greece; sometimes employed as mercenaries by the Athenians.
threnos	A funeral dirge (plural: *threnoi*).
'winged words'	Spoken words, as opposed to words that are only thought and to which we do not 'give wing'.

Suggested Reading

GENERAL READING FOR GREEK HISTORY

Blois, L. de and Spek, van der R.J. *An Introduction to the Ancient World*, London, 1997

Boardman, J. and Hammond, N.G.L. (eds). *The Expansion of the Greek World, Eighth to Sixth Centuries BC, The Cambridge Ancient History III.3*, 2nd edn, Cambridge, 1982

Boardman, J., Hammond, N.G.L., Lewis, D.M. and Ostwald, M. (eds). *Persia, Greece and the Western Mediterranean, c. 525 to 479 BC, The Cambridge Ancient History IV*, 2nd edn, Cambridge, 1988

Boardman, J., Griffin, J. and Murray, O. *The Oxford History of Greece and the Hellenistic World*, Oxford, 1991

Buckley, T. *Aspects of Greek History 750–323 BC. A Source-Based Approach*, London, 1996

Bury, J.B. and Meiggs, R. *A History of Greece: To the Death of Alexander the Great*, 4th edn, Hampshire, 1975

Camp, J.M. *The Athenian Agora: Excavations in the Heart of Classical Athens*, London, 1986

Cartledge, P. (ed.). *The Cambridge Illustrated History of Ancient Greece*, Cambridge, 1998

Demand, N. *A History of Ancient Greece*, New York, 1996

Dillon, M.P.J. and Garland, L. *Ancient Greece. Social and Historical Documents from Archaic Times to the Death of Socrates*, 2nd edn, London, 2000

Dunstan, W.E. *Ancient Greece*, Fort Worth, TX, 2000

Ehrenberg, V. *From Solon to Socrates*, 2nd edn, London, 1973

Fine, J.V.A. *The Ancient Greeks: A Critical History*, Cambridge, MA, 1983

Finley, M.I. *The Ancient Greeks*, London, 1963

Fisher, N. and Wees, H. van. *Archaic Greece*, London, 1998

Hammond, N.G.L. *A History of Greece to 322 BC*, 3rd edn, Oxford, 1986

Hornblower, S. and Spawforth, A. (eds). *The Oxford Classical Dictionary*, 3rd edn, Oxford, 1996

Jeffery, L.H. *Archaic Greece: The City-States c. 700–500 BC*, New York, 1976

Kitto, H.D.F. *The Greeks*, 2nd edn, Harmondsworth, 1957

Levi, P. *Atlas of the Greek World*, Oxford, 1984

Lewis, D.M., Boardman, J., Davies, J.K. and Ostwald, M. (eds). *The Fifth Century BC, The Cambridge Ancient History V*, 2nd edn, Cambridge, 1992

Meier, C. *Athens: A Portrait of the City in its Golden Age*, New York, 1998

Murray, O. *Early Greece*, 2nd edn, London, 1993

Osborne, R. *Greece in the Making, 1200–479 BC*, London, 1996

Pomeroy, S., Burstein, S.M., Donlan, W. and Roberts, J.T. (eds). *Ancient Greece. A Political, Social, and Cultural History*, Oxford, 1998

Powell, A. *Athens and Sparta: Constructing Greek Political and Social History from 478 BC*, London, 1988

—— (ed.). *Classical Sparta: Techniques Behind her Success*, London, 1989

Roberts, J.W. *City of Sokrates: An Introduction to Classical Athens*, London, 1984

Sealey, R. *A History of the Greek City States* ca. *700–338 BC*, Berkeley, CA, 1976
Snodgrass, A. *Archaic Greece. The Age of Experiment*, Berkeley, CA, 1980
Starr, C. *The Economic and Social History of Early Greece: 800–500 BC*, New York, 1977

GODS AND MORTALS

Bremmer, J. *Greek Religion*, Oxford, 1994
Burkert, W. *Greek Religion: Archaic and Classical*, tr. J. Raffan, Oxford, 1985
Dillon, M.P.J. *Girls and Women in Classical Greek Religion*, London, 2002
Dodds, E.R. *The Greeks and the Irrational*, Berkeley, CA, 1956
Easterling, E. and Muir, J.V. (eds). *Greek Religion and Society*, Cambridge, 1985
Garland, R.S.J. *Introducing New Gods*, London, 1992
Guthrie, W.K.C. *The Greeks and their Gods*, Boston, MA, 1950
Jordon, B. *Servants of the Gods: A Study in the Religion, History and Literature of Fifth-Century Athens*, Göttingen, 1979
Luck, G. *Arcana Mundi: Magic and the Occult in the Greek and Roman Worlds*, Baltimore, MD, 1985
Lyons, D. *Gender and Immortality. Heroines in Ancient Greek Myth and Cult*, Princeton, NJ, 1997
Mikalson, J.D. *Athenian Popular Religion*, London, 1983
Parker, R. *Miasma: Pollution and Purification in Early Greek Religion*, Oxford, 1983
——. *Athenian Religion: A History*, Oxford, 1996
Robertson, N. *Festivals and Legends: The Formation of Greek Cities in the Light of Public Ritual*, Toronto, 1992
Simon, E. *Festivals of Attica: An Archaeological Commentary*, Madison, WI, 1983
Zaidman, L.B. and Pantel, P.S. *Religion in the Ancient Greek City*, tr. P. Cartledge, Cambridge, 1992

HUSBANDS AND WIVES

Blundell, S. *Women in Ancient Greece*, Cambridge, MA, 1995
Cameron, A. and Kurht, A. (eds). *Images of Women in Antiquity*, London, 1983
Cantarella, E. *Pandora's Daughters: The Role and Status of Women in Greek and Roman Antiquity*, Baltimore, MD, 1987
Demand, N. *Birth, Death and Motherhood in Classical Greece*, Baltimore, MD, 1994
Dover, K.J. *Greek Homosexuality*, revd edn, London, 1989
Fantham, E., Foley, H.P., Kampen, N.B., Pomeroy, S.B. and Shapiro, H.A. (eds). *Women in the Classical World: Image and Text*, Oxford, 1994
Golden, M. *Children and Childhood in Classical Athens*, Baltimore, MD, 1990
Hawley, R. and Levick, B. (eds). *Women in Antiquity. New Assessments*, London, 1995
Humphreys, S.C. *The Family, Women and Death: Comparative Studies*, London, 1983
Just, R. *Women in Athenian Life and Law*, London, 1989
Keuls, E.C. *The Reign of the Phallus: Sexual Politics in Ancient Athens*, 2nd edn, Berkeley, CA, 1993
Lacey, W.K. *The Family in Classical Greece*, London, 1968
Lefkowitz, M.R. and Fant, M.B. *Women's Life in Greece and Rome*, 2nd edn, Baltimore, MD, 1992
Patterson, C.B. *The Family in Greek History*, Princeton, NJ, 1998
Pomeroy, S.B. *Goddesses, Whores, Wives and Slaves*, New York, 1975

——. *Families in Classical and Hellenistic Greece: Representations and Realities*, Oxford, 1997

Winkler, J. *The Constraints of Desire: The Anthropology of Sex and Gender in Ancient Greece*, New York, 1990

FARMERS AND TRADERS

Austin, M.M. and Vidal-Nacquet, P. *Economic and Social History of Ancient Greece: An Introduction*, Berkeley, CA, 1977

Finley, M.I. *Economy and Society in Ancient Greece*, London, 1981

——. *The Ancient Economy*, 2nd edn, London, 1985

Garnsey, P. and Whittaker, C.R. (eds). *Trade and Famine in Classical Antiquity*, Cambridge, 1983

Garnsey, P. *Famine and Food Supply in the Graeco-Roman World: Responses to Risk and Crisis*, Cambridge, 1985

Hanson, V.D. *The Other Greeks. The Family Farm and the Agrarian Roots of Western Civilization*, New York, 1995

Isager, S. and Hansen, M.H. *Aspects of Athenian Society in the Fourth Century BC*, Odense, 1975

Millett, P. *Lending and Borrowing in Ancient Athens*, Cambridge, 1991

Pomeroy, S.B. *Xenophon's* Oeconomicus. *A Social and Historical Commentary*, Oxford, 1994

Rich, J. and Wallace-Hadrill, A. (eds). *City and Country in the Ancient World*, London, 1991

Tandy, D.W. *Warriors into Traders. The Power of the Market in Early Greece*, Berkeley, CA, 1997

Whittaker, C.R. (ed.). *Pastoral Economies in Classical Antiquity*, Cambridge Philological Society Supplement 14, Cambridge, 1988

Zimmern, A. *The Greek Commonwealth: Politics and Economics in Fifth-Century Athens*, 5th edn, Oxford, 1931

WORKERS AND ENTERTAINERS

Dalby, A. *Siren Feasts. A History of Food and Gastronomy in Greece*, London, 1996

Davidson, J. *Courtesans and Fishcakes. The Consuming Passions of Classical Athens*, London, 1997

Finley, M.I. *Ancient Slavery and Modern Ideology*, Harmondsworth, 1980

Finley, M.I. and Pleket, H.W. *The Olympic Games: The First Thousand Years*, New York, 1976

Garlan, Y. *Slavery in Ancient Greece*, tr. J. Lloyd, Ithaca, NY, 1988

Golden, M. *Sport and Society in Ancient Greece*, Cambridge, 1998

Harris, H.A. *Greek Athletes and Athletics*, London, 1964

Hunt, P. *Slaves, Warfare, and Ideology in the Greek Historians*, Cambridge, 1998

Kyle, D.G. *Athletics in Ancient Athens*, Leiden, 1987

Miller, S.G. *Arete: Greek Sports from Ancient Sources*, 2nd edn, Berkeley, CA, 1991

Morgan, C. *Athletes and Oracles: the Transformation of Olympia and Delphi in the Eighth Century BC*, Cambridge, 1990

Murray, O. (ed.). *Sympotica. A Symposium on the Symposion*, Oxford, 1990

Phillips, D.J. and Pritchard, D. (eds). *Sport and Festival in the Ancient Greek World*, London, 2002

Poliakoff, M.B. *Combat Sports in the Ancient World. Competition, Violence and Culture,* New Haven, CT, 1987

Raschke, W. (ed.). *The Olympics and Other Festivals in Antiquity,* Madison, WI, 1988

Sweet, W.E. *Sport and Recreation in Ancient Greece: A Sourcebook with Translations,* Oxford, 1987

Vogt, J. *Ancient Slavery and the Ideal of Man,* tr. T. Wiedemann, Cambridge, 1975

Wood, E.M. *Peasant-Citizen and Slave: the Foundations of Athenian Democracy,* London, 1988

SOLDIERS AND COWARDS

Adcock, F.E. *The Greek and Macedonian Art of War,* Berkeley, CA, 1957

Anderson, J.K. *Military Theory and Practice in the Age of Xenophon,* Berkeley, CA, 1970

Bugh, G.R. *The Horsemen of Athens,* Princeton, NJ, 1988

Connolly, P. *Greece and Rome at War,* London, 1981

Ducrey, P. *Warfare in Ancient Greece,* New York, 1986

Green, P. *The Greco-Persian Wars,* Berkeley, 1996 (also published as *The Year of Salamis, 480–479 BC,* London, 1970 and *Xerxes at Salamis,* New York, 1970)

Hanson, V.D. *The Western Way of War: Infantry Battle in Classical Greece,* New York, 1989

—— (ed.). *Hoplites: The Classical Greek Battle Experience,* London, 1991

Jordan, B. *The Athenian Navy in the Classical Period,* Berkeley, CA, 1975

Lazenby, J.F. *The Spartan Army,* Warminster, 1985

Parke, H.W. *Greek Mercenary Soldiers,* Oxford, 1933

Pritchett, W.K. *The Greek State at War I–V,* Berkeley, CA, 1971–91

Rich, J. and Shipley, G. (eds). *War and Society in the Greek World,* London, 1993

Snodgrass, A.M. *Arms and Armour of the Greeks,* Ithaca, NY, 1967

Warry, J. *Warfare in the Classical World,* New York, 1980

PHILOSOPHERS AND DOCTORS

Brickhouse, T.C. and Smith, N.D. *Socrates on Trial,* Princeton, NJ, 1989

Colaiaco, J.A. *Socrates Against Athens. Philosophy on Trial,* London, 2001

Cotter, W. *Miracles in Greco-Roman Antiquity,* London, 1999

Edelstein, E.J. and L. *Asclepius: A Collection and Interpretation of the Testimonies I–II,* Baltimore, MD, 1945

Guthrie, W.K.C. *The Greek Philosophers from Thales to Aristotle,* London, 1967

——. *Socrates,* Cambridge, 1971

——. *The Sophists,* Cambridge, 1971

Hope, V.M. and Marshall, E. *Death and Disease in the Ancient City,* London, 2000

Hussey, E. *The Pre-Socratics,* London, 1972

Jouanna, J. *Hippocrates,* Baltimore, MD, 1999

Kerényi, C. *Asklepios: Archetypal Image of the Physician's Existence,* tr. R. Manheim, London, 1960

King, H. *Hippocrates' Woman. Reading the Female Body in Ancient Greece,* London, 1998

Kraut, R. *The Cambridge Companion to Plato,* Cambridge, 1992

Lloyd, G.E.R. *Science, Folklore and Ideology. Studies in the Life Sciences in Ancient Greece,* Cambridge, 1983

Rankin, H.D. *Sophists, Socratics and Cynics,* London, 1983

Romilly, J. de. *The Great Sophists in Periclean Athens,* Oxford, 1992

CITIZENS AND OFFICIALS

Davies, J.K. *Democracy and Classical Greece*, 2nd edn, London, 1993

Ehrenberg, V. *The Greek State*, Oxford, 1960

Finley, M.I. *Politics in the Ancient World*, Cambridge, 1983

Hansen, M.H. *The Athenian Democracy in the Age of Demosthenes: Structure, Principles and Ideology*, Oxford, 1991

Jones, A.H.M. *Athenian Democracy*, Oxford, 1957

Kagan, D. *Pericles of Athens and the Birth of Democracy*, New York, 1991

Murray, O. and Price, S. (eds). *The Greek City from Homer to Alexander*, Oxford, 1990

Ober, J. *Mass and Elite in Democratic Athens. Rhetoric, Ideology, and the Power of the People*, Princeton, NJ, 1989

Osborne, R. *Demos: the Discovery of Classical Attika*, Cambridge, 1985

Ostwald, M. *From Popular Sovereignty to the Sovereignty of Law: Law, Society and Politics in Fifth-Century Athens*, Berkeley, CA, 1986

Sealey, R. *The Athenian Republic: Democracy or the Rule of Law?*, PA, 1987

Sinclair, R.K. *Democracy and Participation in Athens*, Cambridge, 1988

Starr, C.G. *The Birth of Athenian Democracy*, New York, 1990

Stockton, D. *The Classical Athenian Democracy*, Oxford, 1990

Index of Sources

Achilles Tatius, 2.9.1–3: 94
Aeneas the Tactician, *How to Resist Besiegers*, 33.1–4: 181
Aeschines, 1 (*Against Timarchus*), 40–2, 51–2, 58–9: 147–9; 97: 133
Aeschylus, *The Persians*, 65–80: 203; 230–44: 203–4; 272–9: 204; 304–5, 314–17: 205; 337–514: 205–10; 798–831: 210–11; 909–31: 211–12; *Prometheus Bound*, 447–69, 476–83: 235–6; 505–6: 236
Alcman, 77: 165
Anacreon, *Elegy*, 2: 123; *Epigram*, 100d: 215; 102d: 112; 111d: 173; 356 a, b: 123; 373: 124; 388: 120; 395: 27; 412: 124
Antiphon, 5 (*On the Murder of Herodes*), 69: 131–2
Archilochus, 5: 172–3
Aristophanes, *Acharnians*, 544–54: 213; *Clouds*, 1–40: 118–19; 75–216: 228–33; *Frogs*, 1033–6: 279; *Lysistrata*, 99–237: 193–8; 403–30: 88–9; 706–80: 198–201; *The Seasons*, Fragment 577: 132; *Wasps*, 54, 64–167: 251–5; *Wealth*, 160–8: 113–14; *Women at the Festival of the Thesmophoria*, 383–432: 83–5; 466–519, 531–67: 85–8; *Women in Assembly*, 214–44: 249–50
Aristotle, *Constitution of the Athenians*, 50.1–2: 146; *Oeconomicus*, 1344a23–b21: 128–9; *Politics*, 1253a2–3: 247; 1253b14–54a17: 134–5; 1254b24–b34, 1255a1–a12: 135–6; 1255b31–b37: 136; 1275a1–a33, 1275b17–b21: 264–5; 1277b33–78a2, 1278a6–a13, 1278a17–a26: 265–6; 1326a40–b11, 1326b14–b24: 263–4
Arrian, *The Expedition of Alexander*, 2.3.6–8: 240; 2.18.1–19.6: 182–3; 4.18.4–19.5: 191–2; 6.9.1–11.2, 6.13.4–5: 188–91; 7.14.1–10: 29–31
Athenaeus, *The Wise Men at Dinner*, 412e–f: 159; 573c–e: 143; 590d–591d: 144–5

Bacchylides, *Paean*, 4.61–72, 75–80: 167–8; *Processionals*, Fragments 11–12: 238; *Victory Ode* 4, lines 1–6: 6; 5, lines 1–2: 6; 5.37–49: 155–6; 9.21–38: 156–7; 10.15–28: 156; 19.1–8: 7–8; *Fragment* 24: 240; 20b, lines 6–16: 160–1; 21: 161; 25: 238

Callimachus, *Hymn to Artemis* (3), 1–25: 40–1; *Hymn to Demeter* (6), 1–6, 118–38: 41–2

Demosthenes, 24 (*Against Timocrates*), 124: 131; 27 (*Against Aphobus* 1), 9: 133; 32 (*Against Zenothemis*), 4–9: 108–10; 43 (*Against Macartatus*), 66: 45; 47 (*Against Evergus and Mnesibulus*), 55–6: 131; 53 (*Against Nicostratus*), 16: 130; 59 (*Against Neaera*), 29–32: 145–6

Empedocles, Fragments 11, 112, 134: 219
Epicharmus of Syracuse, Fragments 8, 48, 49, 64: 219

Epicrates, *Hard to Sell*, Fragment 5: 133
Euripides, *Alcestis*, 280–356, 416–44, 463–4: 63–7; *Autolycus*, Fragment 284: 150–1; *Andromache*, 445–9: 7; *Ion*, 226–9: 44; 299–304: 45; *Medea*, 225–65: 67–8; 569–75: 68–9; 1070–80: 69; 1090–115: 69–70; 1236–50: 70; 1323–85, 1415–19: 71–3; *Suppliant Women*, 267–9: 132; Fragment 755: 151

Fraenkel, M. (ed.), *Inscriptiones Graecae* (Berlin, 1902), vol. IV.1, 2nd edn, nos 121–2, cures 3, 5, 6, 7, 16, 39: 245–6
Friedländer, P. *Epigrammata. Greek Inscriptions in Verse* (London, 1948), no. 1: 32; 2: 32; 25: 32; 135: 32–3

Gaertringen, F.H. de (ed.), *Inscriptiones Graecae* (Berlin, 1939), vol. XII.3, no. 536: 95; 538: 95; 540: 95

Heraclitus, Fragments 12, 27, 30, 35, 49, 49a, 89, 93, 97, 102, 135, 136: 218–19; 58: 240–1
Herodotus, Preface: 282; 1.5.4: 282; 1.30.1–32.2, 32.4–5, 32.9, 33–34.1: 220–2; 1.53.1–3: 222; 1.86.1–5: 222–3; 2.53.2: 283; 3.40.1–43.2: 33–4; 3.80.1–82.4: 267–9; 5.92η1–4: 24–5; 6.79.1: 185–6; 6.126.1–130.1: 59–61; 7.153.2: 282; 7.208.1–209.4: 171–2; 9.62.2–63.2: 184–5
Hesiod, *Works and Days*, 168–73: 20; 213–64: 112–13; 302–20: 127; 342–51: 96–7; 369–70: 123; 458–82: 104–5; 519–24: 58–9; 582–96: 122; 618–34, 641–5, 663–77, 689–94: 110–11; 724–6: 17–18; 760–4: 83
Hippocrates(?), *Regimen in Health*, 1.2–3: 241
'Hippocratic Oath', 241–2
Homer
   Iliad, 1.1–5: 165; 1.8–32: 11–12; 1.33–129: 12–15; 2.198–270: 269–72; 5.280–93, 296: 169; 6.390–493: 139–42; 9.433: 91; 9.485–98: 91–2; 9.499–514: 15–16; 12.310–28: 168–9; 16.7–11: 52; 18.490–606: 100–3; 22.306–54, 361–6, 395–415: 186–8; 22.482–515: 89–91; 23.30–4, 59–107: 28–9; 23.664–99: 152–3
   Odyssey 3.430–63, 470–2: 16–17; 4.1: 2; 4.219–31: 35; 6.25–109: 54–7; 6.149–59: 57; 6.251–88: 57–8; 9.106–39: 106–7; 10.229–48: 35–6; 10.410–14: 104; 10.388–99: 36; 11.23–80: 20–2; 11.140–53: 22; 11.204–22: 23; 11.576–600: 23–4; 17.290–327: 162–4; 17.322–3: 125; 22.1–25: 74–5; 22.65–98: 75–6; 22.241–309: 76–8; 22.399–418: 78–9; 23.289–301: 79–80; 24.1–18: 19–20; 24.125–50: 73–4
Homeric Hymn to Aphrodite, (5), 1–41: 42–4
Hyperides, 6, *Funeral Oration*, 4–5: 259–60; 41–3: 31–2

Inscriptiones Graecae, *see* Fraenkel, Gaertringen, Kirchner
Isocrates, 17 (*Trapeziticus*), 13–14: 130

Index of Illustration Citations

Index

References to illustrations are given in italics.